DEDICATION

*To my son Jonathan and to all the people who want
to know what is going on with their Bibles.
And especially to all the pastors who haven't
noticed what has happened yet.*

TABLE OF CONTENTS

Limit of Liability/Disclaimer of Warranty

Introduction

The Mandela Effect is a supernatural phenomenon that has been mislabeled as "collective misremembering". Never before has the culture at large all remembered the same things in the past, and then been told they are all wrong, largely by the media and misled professionals that have been lying to us for our entire lives. What they fail to investigate and even address is the prolific amount of residual, or evidence, that we remember, showing that our memories are in fact valid. Nor do they query the idea that it is statistically impossible for thousands, if not millions of people to misremember the same thing in total error. If there were true misremembering, the errors would be scattered. So the questions arises - why are they covering it up?

Reasons for the Mandela Effect range from us sliding between parallel universes, to accessing different dimensions to living in a simulation to Satanic black majick or to God. As my perspective comes from a Biblical worldview, I explain what I believe is the source and reasons the supernatural changes are taking place. Having documented the Bible changes for 5 years, I have a large database and include various lists of Bible changes throughout the Old Testament as well as have put the entire New Testament changes in order, starting at Matthew One, and going through to the end of Revelation. There are over 200 pages of Bible changes in this large 8" X 10" book. Use it as a handy companion to reading the Bible, should you spot an anomaly and wish to cross reference it as a possible change.

In the spirit of timeline deception, there is an in-depth chapter devoted to the concept that the architectural evidence points to a past Millennial Reign of Christ, putting us in Satan's Little Season.

It also validates your experience as you see how your recollection of Bible passages compares with others who believe they are now different. The book also has numerous photographs of residual. Bible and music quizzes are included in order to help you share the Mandela Effect with others.

If nothing else, this book will make you realize you are not alone, and definitely not crazy. I have known about the Mandela Effect for 5 years now, and have been literally obsesses with finding out what is going on. I have written hundreds of blog posts for MandelaBibleChanges.com and now TheSupernaturalBibleChanges.Com website. I have listened to the online communities livestreams on a daily basis for the past 5 years I know what people are thinking and the different theories, but primarily, I know how the Bible has changed.

I have had readers send me hand written pages of the entire Bible and posted it online at the first website mentioned. Then it was mysteriously removed. I still have the pages, but not in order. I have come to find out that even the written pages can be changed, as do photographs.

Having read the Bible extensively over the course of 40 years and attended both a Christian high school and college where Bible study of the King James Version was required, I know what was in the Bible. I have listened to hundreds, maybe thousands of sermons as well. And I have a brain and a memory and a desire to get to the truth.

The Mandela Effect Bible changes are the most monumental occurrence since the birth of Christ, in my opinion. We have not seen a supernatural manifestation in our lifetimes of this magnitude, nor have heard of any in recent history. And the authorities are not acknowledging it. Of the ones that are, many are not Christian and are espousing some fantastic theories. If you cannot ascribe to us living in a simulation or bouncing from one universe to another, then this book is for you.

I give you a Biblical viewpoint of the Mandela Effect as well as outline the changes in the entire New Testament in order of book and verse, so you can easily look up a changed verse, totaling over 200 pages of documented Bible changes and how they used to read before.

There is a whole chapter on residual consisting mainly of illustrations. Also there are two quizzes for your use to help others understand the Mandela Effect. One is a Biblical quiz of 50 Bible changes, and the other is a musical quiz.

The changes to the Bible are continually occurring, so it is literally impossible to document them all. Understand that there are so many thousands of changes to the Bible that I could not document them all. Also, my Old Testament chart was lost when the first website was mysteriously removed from the internet.

Yes, the Mandela Effect bible changes are quite a dilemna. And for those who are wondering why I'm spelling dilemna wrong - that's how it used to be spelled less than 10 years ago. Yet another example of the Mandela Effect.

All Biblical references are from the *King James Version* Bible unless specifically noted otherwise.

Chapter 1

What is the Mandela Effect?

—◆—

*"Any sufficiently advanced technology
is indistinguishable from magic."*

Arthur C. Clarke

John was a devout Christian who loved reading the Bible every day. He was brought up in a church that only preached from the King James Version, which he believed was the most accurate and faithful to the original manuscripts. He had memorized many verses and passages, and often quoted them to his friends and family.

One day, he decided to read the Gospel of Matthew, which he had not read in a while. He opened his KJV Bible and started from the first chapter. In the very second verse he was surprised to see that the genealogy of Jesus had changed.

Instead of listing Jesus lineage as coming from Judah, he saw that Jesus now came from the line of Judas. He wondered how he could have missed that before.

He read on, and came to Matthew 6:9-13, the Lord's Prayer. He was shocked to see that it had changed drastically. Instead of saying "forgive us our trespasses, it now read "forgive us our debts". Other words seemed odd as well. "Our Father *which* art in heaven, Hallowed be thy name. Thy kingdom come, Thy will be done *in* earth, as it is in heaven. Give us this day our daily bread. And forgive us our *debts,* as we forgive our *debtors. .*" He read on. In Matthew 10:12

And when ye come into an house, **salute** it. Salute it? He never heard that word in the Bible before. Wasn't it *greet,* he thought? He flipped the pages to the book of Luke. Maybe he had remembered Matthew as actually reading like one of the other gospels, as there are 4: Matthew, Mark, Luke and John, which all give the same account of Jesus life and teachings from different readers' viewpoints.

He flips the page to Luke 12:24 Consider the **ravens**: for they neither sow nor reap; which neither have storehouse nor barn; He knows that it was consider the **sparrows**, as he did a Bible study on that verse, and the church had made a set of cups that said "consider the sparrows" to give out to the Bible study attendees. In fact, he still had that cup. He ran into the kitchen and found it, "Yes, it says sparrows! I know I'm not going crazy!"

John felt a chill run down his spine. He could not believe what he was reading. He had learned the Lord's Prayer by heart since he was a child, and he had always recited it the way he remembered it. He knows the Bible said "sparrows" where it now reads "ravens." He wondered if his Bible was defective, or if someone had tampered with it. He decided to check his other Bibles, specifically his grandmother's 160 year old King James Bible, to see if they had the same changes.

He went to his bookshelf, and took out the aged Bible, removing the elastic band that held the binding on, opening it to Matthew 6:9-13. To his dismay, it read the same way. He looked for the other verses and saw that they all said the same thing. He felt a surge of panic. He wondered if he was going crazy, or if he was dreaming. He pinched himself, but he felt the pain. He was awake, and this was real.

He decided to call his pastor, and ask him if he knew anything about the words in the Bible changing. He picked up his phone, and dialed the number. His pastor answered and asked how he could help.

"Pastor, I wanted to let you know that I was just reading my Bible and there are words there that never used to be there. I want to know what is going on!"

"I'd be glad to help, John. What passage are you concerned about?

"Well, for one, the passage in Luke 12: 24 says "ravens" and I know it was "sparrows"!

"John, the passage says "ravens" and I'm sure you are thinking it was "sparrows" because they are both birds. I just looked up the word in the Greek Lexicon, and it says "ravens."

John is aghast, "But I remember giving a study in Sunday School on that verse. I even made cups and still have one that says "consider the sparrows"!

"John," remarked the pastor, "I'm sure it was an honest mistake. Like I said, they are both birds. It's an easy mistake to make."

John continued, "But what about the verse saying you are to **salute** when entering a house? That was never there!"

"Yes, it was always there, John. Perhaps you just never noticed it." John left the conversation befuddled. He decided to try to find someone who could help him, or at least explain what was going on. He remembered listening to a podcast from an author, Fritz Springmeier, who gave out his email for anyone to contact him. He had given a great talk on how freemasonry had infiltrated the church with Luciferian doctrines. He decided to email him.

The night was long, as John felt a wave of horror. He realized that he had entered a nightmare. He wondered if he had somehow crossed into a parallel reality, where everything was different. He wondered if there was a way to go back, or if he was stuck here forever. He spent the entire night putting in the search words. "the Bible is changing" but only came up with articles of different translations. He barely slept, eagerly awaiting a response from Mr Springmeier.

Finally, around noon the next day, he gets the email and reads it. Fritz empathized, and said:

"I'm afraid you're not the only one who's confused. Many people are experiencing the same thing. The Bible is changing, as well as the world is changing. It's all part of the great deception, the end times, the fulfillment of prophecy."

"It's hard to explain, but I'll try. You see, the fallen angels, the Illuminati, the elite. All have the power to manipulate reality, to alter history, to change the past, the present, and the future. They use advanced technology, such as quantum computers, CERN, D-Wave, to access and exploit parallel realities, to create and destroy timelines, to rewrite the script of the world. They are the masters of illusion, the lords of chaos, the agents of Satan. They are the ones who are changing things. They are the ones who are deceiving the masses, leading them astray, preparing them for the Antichrist, the beast, the false prophet. They are the ones who are fulfilling the prophecy of Revelation, the mark of the beast, the great tribulation, the Armageddon. They are the ones who are paving the road to hell, the end of individual choice, the end of free will, the end of humanity."

"They want to be gods. They want to overthrow the true God, the Creator, the Father. They want to create their own reality, their own kingdom, their own heaven. They want to enslave humanity, to make them their servants, their worshipers, their sacrifices. They want to destroy everything that is good, true, and beautiful. They want to unleash evil, darkness, and misery. They want to bring about the new world order, the one world government, the one world religion, the one world currency.

John thought to himself,

> *"This is the strong delusion! "*

That story is fictional based on true events which illustrate the Mandela Effect. The following is a true story and my account of things that happened to me, which I attribute to the Mandela Effect:

My Story

I attended a Baptist Bible Camp at the age of 11, where I accepted Jesus. After that, I became truly sincere about learning about the Bible. I took a formal Bible study and read it on my own, always from the only Bible I had, a King James Version. I read it a few times before attending a Christian College, where we had

9

to go to sermons every Monday and Friday nights, as well as take a formal Bible class, all from the KJV Bible. By the time I was 21, I pretty much heard and read the Bible pretty thoroughly.

Throughout my adult life, I attended church pretty regularly, hearing sermons and always following along in my same Bible. After the birth of my child, I did become less regular, as I was extremely busy trying to work full time and raise a son pretty much on my own, having gone through a divorce due to pervasive abuse. The devil has tried to take me down and put me out many times in my difficult life; yet I am still here, thanks to God.

With that said, I rarely cracked open the Bible in the past few years leading up to 2018, but still listened to sermons on Sunday TV. It was in 2017 that I became more serious about seeking God, again, when Hurricane Irma hit my state of Florida.

It was a monster storm barreling towards South Florida with a wind speed of 185 mph. Hurricane Irma was the strongest, most intense hurricane ever to exist in the Atlantic Basin, with sustained winds of 185 mph and an atmospheric pressure of 913. Unheard of. Unprecedented. Apocalyptic.

Was God showing us His power? Was it a regular hurricane exacerbated by HAARP? Was it a man-made hurricane aimed at revenging the Trump voting state of Florida? As a long time Florida resident, I know the devastation caused by Hurricane Andrew in the 1990s, a Category 5 with winds of 145 mph, and that was a tiny speck of a storm compared to Irma. Irma was projected to be 100 times stronger, as wind speeds increase the strength of a hurricane exponentially. Puerto Rico was totally devastating from the preceding storm of the 2017 season, Maria, with wind speeds of 175 mph. Utterly destroyed.

So imagine my panic when this hurricane with 185 mph winds was headed right towards us. The fact is, I could barely eat and slept but only 3 hours each night for about 10 days straight.

I even had a dream with an image of a swirling hurricane and the numbers 185 in the center, and God said he would protect me in the center of the hurricane like He did with Shadrach, Meshach, and Abednego in the furnace. But still, I was panicked, as was everyone else.

The entire cities of Key West, the Upper Keys and Miami Beach were evacuated 4 days prior to the storm, with over 700,000 people on the highways trying to get out of Dodge. Within the next couple of days, 5.6 million people were evacuated, the largest evacuation order the country has ever seen.

I had to throw everything I ever expected to own again into the back of my SUV and drive myself out of the West Palm Beach area, navigating the back roads of rural Florida.

> *Everyone was in panic mode, with neighbors throwing their belongings into garbage bags and tossing them into their cars, then jumping in - and hauling ass as fast as they could.*

I can't tell you the ultimate stress of it all. It was like a scene out of the movie Independence Day, when Will Smith shuffled outside to grab his morning paper and noticed all his neighbors throwing their belongings in their cars and then racing down the streets, as a huge alien spaceship hovered above.

Before evacuating from the east coast, I had grabbed some CDs from my husband's huge collection and threw them in the car. I had put 5 CDs. He likes rock music, and has hundreds of CDs, all rock.

I didn't choose them, look at them or know what they were. It was so frantic trying to pack to evacuate. Neighbors were just throwing stuff into garbage bags in their cars.

As I couldn't get a radio station that wasn't in Spanish, I turned on the CD player. Instantly I started getting messages from God. I was like, Wow, God is giving me encouragement to make it across the state. But it was more than that. For the next 3 hours, every song had spiritual messages, even prophetic, in them. I couldn't believe it. How could these rock songs have spiritual messages? They aren't Christian music at all. Not one. Interpretations flooded my head of what the songs meant...It was non stop. I felt like my brain was a sparkler, with strong messages firing all over the place.

After about an hour of this, I thought for sure that the next song would be just regular rock, but NO. One after the other. When yet another CD loaded and started with new messages, I just laughed because at this point, it was pretty evident that God had this all planned out.

Here are some of the actual lyrics that played:

We just run with the wind
And we'll fly with the rain
We don't know where we'll get to,
Or if we'll get back again
We just run with the wind
And we fly through the rain

What if the engine dies
These are no friendly skies
My heads spinning round

The other thing was, my teenage son refused to leave his apartment and evacuate, so I left him behind with a gun. His dad had also died a few years back, so he was "half an orphan" I guess you could say. Nevertheless, these lyrics were spot on to that situation:

You must leave now, take what you need, you think will last
But whatever you wish to keep, you better grab it fast
Yonder stands <u>your orphan with his gun</u>
Crying like a fire in the sun

Look out the saints are comin' through
And it's all over now, baby blue
The highway is for gamblers, better use your sense
Take what you have gathered from coincidence

The empty-handed painter from your streets
Is drawing crazy patterns on your sheets
This sky, too, is folding under you
And it's all over now, baby blue

You have got to be kidding, God.

My husband had stayed behind to put up the hurricane shutters, as they made him stay at work up until the day before the Hurricane hit. He later met me at his brother's house in Tampa, and by the grace of God, the Hurricane that Was Headed for Us Dead On TURNED AWAY, just a few miles before it hit.

I seriously was prepared to die. I'm relaying this story only to let you know that I was literally brought to my knees by that hurricane. I prayed like I never prayed before, and God spoke to me for hours, through music of all crazy things, as I was alone and traveling in a very precarious situation. You learn to understand what's important and what's not when you are faced with great struggle or death.

> *What's important is that we have a choice as to whether we want to be on the right side, the side of truth and light - God's side, or on the other side: lies, deception and darkness. There is no middle ground.*

I was very strongly impressed that it was God who allowed this storm to get that big, in order to bring people to repentance and understand that the time is short before His son, Jesus, will come again, returning in the clouds.

After the hurricane is often the worst time. We got a phone call from the alarm company saying our house had been broken into, so my husband bolted in the car to go home, even though the roads were still closed. I was too tired to even pack the car up, so stayed behind and decided to return the following day. Of course, I only got 3 hours sleep again, as the generator was running all night making a great deal of noise.

So I woke up at 1 am, pretty much exhausted and wondering how I would be able to drive alone , across the state. But it had to be done, before the millions of evacuees started to clog the roads.

Looters were already out in full force, knocking on people's doors, saying they were the Light Company or FEMA, sticking guns in people's faces, then stealing everything in their home. The police were too busy to even respond.

Driving in the dark of night, criminals could easily cut me off the road and stick a gun in my face, as well. So I prayed. Should I stay or should I go? Could I even make it, being so tired?

It's then that God started talking to me through music again. I turned on the radio and instantly a song came on, called *"Hold Your Head Up" by Steppenwolf. The lyrics said:*

And if it's bad
Don't let it get you down, you can take it
And if it hurts
Don't let them see you cry, you can make it

Hold your head up, oh, hold your head up, oh
Hold your head up, oh hold your head high

And if they stare
Just let them burn their eyes on you moving
And if they shout
Don't let it change a thing that you're doing

Hold your head up, oh, hold your head up, oh
Hold your head up, oh hold your head high

Another song played with the following lyrics:

There's a warning coming in
Storm coming overhead
Stop lying in your bed
There's nowhere to hide
There's lightning in the sky
Storm coming in the night
Stop running, stand and fight
Hold your head high
Hold your head high

If that isn't an answer to prayer on what I should do, I do not know what was! So I got out of bed and packed for 3 hours, then dressed up like a man with a cap on , hiding my hair, with 2 guns in my car, and hit the road at 4 am. It is about a 5 hour drive from Tampa to Boynton Beach.The blessing was I was the only one on the road, and got there fine.

So, what does that have to do with the Mandela Effect? Not much, except that it was the beginning of the awakening process God was putting me through. In less than a year, in June of 2018, I was watching videos on Youtube and saw some some great ones put out by Truthshock TV and Mr. E. The latter was exposing how many of the Hollywood actresses are transgender and the video and forensic proof he had was undeniable. He was taken off of Youtube by the Thought Police but can still be found at Apocalypse_Watchman by MrE on Bitchute. TruthShock TV also put out some great transgender expose videos which were Christian - oriented and educational. I was shocked but had to acknowledge the forensic evidence was undeniable. Then one day, I was watching TruthShock TV on Youtube and he was going over how the Bible was being changed. I was intrigued and decided to check it out for myself, in my own 40-some-odd-year-old Bible, worn and used from years of use. I checked out the passages he cited and started reading more. I couldn't believe what I was reading. New words that I had never ever seen before were popping up all over the place: *Peraventure, god-ward, us-ward, alway, the first initial of God's names were no longer capitalized, astonied, lawyers* was in there, as well as *banks!* I had never read those words in the Bible, nor even heard them in sermons! What was going on?

Well, instantly the Holy Spirit struck me and not in a good way. I was devastated, shocked and instantly aware of the idea that this had to be the end of time, the last days, as something this diabolical could only happen under those circumstances. I was so gobsmacked that I believe I actually went into shock as I began crying and praying and searching on the internet for information, to not much avail. Bill Bean was an exorcist who spoke out on how he saw the Bible changes, and himself admitted he almost fell out of his chair when he opened his Bible and read a passage that he absolutely knew was different.

My symptoms continued for weeks, and I could not work or do much of anything, except lie in the backyard lounge chair and stair at the palm trees. My brain felt like it was going to split in two and I thought I was having some sort of a nervous breakdown. My husband believed me, but had no frame of reference, not being a former Bible student. So I endured for 3 weeks in this incapacitated state, wishing I had someone to speak to that understood. That never happened, so I sought out a couple of pastors that I previously attended church, to speak to.

Not to go into detail, but they outright dismissed my claims. One said I probably needed a new set of glasses, and the other said to not engage in foolishness and quoted 1 Timothy 6:20: O Timothy, keep that which is committed to thy trust, avoiding profane and vain babblings, and oppositions of science falsely so called:

Not even noticing that *oppositions of science* was never previously there. So he was essentially telling me I was talking a bunch of nonsense. I ended up finding online groups of believers that gathered together to share their own testimonies of how they believed the Bible had been changed.

Then one morning, I woke up and as I was making breakfast in the kitchen, I threw the eggshells into the trashcan. A trash can of a find that I bought at a thrift store months prior. After I buy a treasure from a thrift store, I love to look up the product online, to see how much it really cost. I had looked it up on the internet according to the metal stamped words on the lid, which read "Simply Human". The trash can was about $150 dollars, so I was happy I got it for $30. Pretty much every day I would look at the name Simply Human on the lid as I threw away garbage. But this morning was different: the lid said, *Simple Human.* I gasped in horror!

I ran to the internet and looked it up. I saw that the name was now officially Simple Human, but I saw some retail websites where it listed the cans for sale as

> *That is an example of what we call "residue" which is another name for "circumstantial evidence".*

"Simply Human" the way I remembered. Why would they do that?

Several years passed, and I grew weary of people not caring or noticing the Mandela Effects. I prayed to God and asked him to show me one again, just to justify to myself that I wasn't crazy. Not only did he answer my prayer the very next day, he gave me two Mandela Effects!

I went out to the car to do some errands. There was always a button on the dash that was poorly placed, as it blocked the numerical information behind it, being in the middle. When you pushed the button to find out the odometer reading, or the gas mileage, your hand would hide the numerics behind it, so it was a bad design. I immediately noticed the button was way over on the left side. I was gobsmacked! It moved! I pressed the button and could see the display in the center clearly. But when I pressed it again, the gas mileage reading never came up. Now it only reads the odometer and the trip mileage, so I guess when you pray, be careful what you pray for!

Not only that, but I later went on my computer to do a blog post with a graphic, and the Print Screen function wouldn't work. I fiddled with it for a long time, until I happened upon that fact that instead of pressing Control , Print Screen, now I had to press FN print screen. Not only did the keys change, but now I had the capability to crop it as well as shoot the screen. Believe me, I used that function every day for the past 3 years, and I know what I used, and it changed!

Be careful what you pray for. In the subsequent months, my journey of truth (apocalypse) continued. The next year a friend told me how he just learned the earth was flat. I looked into that and saw the evidence did in fact, prove that idea. And now, I am learning that the Millennial Reign of Jesus may have already happened during what was labeled, "The Dark Ages" which would be a perfect satanic inverted label. We may be actually living in the Little Season of Satan, a time of great deception. Can you deny we are in a period of great deception?

So, you may be thinking -- she is really gullible! No, I am not that gullible, and I happen to be very educated and have an open mind. What I think may be the trait that all truthers have is, we seek the truth, wherever it may lead.

I think the people we call "normies" who don't want to even investigate alternate claims, are the gullible ones. They accept lies as truth, with no critical thinking whatsoever. And let me be clear: Jesus commanded us to not be deceived. Yes, Christians, it is ok to look on the internet to gather information. It is okay to read books and have questions about the history of the earth, the shape of the earth, the origin of the dinosaurs, the existence of giants, the meaning of melted buildings, the age of architecture, and anything else your curious mind feels needs an answer to.

Luke 21:8

And he said, Take heed that ye be not **deceived**:

1 Corinthians 15:33

Be not **deceived**:

Galatians 6:7

Be not **deceived**;

2 Timothy 3:13

But evil men and seducers shall wax worse and worse, deceiving, and being **deceived**.

Revelation 18:23

And the light of a candle shall shine no more at all in thee; and the voice of the bridegroom and of the bride shall be heard no more at all in thee: for thy merchants were the great men of the earth; for by thy sorceries were all nations **deceived**.

Revelation 20:10

And the devil that **deceived** them

So many people turn up their noses at the Mandela Effect, saying it is not important and who cares? After all, they only see the minor spelling changes occurring in company names or products. Would they feel that way if they knew the human body has changed or that people have come back from the dead?

Have they stopped to consider that if one little thing changes,
that means that everything can change?

Maybe you have bought this book because you are concerned about the changes you've seen in the Bible that you have read for many years. You may have thought that you are just misremembering, but you are real sure about a lot of the passages that you used to know.

I am here to reassure you that you are not losing your mind nor your memory. When thousands of other people remember the same thing as you, it is not collective misremembering, as the popular culture would have you believe, but it is a statistical anomaly that points to a phenomenon. It has never occurred in history that millions of people misremember the exact same thing - until now.

What is more alarming is that the changes are occurring in the Bible. It is one thing to know that Chic-Fil-A now has a K added at the end of Chic, but it is another thing to realize that God's inspired words are being changed. How could God let that happen?

In the Old Testament, Israel strayed from God's laws over and over and over , and God sent them plagues and judgments and wicked kings. It is no different today. You can't expect to remove God from American society and replace the moral Christian culture with abortion, transvestism, homosexuality, satanic ritual abuse, Godlessness in schools, pedophilia, transhumanism, bodily mutilation, perversion on every front and depraved morals and expect God to bless the country. We are getting what we deserve, and that is a removal of God's protective hand.

Yes, Satan is running amuk. He is not only in control, he is having a field day. On every single front, he is effecting deception. It is so bad, that it seems as if we are living in a horror movie.

When you realize that NASA has lied to us about going to the moon and the general shape of the earth, you know that the deception started a long time ago. When you realize that Freemasons literally run the world, and they really are Luciferians, you know that evil is prevailing. When you realize that a phenomenon called the Mandela Effect is changing reality as your see it, you not only are shocked, but you can't even make sense of it. And when you realize that the Mandela Effect is changing the written Holy Bible, the inspired words of God, you know you are not in Kansas anymore.

Many have considered that maybe they have died and gone to hell. Others think that we are jumping from one universe to another. Still others are convinced that time travel is in play. Christians are not able to jump on those bandwagons in light of what God has taught about living our one life and then having a judgement.

We know that God is real through the experiences that we have had with Him, and how He has revealed Himself to us. We are grateful that He has put up with us and many of us attribute our very lives to Him. We would otherwise be dead. So no, we are not going to jump onto the New Age theories of evolved consciousness and thought manifestation, as we know where those theories come from and how they are of the dark side. So what do we make of this supernatural phenomenon called the Mandela Effect? How do we square it with the Bible?

What can we make of looking in our Bibles and seeing that Luke 6:49---when Jesus spoke of not building your house on shifting sand but on the rock....now sand has been changed to EARTH.

Mark 13:10----the word "preached" replaced by PUBLISHED

Luke 8:39...."proclaimed" replaced by PUBLISHED Luke 17:31 ---the word "possessions" replaced by STUFF

In Numbers and Exodus...the word "womb" is mentioned 24 times and has been replaced by MATRIX

Job 19:23...."written in a scroll" replaced by PRINTED IN A BOOK Revelations 5..."scroll" replaced by BOOK

Genesis 1:1...."heavens" replaced by HEAVEN

Isaiah 11:6...instead of the Lion lying with the Lamb it is now the WOLF lying with the Lamb

Isaiah 65:25...again WOLF instead of Lion

Matthew 6:9-13...."on earth" now IN EARTH. "trespass" and "trespasser" now DEBT and DEBTORS

Matthew 9:17..."wineskins" changed to BOTTLES

Mark 2:22..."wineskins" changed to BOTTLES

23

Luke 19:23..."those who lend" has been changed to TAKE IT TO THE BANK

Luke 19:27....SLAY THEM BEFORE ME has been inserted. It has never said that.

Deuteronomy 17:1...."defect" was replaced by EVILFAVOUREDNESS (I don't think that's a word)

Ecclesiastes 3:11...."eternity" replaced by WORLD

Matthew 13:15...."waxed cold" replaced by WAXED GROSS

Job 21:24..."his pails" are full of milk has been replaced with HIS BREASTS ARE FULL OF MILK

Numbers 11:12...."as a father beareth the sucking child"..now says AS A NURSING FATHER

Luke 1:35..."holy one" replaced by HOLY THING

Luke 5:19 and 5:24..."bed" replaced by COUCH

Acts 12:4..."Passover" replaced by EASTER

Revelation 12:12...."inhabitants" replaced by INHABITERS and AND THE SEA inserted---never there before.

Revelation 22:21...added. It previously ended with verse 20.

Ruth 4:4..."tell" replaced by ADVERTISE

Numbers 24:14.."advise" replaced by ADVERTISE Genesis 40:1..."cupbearer" replaced by BUTLER

Romans 5:4...."patience" replaced by EXPERIENCE

This chart from Statista.com shows how 1/3 of Christians NEVER read the Bible, and of those who do, they comprise less than 20%. And of those 20% that do read it, how many are reading from *other versions?* That is important, because the vast majority of Bible changes are occurring only in the King James Version.

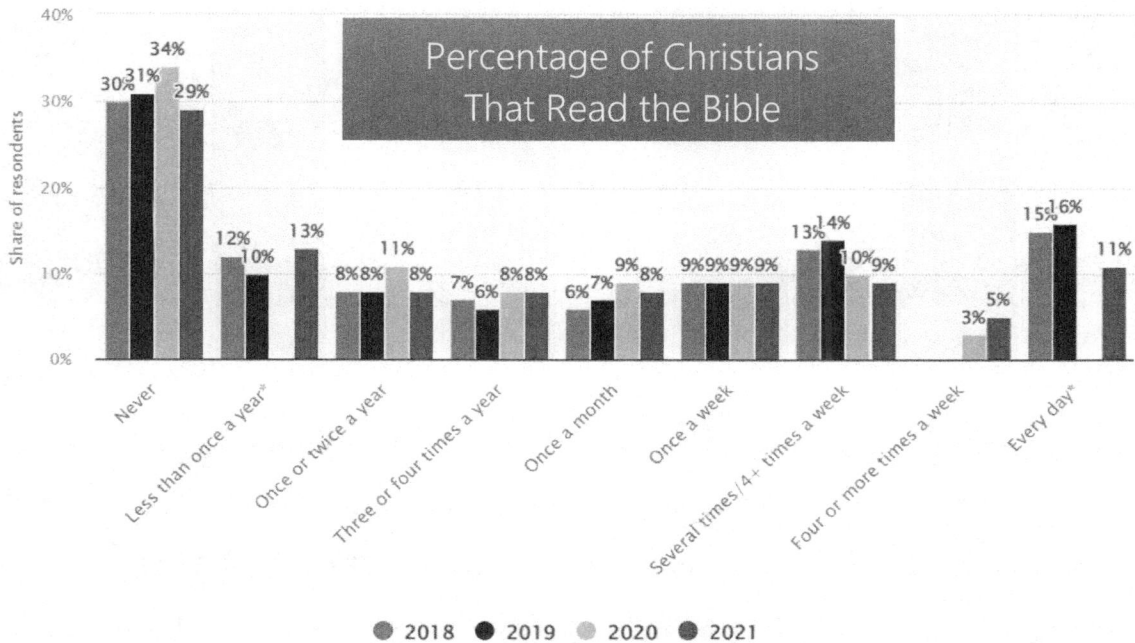

Percentage of Christians That Read the Bible

As the King James Version is the only Bible I ever read for decades, any foreign language in it sticks out like a sore thumb.

Although I do not believe that God is creating the changes, I think he is allowing Satan and his emissaries on this earth to do so. God may be allowing it as a means to wake up his church.

There is an important distinction to be made between God *controlling* evil and God *creating* evil. God is not the author of sin, but He can use sinful men to attain an objective. Romans 8:28 says, "For those who love God all things work together for good, for those who are called according to his purpose."

Amos 8:11

> *Behold, the days come, saith the Lord GOD, that I will send a famine in the land, not a famine of bread, nor a thirst for water, but of hearing the words of the LORD:*

The above passage describes a time there will be a famine in the land for the words of the Lord, which perfectly describes what the Mandela Effect Bible Changes are causing. Has God sent it, or is He allowing it? Is He making the changes, or is Satan and his minions? These are the topics that will be explored.

Chapter 2

Residual

Residual is the circumstantial evidence for the Mandela Effect

One of the enigmatic characteristics of the Mandela Effect is the existence of a great deal of "residue" or "residual", which is synonymous with "circumstantial evidence." Take, for example, the very common Mandela Effect regarding the "Lion and the Lamb" phrase that is

"Then the lion shall lay down with the lamb, and the bear shall eat grass like the ox, and the child shall play on the hole of the asp, and nothing shall hurt nor destroy in all My Holy Mountain!"
~Isaiah 11:6~

remembered being in the Bible.

The Lion and the Lamb

Many remember Isaiah 11:6 as reading that the "lion shall lie down with the lamb" and not "the wolf" as it now reads. Numerous pastors repeat that phrase in their sermons, including John Hagee's sermon on the millennium, saying the "lion shall lie down with the lamb" *ten* times!

Listen to hear him repeat the lion and lamb in the following video titled *Pastor John Hagee - TEN times with Hagee - Isaiah 11:6 Residue - Compilation by Bluepacman 13 on Youtube*   https://www.youtube.com/watch?v=_aakMEuSUrI&t=473s

Other pieces of residual, or circumstantial evidence, go as far back as the early 1800s in this video titled *They Say We Don't Do Our Research by That Flat Fellow by Brian S. Staveley on Rumble:*

https://rumble.com/v1djwda-they-say-we-dont-do-our-research-by-that-flat-fellow.html

Not only countless businesses worldwide are named "Lion and Lamb" but also artifacts

Screenshot from the book Space Time: *The Mathematics of Faith* by Paulson p.211:

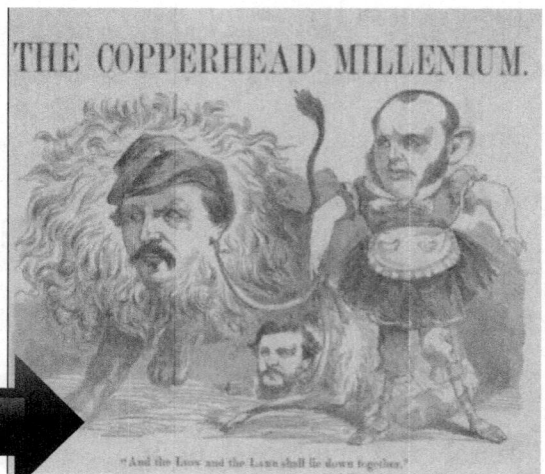

And the lion and the lamb shall lie down together

THE COPPERHEAD MILLENIUM.

"And the Lion and the Lamb shall lie down together."

uses an interval of one thousand years to enumerate the interval of the rest period, as previously discussed (Isaiah also prophecied of this era, an era of peace, in which the lion shall lay down with the lamb [Isaiah 11:6-8]). According to the discussion in the chapter "Chronology of the Abrahamic People," we see that we are nearing the end of the sixth period if that is the case.

An important conclusion of this investigation is that God is leading national Israel through history (and we who are Gentiles as well). His leadership has resulted in many periods that concern the number 7 for that nation. It is instructive to go through the Bible and discover all the places wherein God makes use of the seven-unit period with respect to Israel: the

Evidence as to how things "used to be" is called *residue* or *residual*, and we use it as evidence to bolster what we remember as being fact. Why would all this evidence in the 1800s for lion and lamb be found, and none for the wolf and the lamb?

Note that very recently, images have come up on internet searches that show the wolf and the lamb, but they were created in the last couple of years, as I searched for them 3 years ago and could find NONE

In 1922 Thomas Osborn wrote a book called *The Lion and the Lamb: A Drama of the Apocalypse.*

Other residue is found in tattoos:

The VW symbol has no line in the center like it used to have.

Beam me Up Scotty - a phrase that they say never existed

Haas avocados which is now "H**ass**", like an "**ass**". The devil is so adolescent in his thoughts and loves to focus everything on sex.

Hello, Clarice was never said in the *Silence of the Lambs and* Tinkerbell never flew around the Disney castle with fairy dust as these tattoos portray.

The Bible Trivia Game

The Bible Trivia game states it's "the game where trivia is not trivial" produced in 1984. It is rightfully presumed that a game creator would take the time to check and recheck the answers in the Bible before spending time and money in printing hundreds, if not thousands, of games. Not only are the questions and answers rife with mistakes, but even the Bible text printed on the front cover is wrong. In fact, the wording presented is not found in any version of the Bible. The game cover reads: *For wisdom is better than rubies, and all things that may be desired are not to be compared with it.* Proverbs 8:11

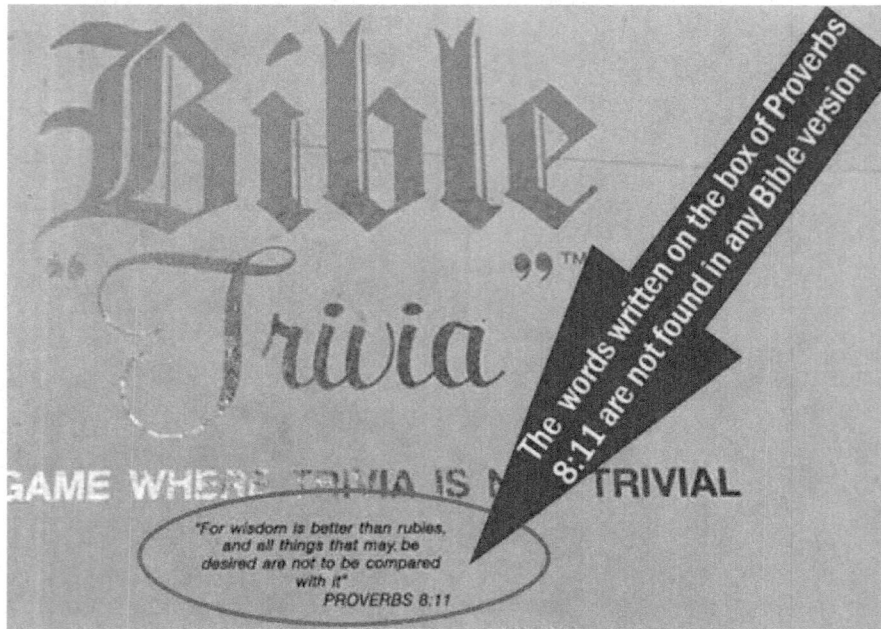

Yet now we see that this game has numerous errors. and apparently that matter "is trivial" to many Christians and pastors.

The Mandela Effect, or quantum effect has changed thousands of observable items in this reality, with the Bible being the most consequential. See all the blatant changes in this video: https://www.youtube.com/watch?v=0PSuf1udvwA&t=2s

Unexplainable Changes to painting *The Creation of Man* by Michelangelo

The following list of supernatural Bible changes was compiled around the year 2017. As the Bible is consistently being changed, you may notice some differences from this chart to your physical Bibles today. In fact, there are many more thousands of changes now than in 2017.

Being a designer, I went to a 4-year university to study art. That included an extensive Art History course, which I thought was the most difficult of all the art classes. It involved a great deal of memorization for each art piece, including the date, period of art, details of why the piece looked the way it did, etc.

For example, we learned why each piece was standing or looking in a certain direction, who were the ancillary characters, what the symbolism was, how it related to the culture of the time period, why certain colors were used, and on and on. Needless to say, I spent most of my time that semester memorizing from this 1,000 page Art History book. Suffice to say, I know a little bit about art.

I remember the discussion around Leonardo DaVinci's Mona Lisa, and how no one knew if she were smiling or not, as the painting was so ambiguous that it could be seen either way.

In fact, about 3 years ago, when I saw Michelangelo's painting, which they now call "The Creation of Adam" I was like, wait- I memorized it as "The Creation of Man" . It wasn't until 3 years later that I actually found residual evidence of that title, proving that our memories are reliable, as I took that class 35 years ago.

Yet, many art sites and even Wikipedia, name the title as "Creation of ADAM". So, which is it?

"The Creation of Adam (Italian: *Creazione di Adamo*) is a <u>fresco</u> painting by Italian artist <u>Michelangelo</u>, which forms part of the <u>Sistine Chapel's ceiling</u>, painted c. 1508–1512. It illustrates the <u>Biblical</u> <u>creation narrative</u> from the <u>Book of Genesis</u> in which <u>God</u> gives life to <u>Adam</u>, the first <u>man</u>." Wikipedia.

Additionally, the proportions of the painting have been altered. This painting appears on the ceiling of the Sistine Chapel, where it was painted in the year 1508-1512, as it took 4 years to do. The above images depict how the painting now appears on the ceiling of the Sistine Chapel. So what is the problem, you ask? Well, I immediately noticed how God's hand was now lower than Adam's and also how it is smaller. The original discussion in college was that God was positioned higher than man because he is in heaven and we are on earth.

The direction of God's hand was on a diagonal, reaching down to touch man's hand. The fact that God's hand was larger indicated that God was more powerful than man. But now, for some reason, none of that discussion can be found anywhere on the internet.

Now, the fact that man's hand is higher than God's and that Adam's hand is now larger than God's, plays into the narrative of the

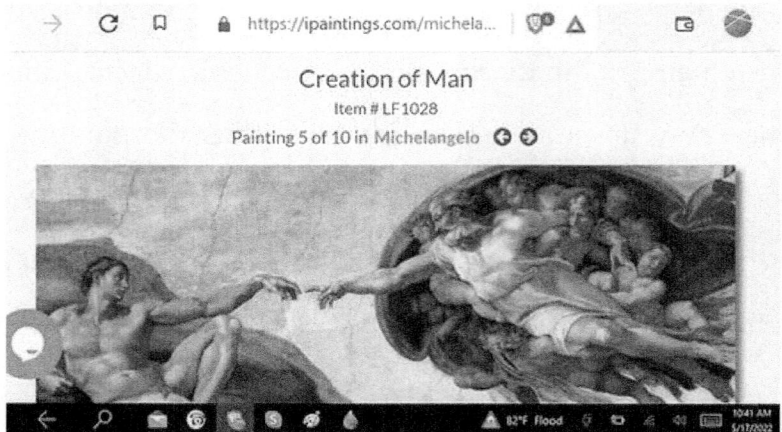

lowering and denigration of God and His character, a minimization of God and his power.

Yet, many art sites and even Wikipedia, name the title as "Creation of ADAM". So, which is it? The above image depicts how the painting now appears on the ceiling of the Sistine Chapel. So what is the problem, you ask? Well, I immediately noticed how God's hand was now lower than Adam's and also how it is smaller. The original discussion in college was that God was positioned higher than man because he is in heaven and we are on earth.

The direction of God's hand was on a diagonal, reaching down to touch man's hand. The fact that God's hand was larger indicated that God was more powerful than man. But now, for some reason, none of that discussion can be found anywhere on the internet.

Now, the fact that man's hand is higher than God's and that Adam's hand is now larger than God's, plays into the narrative of the lowering and denigration of God and His character, a minimization of God and his power.

I created the following art piece to depict the way the Creation of Man by Michelangelo used to look and the way that I remember it to be.

Discussions around this in college told how God's hand is bigger than man's, to show God's supremacy. The idea that He was coming from above and reaching down to man also showed his Diety.

Here is some residual found in tattoos:

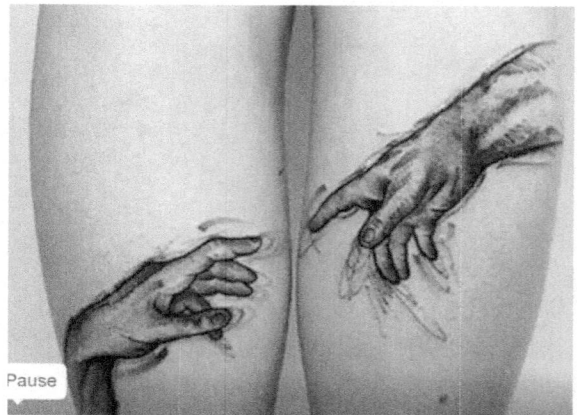

Pause

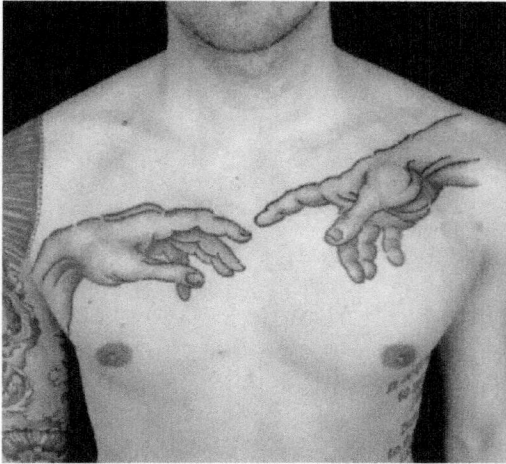

Rodin's *The Thinker* statue has been changed several times incrementally. It used to be that his hand was on his head, then it changed to his chin with a closed fist with his right hand on his right knee. Then it switched to the current totally awkward position of his right hand on his left knee. There have also been flip-flops in which they change, then change back. This has occurred with Tidy Cats/Cat, the movie line Houston-We/We've have a problem and the Flin(t)stones.

Getting on to the Bible

I found out about the cultural Mandela Effects before the Bible, and while they are indeed compelling, the changes to the Bible had a profound effect on me. My thought was that if God allowed this to happen to the scriptures, then that is very, very serious. The whole of Christendom would be impacted and not in a good way.

Because the name of Chic-Fil-A has been changed to Chick-Fil-A, you may think – no big deal. It's just one letter. In movies, it's just one word. That doesn't hurt anybody.

The fact of the matter is, being able to change anything in our reality is MONUMENTALLY HUGE. Just try to wrap your mind around how one day the

Bible can say "trespasses" in the Lord's Prayer, and the next day, that Bible sitting on your table now says "debts" in its place.

> *If they can change one thing – they can change EVERYTHING.*

When we look at all the things that have been changed, the object that has incurred the most changes has been the Bible. Thousands of words have been eliminated and switched and the grammar is horrendous. This is a criminal case, and to find the perpetrator, we can look to motive. There seems to be no apparent motive in changing minor spellings in the titles of company names. But when it comes to the Bible, there is plenty of motive that points to the culprit. Who else would want to change the Bible, except the hater of God – Satan himself?

There are those who think that God is making the changes, but if that is true, why would God defile His own Bible by denigrating himself and inserting foul language and connotations?

Many of the Mandela Effects are innocuous in nature, however many more are negative and actually put God and Jesus in a much lower position. For example, the language being used to describe Jesus has sexual undertones, even implying transgenderism. Is that coincidental considering the state of the world in which transgenderism and perversity is being pushed so hard that everyone is literally traumatized? I can't look at a picture of two men being close together without thinking they are about to kiss each other, due to seeing it all over the media now. I never would have thought that just ten years ago. In fact, it was taboo to show gay interactions up until recently. When the movie Brokeback Mountain surfaced in 2005 it was shocking to everyone. So now Jesus is being depicted pejoratively whenever the scriptures can be twisted to do so.

Chapter 3

The Denigration of God and Jesus in the Bible

"Wherever there is degeneration and apathy, there also is sexual perversion, cold depravity, miscarriage, premature old age, grumbling youth, there is a decline in the arts, indifference to science, and injustice in all its forms."
-Anton Chekhov

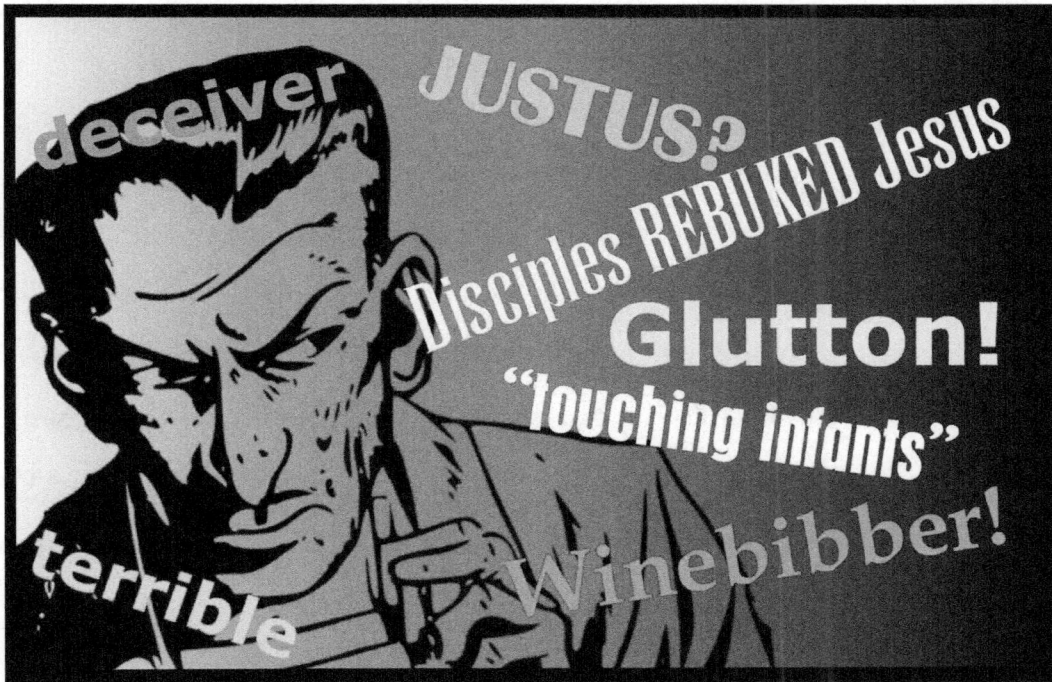

Since the supernatural Quantum Bible Changes started several years ago, we've noticed that grammar errors are all over the place, and that Jesus' and God's names and pronouns are not capitalized like they used to be. Word switches have occurred, with obscure Old English terms that mean the same, but sound foreign. But does that really matter? If a word still means the same, then what is the purpose behind these Bible changes?

That's very simple. The Bible is being rewritten to lay the foundation for the upcoming One World Religion. Jesus will be shown to NOT be the Saviour, at least the Jesus that was written about in the Bible.

Muslims believe that Jesus was a prophet, not the Son of God. According to the way the Bible is being rewritten, this will be shown to be the case and the Antichrist will be heralded in as the REAL MESSIAH. The Jews are also awaiting Jesus first return, so the Word of God for Christians to go along with it.

Christians are Satan's ultimate target, so what better way to get them on board to accept the Mark of the Beast, than to back up the New World Order One Religion's philosophy with the Bible?

These changes are happening to make the Bible appeal to the Luciferians dream and goal for a One World Religion, in which everyone – Christians, Muslims, Buddhists, will be part of. In order to appeal to these different sects, there must be substantiation in The following verses show that the character of Jesus/God is being downgraded and portrayed as less than holy, with the purpose of showing that He is NOT the Son of God. If Jesus/God is not the holy, supreme being, then WHO IS?

Lucifer could step into that spot easily if it is shown that Jesus is not the holy Supreme being, the Creator of the world. We know that Luciferian satanic worship is rampant in today's world.

I have spoken to a couple of ministers who do not believe the Bible has been changed, but attribute it to my remembering "different versions". Perhaps it's them who remember "different versions" because I have been reading the same King James Bible for 40 years. It appears that the deception is working just great, as even Christian ministers have not caught onto it.

Changed Scriptures Denigrate God and Jesus

Revelation 3:14
And unto the angel of the church of the Laodiceans write; These things saith the Amen, the faithful and true witness, the beginning of the **creation of God;**
This implies someone created God.

Isaiah 45:14
… and they shall fall down unto thee, they shall make supplication unto thee, saying, Surely God is in thee; and there is none else, **there is no God.**
It used to read "there is no other God"

GOD HAS A FATHER?
Revelation 1:6
And hath made us kings and priests unto God and **his Father;** to him be glory and dominion for ever and ever. Amen.

It used to be: God the Father

GOD'S NAME IS JEALOUS?

Exodus 34:14

For thou shalt worship no other god: for the Lord, **whose name is Jealous,** is a jealous God: (*It never said that God's name was Jealous!*)

JESUS WASN'T RAISED FROM THE DEAD?

1 Corinthians 15:15

Yea, and we are found false witnesses of God; because we have testified of God that he raised up Christ: **whom he raised not up,** if so be that the dead rise not.

God did not raise up Christ? He is not capitalized.

JESUS IS THE FIRST BEGOTTEN OF THE DEAD?

Rev 1:5

And from Jesus Christ, who is the faithful witness, and **the first begotten of the dead,** and the prince of the kings of the earth. Unto him that loved us, and washed us from our sins in his own blood,

It used to be: Jesus is the firstfruit of the resurrection.

JESUS DOES NOT CARE FOR MEN?

Mark 12:14

And when they were come, they say unto him, Master, we know that thou art true, and **carest for no man:**

Matthew 22:16

And they sent out unto him their disciples with the Herodians, saying, Master, we know that thou art true, and teachest the way of God in truth, **neither carest thou for any man: for thou regardest not the person of men.**

JESUS DESCENDED FROM JUDAS?

Matthew 1:2

Abraham begat Isaac; and Isaac begat Jacob; and Jacob begat **Judas** and his brethren;

Yet on Bible.com, it still says Judah:

Search results for: *matthew 1:2*

Bible	King James Version (KJV)	▾
Users		
Plans	Matthew 1:2 (KJV)	
	Abraham begat Isaac; and Isaac begat Jacob; and Jacob begat Judah and his brethren;	

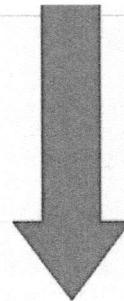

Matthew 1:3

Search results for: *matthew 1:;3*

Bible

Users

Plans

King James Version (KJV)   ▾

Matthew 1:3 (KJV)

And Judah begat Phares and Zara of Thamar; and Phares begat Esrom; and Esrom begat Aram;

Matthew 3:1 (KJV)

In those days came John the Baptist, preaching in the wilderness of Judaea,

And Judas begat Phares and Zara of Thamar; and Phares begat Esrom; and Esrom begat Aram; Yet on Bible.com, it still says Judah.

JESUS IS A PEDOPHILE AND HIS DISCIPLES HAD TO KEEP HIM IN CHECK?

Luke 18:15- And they brought unto him also **infants, that he would touch them:** but when his **disciples saw it, they rebuked them.**

Matthew 19:14 - But Jesus said, **Suffer little children,** and forbid them not, to come unto me: for of such is the kingdom of heaven.

It should read: Suffer the little children

JESUS IS A PERVERT ?

Luke 23:14

… Ye have brought this man unto me, as one that **perverteth the people**: and, behold, I, having examined him before you, have found no fault in this man **touching those things whereof ye accuse him:**

(The real meaning for touching those things is more like "pertaining to") Here is the Greek definition of the phrase "touching those things": The Greek definition is a pronoun "which, or who" not a VERB: TOUCHING! How could the translators be so OFF?

JESUS IS A GLUTTON AND A WINEBIBBER?

Matthew 11:19

The Son of man came eating and drinking, and they say, Behold **a man gluttonous, and a winebibber,** a friend of publicans and sinners.

Psalm 78:65

65 Then the Lord awaked as one out of sleep, and like a mighty man that **shouteth by reason of wine.**

Awaked? What kind of English is that?

Acts 17:30

And the times of this ignorance **God winked at;** but now commandeth all men every where to repent:

Someone who winks their eye is planning ·evil , perverse things

Jer 4:10

Then said I, Ah, Lord GOD! **surely thou hast greatly deceived this people and Jerusalem,** saying, Ye shall have peace; whereas the sword reacheth unto the soul.

JESUS IS NAMED JUSTUS?

Colossians 4:11

And Jesus, which is called Justus, who are of the circumcision.

Not only is Jesus NOT called Justus, the grammar is wrong. WHO ARE refers to TWO or MORE people.

JESUS IS "VERY CHRIST"?

Acts 9:22

But Saul increased the more in strength, and confounded the Jews which dwelt at Damascus, proving that **this is very Christ.**

Used to be : indeed the Christ

The sentence makes no sense now. Very Christ? Maybe "very Christlike" would make sense, but not this.

THIEF ON THE CROSS REVILED JESUS?

Mark 15:

32 Let Christ the King of Israel descend now from the cross, that we may see and believe. And **they that were crucified with him reviled him.**

What about the thief hanging next to Jesus, whom Jesus granted eternal life? Did he also revile him, as this passage says?

JESUS IS A MURDERER?

Luke 19:27

27 But those mine enemies, which would not that I should reign over them, bring hither, and **slay them before me.**

JESUS IS TERRIBLE?

Psalm 47:Too

For **the Lord most high is terrible;** he is a great King over all the earth.

GOD DOES NOT FORGIVE YOUR SINS?

Joshua 24:19

And Joshua said unto the people, Ye cannot serve the Lord: for he is an holy God; he is a jealous God; **he will not forgive your transgressions nor your sins.**

MESSIAS INSTEAD OF MESSIAH

John 1:41

He first findeth his own brother Simon, and saith unto him, We have found the **Messias,** which is, being interpreted, the Christ.

John 4:25

The woman saith unto him, I know that **Messias** cometh, which is called Christ: when he is come, he will tell us all things.

The words him and he should be capitalized since it is referring to Christ.

Messias is a misspelling. Should be Messiahs. The Old Testament (and New Testament) never taught the idea of messiahs plural. It only pointed to one Messiah.

GOD DOES NOT RESPECT PEOPLE

Colossians 3:25

But he that doeth wrong shall receive for the wrong which he hath done: and **there is no respect of persons.**

2 Corinthians 11:4 (KJV)

4 For if he that cometh preacheth another Jesus, whom we have not preached, or if ye receive another spirit, which ye have not received, or another gospel, which ye have not accepted, ye might well bear with him.

Let's simplify this sentence for clarity sake.

"For if he that cometh preacheth another Jesus... ye might well bear with him."

Knowing that verses are changed in this disturbing fashion we can see that Jesus the Messiah is being questioned. Also, another Jesus is to be followed. Perfect setup for the antichrist.

To make matters worse we now find the scriptures saying that **Jacob begat Judas!**

Matthew 1:2

Abraham begat Isaac; and Isaac begat Jacob; and Jacob begat **Judas** and his brethren;

3 And **Judas** begat Phares and Zara of Thamar; and Phares begat Esrom; and Esrom begat Aram;

There is so much wrong with this change. The name Judas has become synonymous with high treason. It goes without saying that Jesus is/was no traitor!

The bloodline of Jesus matters. He is the Lion of the tribe of Judah, not Judas! He is also the Root of David.

Revelation 5:5

And one of the elders saith unto me, Weep not: behold, the Lion of the tribe of Judah, the **Root of David**, hath prevailed to open the book, and to loose the seven seals thereof.

If Matthew 1:2-3 is correct then Jesus is not from the tribe of Judah. This would make God a liar, and we know that God cannot lie.

So far we have seen that the Bible corruptions have called into question Jesus' claim to be the one and only Messiah, and also His lineage. This perversion not only says that Jesus is not from the tribe of Judah, but is not the Root of David.

Hebrews 3:1

Wherefore, holy brethren, partakers of the heavenly calling, consider the **Apostle** and High Priest of our **profession,** Christ Jesus;

This verse used to say Lord instead of Apostle, and confession instead of profession. Profession is a Catholic ritual. Below is an excerpt from the:

CATHOLIC PROFESSION OF FAITH

With firm faith, I also believe everything contained in the word of God, whether written or handed down in Tradition, which the Church, either by a solemn judgment or by the ordinary and universal Magisterium, sets forth to be believed as divinely revealed.

I also firmly accept and hold each and everything definitively proposed by the Church regarding teaching on faith and morals.

Moreover, I adhere with religious submission of will and intellect to the teachings which either the Roman Pontiff or the College of Bishops enunciate when they exercise their authentic Magisterium, even if they do not intend to proclaim these teachings by a definitive act.

Can you imagine Jacob, the son of Isaac declaring that the house of God, and the gate of heaven is dreadful? He didn't! But, your Bibles now say that he did.

Genesis 28:17

And he was afraid, and said, How **dreadful** is this place! this is none other but the house of God, and this is the gate of heaven. Dreadful should be **awesome**, and the word **this** should be capitalized since it begins a new sentence.Likewise, can you imagine the prophet Jeremiah calling the Lord a deceiver? Of course not! He does now:

Jeremiah 4:10

Then said I, Ah, Lord God! surely thou hast greatly **deceived** this people and Jerusalem, saying, Ye shall have peace; whereas the sword reacheth unto the soul. And,

Jeremiah 20:7

O Lord, thou hast deceived me, and I was **deceived**; **thou** art stronger than I, and hast prevailed: I am in derision daily, every one mocketh me.

This also suggests that Jeremiah was a false prophet deceived by God. Thou should be capitalized since it is referring to the Lord God. Also the words **every one** should be one word – **everyone**.

Let's take a look at verses that now say that God is dreadful. First let us note that dreadful is used in other verses correctly, and it means terrible, or horrible. The prophet Daniel speaking of the beast:

Daniel 7:7

After this I saw in the night visions, and behold a fourth beast, **dreadful** and terrible…

So, we know that the editors of the Bible, and Daniel knew what the word dreadful meant. Can you just imagine the prophet Daniel calling the Lord dreadful? Here we go:

Daniel 9:4 (KJV)

And I prayed unto the Lord my God, and made my confession, and said, O Lord, the great and **dreadful** God, keeping the covenant and mercy to them that love him, and to them that keep his commandments;

Dreadful was, and should be **awesome**. The words him and his should be capitalized since he is referring to God.

Next we have king David calling the Lord terrible!

Psalm 47:2

2 For the Lord most high is **terrible;** he is a great King over all the earth.

Terrible should be **awesome**, and the word **he** should be capitalized.

Another,

Psalm 66:3

Say unto God, How **terrible** art thou in thy works! through the greatness of thy power shall thine enemies submit themselves unto thee.

Terrible should be **awesome**, and the word **through** should be capitalized.

One more,

Psalm 99:3

Let them praise thy great and **terrible** name; for it is holy.

Terrible should be **awesome**, and the word **thy** should be capitalized.

It is not just in Psalms where the scriptures now say God is terrible, Isaiah;

Isaiah 64:3

When thou didst **terrible** things which we looked not for, thou camest down, the mountains flowed down at thy presence.

Terrible should be **awesome**, and the words **thou** and **thy** should be capitalized.

Unfortunately most Catholics and Christians likewise do not verify what they are taught in churches and cults by comparing and confirming these things in scripture. We know from history that this gullibility is very deadly. It will be even more so during the Tribulation. Ignorance is not just deadly in the physical, but especially in the spiritual realm.

As we shall see the Bible has been changed to read that there is no God. Only the corrupt heart of a strident fool would believe such absurdities. But, believe they will.

Scriptures now Say – Christ will NOT Defeat Satan!

Due to the satanic Mandela Effect, your Bibles now say that Jesus will not defeat Satan and his kingdom. This is a scriptural change of great significance. It is not only an abomination, but a brazen evil lie!

Unfortunately, many Christian leaders and scholars today would not be moved much (if at all) by these malevolent changes. Their passions and allegiances lie elsewhere. No longer are they interested in such inconvenient things as truth, scriptural integrity, or resisting the enemy.

Many of them teach and speak directly against God's laws, precepts, covenants, truths and doctrines. Just think of the absurdity of it – Christians against Christ! That is exactly what it has come down to.

We have already seen how scriptures now declare that there are multiple messiahs, and to follow them instead: And,

2 Corinthians 11:4

For if he that cometh preacheth another Jesus, whom we have not preached, or if ye receive another spirit, which ye have not received, or another gospel, which ye have not accepted, ye might well bear with him.

If this doesn't grieve your spirit I just don't know what will. Let's move on and take a look at the subject of this article. Genesis 3:15 is the first universally recognized messianic prophecy in the Old Testament. Originally it predicted that the head of the serpent would be crushed by Messiah. That old serpent (Satan) would be destroyed. Not anymore!

Genesis 3:15

And I will put enmity between thee and the woman, and between thy seed and her seed; **it** shall **bruise thy head**, and thou shalt bruise **his** heel.

53

So, now the verse calls Jesus "it" and does not capitalize the word his. Jesus is not an IT… ever! The scholars who wrote the King James would never have referred to Jesus as it.

This is also very similar to a corrupted verse in Luke 1:35 referring to the Christ child as a holy thing.

Luke 1:35

And the angel answered and said unto her, The Holy Ghost shall come upon thee, and the power of the Highest shall overshadow thee: therefore also that **holy thing** which shall be born of thee shall be called the Son of God.

Do you see the pattern of denigrating Jesus, the Creator of the heavens and the universe? I have written about these changes and many more in greater detail in previous articles.

As many of you know, along with these supernatural verse changes are grammatical and punctuation errors. This instance is no exception.

Next, the second corruption we have in the New Testament denying that Jesus will defeat Satan:

Romans 16:20 (KJV)

And the God of peace shall **bruise** Satan under your feet shortly. The grace of our Lord Jesus Christ be with you. Amen.

Let us get back to the main subject of the unquestionable victory of Christ over Satan. Genesis 1:15 and Romans 16:20 have been deliberately altered to state that Jesus only bruises the head of the serpent, not crushes. These are two entirely different things. One is to wound, and the other is to destroy.

Chapter 4

Transgenderism in the Bible

If you look back today over the last 25 years, it is a fact that we have had a progressive degeneration of our intelligence community in general; in particular in the field of human intelligence. -Paul Bremer

1 Corinthians 6:9

Know ye not that the unrighteous shall not inherit — — — the kingdom of God? Be not deceived: neither fornicators, nor idolaters, nor adulterers, nor effeminate, nor abusers of themselves with mankind,

Used to be: homosexuals . Effeminate just means more womanly qualities

One huge problem with some of the Bible changes is the transgendering of the Bible. Men with breasts full of milk that nurse babies, and men sleeping together are now described in the Bible.

The Bible is very clear on God's stance on homosexuality as demonstrated with his destruction of Sodom and Gomorrah. This article is not meant to disparage homosexual or transexual people, as all of us have various sins in our lives. If we come to God through Jesus Christ and confess our sins and turn from our ways, God will hear and heal us.

> *Leviticus 18:22*
>
> *Thou shalt not lie with mankind, as with womankind: it is abomination.*

There is a monumental push to not only normalize homosexuality and transgenderism, but to encourage and promote it. This accomplishes several goals for Satan:

➤ to pervert God's creation of man and woman's natural procreation ability

➤ destroy the family unit

➤ cause men and women to commit sexual sin

When there is a strong family unit, people are more self-reliant, and less apt to depend on government assistance, and be more self sufficient. This is antithetical to the New World Order. Also, Satan just loves to destroy God's creation in any way he can.

The following scriptures point out how the Bible is now replete with absurd descriptions of men having breasts that nurse (lactate) and even Jesus as having breasts, which supports transgenderism.

Luke 17:34

I tell you, in that night there ————-shall be **two men in one bed;** the one shall be taken, and the other shall be left.

(The Greek does NOT say "men", just "two in one bed"!

Luke 17:35

Two women shall be grinding together; the one shall be taken, and the other left.

James 2:3

And ye have respect to him that **weareth the gay clothing.**

Job 21:24

His breasts are full of milk, and his — —–bones are moistened with marrow.

Numbers 11:12

Have I conceived all this people? have I begotten them, that thou shouldest say unto me, Carry them in thy bosom, as **a nursing father beareth the sucking child,** unto the land which thou swarest unto their fathers?

Isaiah 49:23

And kings shall be thy **nursing fathers,** and their queens thy nursing mothers:

Isaiah 60:16

Thou shalt also suck the milk of the Gentiles, and — — —– **shalt suck the breast of kings:**

Luke 17: 26-30

26 And as it was in the days of **Noe,** they did eat, they drank, they married wives, **they were given in marriage,** until the day that Noah entered into the ark, and the flood came, and destroyed them all.

28 Likewise also as it was in the days of Lot; they did eat, they drank, they bought, they sold, they planted, they **builded;**

29 But the same day that Lot went out of Sodom it rained fire and brimstone from heaven, and destroyed them all.

30 Even thus shall it be in the day when the Son of man is revealed.

Should be: Noah, they gave and were given in marriage, built, comes again

Jesus Portrayed as Having Breasts and Wearing a Girdle

Is Jesus transgendered in the Bible now?

Revelation 1:13

And in the midst of the seven candlesticks one like unto the Son of man, clothed with a garment down to the foot, and **girt about the paps with a golden girdle.**

As we can see in the only other 2 Bible texts mentioning "paps" they are both describing women's breasts:

The Greek word is **mastos**, from which mammograms and mammary glands, which refers to women's breasts, is derived. Moreover, even if the word derivation means a man's nipple, the Bible usage is wrong, as men's nipples don't emit milk, so can't be **"sucked".**

Revelation 15:6
And the seven angels came out of the temple, having the seven plagues, clothed in pure and white linen, and having **their breasts girded with golden girdles.**

Luke 11:27

And it came to pass, as he spake these things, a certain woman of the company lifted up her voice, and —————said unto him, Blessed *is* the womb that bare thee, and the **paps which thou hast sucked.**

Luke 23:29

For, behold, the days are coming, in the ————-which they shall say, Blessed *are* the barren, and the wombs that never bare, and **the paps which never gave suck.**

Job 21:24

His breasts are full of milk, and his bones are moistened with marrow.

Numbers 11:12

Have I conceived all this people? have I begotten them, that thou shouldest say unto me, Carry them in thy bosom, as a nursing father beareth the sucking child, unto the land which thou swarest unto their fathers?

Isaiah 49:23

And kings shall be **thy nursing fathers,** and their queens thy nursing mothers:

GENDER Now in the Bible
 Curiously, now we have the word "gender" in the Bible, making the sentences sound nonsensical:

Leviticus 19:19

Ye shall keep my statutes. Thou shalt not let thy cattle **gender** with a diverse kind: thou shalt not sow thy field with mingled seed: neither shall a garment mingled of linen and woollen come upon thee.

Job 21:10

Their bull **gendereth**, and faileth not; their cow calveth, and casteth not her calf.

Job 38:29

Out of whose womb came the ice? and the hoary frost of heaven, who hath **gendered** it?

Galatians 4:24

Which things are an allegory: for these are the two covenants; the one from the mount Sinai, which **gendereth** to bondage, which is Agar.

2 Timothy 2:23

But foolish and unlearned questions avoid, knowing that they do **gender** strifes.

Used to be: **generate**

Sexually Suggestive Language

Mark 15:43

Joseph of Arimathaea, **an honourable counsellor,** which also waited for the kingdom———— of God, came, and went in boldly unto Pilate, and **craved the body of Jesus.**

Used to be: a member of the Sanhedrin, asked for Jesus' body

John 5:7

The **impotent man** answered him, Sir, **I have no man,** when——— the water is troubled, to put me into the pool: but while **I am coming,** another steppeth down before me.

Used to be: **lame, I am going**

James 2:3

And ye have respect to him that **weareth the gay clothing**

It should be: fine clothing

Exodus 28:40

And for Aaron's sons thou shalt make coats, and thou shalt make for them **girdles, and bonnets** shalt thou make for them, for glory and for beauty.

Exodus 29:9

And thou shalt gird them with **girdles,** Aaron and his sons, and put the **bonnets** on them

Mark 6:8

And commanded them that they should take nothing for their journey, save a staff only; no scrip, no bread, no money in their **purse:**

Deuteronomy 22:30

A man shall not take his father's wife, nor discover **his father's skirt.**

Deuteronomy 27:20

Cursed be he that lieth with his father's wife; because he uncovereth his **father's skirt.**

Acts 22:25

And as they bound him with **thongs**, Paul said unto the centurion that stood by, Is it lawful for you to scourge a man that is a Roman, and uncondemned?

Acts 9:5

And he said, Who art thou, Lord? And the Lord said, I am Jesus whom thou persecutest: it is hard for thee to **kick against the pricks.**

Deuteronomy 23:1

He that is **wounded in the stones,** or hath **his privy member cut off,** shall not enter into the congregation of the Lord.

Isaiah 27:12

And it shall come to pass in that day, that the Lord shall **beat off** from the channel of the river unto the stream of Egypt, and ye shall be gathered one by one, O ye children of Israel.

The fact of the matter is we are rapidly sliding down the slippery slope. The gay movement slid into the TRANS movement, which will slide into:

➢ **Transgender**

➢ **Transgene – modification of your genes**

➢ **Transhumanism,** which is the ultimate goal of Luciferian doctrine.

By humans merging with machines, introducing nanobots into their bodies, and having their genetic codes altered along with a neural lace mesh encompassing their brain (connecting their brains to the AI god, superbrain internet connection to everyone in the world) The satanic religions will achieve what they believe is their *trans*formation into being *gods.*

Chapter 5

Various Bible Changes Due to Mandela Effect

The Mandela Effect is the greatest miraculous manifestation of power displayed since the parting of the Red Sea.

L et's begin with the most well known verse of the New Testament in the Bible, one in which I had memorized for 40 years and taught to my son. So I know what it said. And the sly, subtle devil has changed one very important word: **should**

John 3:16
For God so loved the world, that he gave his only begotten Son, that whosoever believeth in him <u>should</u> not perish, but have everlasting life.

That word "should" used to be "shall". When you go to law school you learn that the word **shall** means it is imperative, the way it is, and will happen. However, the word should is a *maybe* word. Should you go to the store? Maybe you should, if you need something, maybe you shouldn't if it is snowing out. Get my drift?

So the word should in this verse means, well- maybe you *should* have everlasting life, but you probably won't, as you are a sinner. It could be read that way!

Whilst John 3:16 is the most well known verse in the New Testament, it is not the most well known verse in the Bible, which is Genesis 1:1.

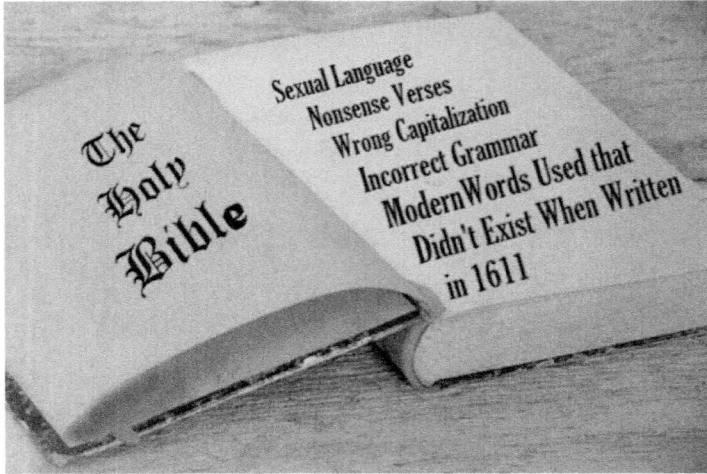

Genesis 1:1

In the beginning God created the **heaven** and the earth.

Here it is, Genesis 1:1, the most well known verse in the entire Bible, and what do you know it HAS been changed!

Heaven used to be heavens - plural. We know it was heavens plural before because the Bible teaches at least three heavens. It seems the only ones who don't understand this are the scoffers.

If you say it out loud with the new heaven singular, it doesn't roll off the tongue the way it used to. Heaven singular is not grammatically correct.

We also have the support of other scripture to attest to the fact that the Mandela Effect has changed this verse from heavens to heaven. Take a look at these verses from Genesis chapter two:

Genesis 2:

1 Thus the **heavens** and the earth were finished, and all the host of them.

4 These are the generations of the **heavens** and of the earth when they were created, in the day that the LORD God made the earth and the **heavens,**

And,

1 Chronicles 16:26

For all the gods of the people are idols: but the LORD made the **heavens.**

And,

Psalms 19:1

(To the chief Musician, A Psalm of David.) The **heavens** declare the glory of God; and the firmament sheweth his handywork. (It used to be spelled "handiwork.)

And,

Psalms 33:6

By the word of the LORD were the **heavens** made; and all the host of them by the breath of his mouth.

The Lord's Supper Painting by DaVinci

Not only is the Holy Grail missing, the glasses used to drink from. appear to be modern day glassware. In Jesus' day they would have been earthen.

Let's try an experiment with a very, very well known passage. Please fill in the blanks in this verse. (don't feel bad if you can't)

1 Peter 4:8

8 And above all things have fervent _____ among yourselves: for _____ shall cover a multitude of sins.

Did you fill in the blanks with the word love? That is the correct answer that we (long time Christians) all know and remember. This is how it reads today:

1 Peter 4:8 (KJV)

8 And above all things have fervent charity among yourselves: for charity shall cover the multitude of sins.

I have never met anyone who remembers "charity shall cover the multitude of sins". The scoffers will even give you the same correct quote from memory. But, when shown the Bible corruption they will say that it has always read charity in that verse, even though

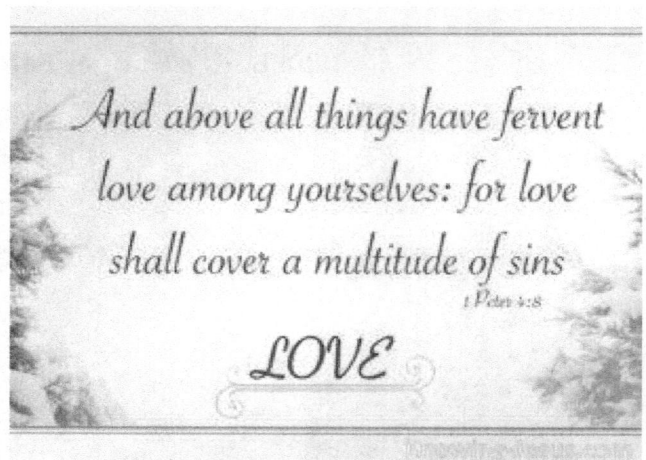

And above all things have fervent love among yourselves: for love shall cover a multitude of sins
1 Peter 4:8

LOVE

they just got done quoting the correct verse – Astounding!

They will ever so predictably explain that people have just been accustomed to saying love instead of charity. They'll even give an anecdotal story to support their claim. They'll tell you that somebody hundreds of years ago said love instead of charity and it spread and stuck to this day. No really, that's what they say!

This verse has been read aloud to church goers hundreds of millions of times through the centuries by pastors, ministers, and teachers and no one ever thought to correct it?

Preposterous! These are the levels that the scoffers stoop to.

There is a pattern of changing out love for charity in well known verses. The Apostle Paul's very famous "Way of Love" is completely gutted. Sorry scoffers, but this is a very well known passage. The title above 1 Corinthians 13:13 says "The Way of Love" It is correct there, but not in the chapter. It now reads:

1 Corinthians 13:1-2

Though I speak with the tongues of men and of angels, and have not charity, I am become as sounding brass, or a tinkling cymbal. And though I have the gift of prophecy, and understand all mysteries, and all knowledge; and though I have all faith, so that I could remove mountains, and have not charity, I am nothing.

1 Corinthians 16:15

I beseech you, brethren, (ye know the house of Stephanas, it is the firstfruits of Achaia, and that they have **addicted** themselves to the ministry of the saints,)

Used to be: first converts of Asia, devoted

Acts 12:4

And when he had apprehended him, he put him in prison, and delivered him to four **quaternions** of soldiers to keep him; intending after **Easter** to bring him forth to the people.

It used to be **Passover**

Origin of Easter – Its Pagan Roots

The origin of Easter dates back to ancient times, not long after the global Flood recorded in Genesis 6-9 of the Bible. Nimrod, a grandson of Noah, had turned from following his grandfather's God and had become a tyrannical ruler. According to the biblical record, as king, Nimrod created Babel, Ninevah, Asshur, Calla and other cities, all known for lifestyles that promoted unspeakable evil and perversion.

When Nimrod died, his wife, Queen Semiramis, deified him as the Sun-god, or Life Giver. Later he would become known as Baal, and those who followed the religion Semiramis created in his name would be called Baal worshippers. They became associated with idolatry, demon worship, human sacrifice and other practices regarded as evil.The origin of Easter involves the birth of Semiramis' illegitimate son, Tammuz. Somehow, Semiramis convinced the people that Tammuz was actually Nimrod reborn.

Since people had been looking for the promised savior since the beginning of mankind (see Genesis 3:15), they were persuaded by Semiramis to believe that Tammuz was that savior, even that he had been supernaturally conceived. Before long, in addition to worshiping Tammuz (or Nimrod reborn), the people also worshiped Semiramis herself as the goddess of fertility. In other cultures, she has been called Ishtar, Ashtur and yes, Easter."

2 Corinthians 6:15

And what **concord** hath Christ with Belial? or what part hath he that believeth with an **infidel?**

Used to be: harmony, unbeliever

Eat the Passover?

Mark 14:12

And the first day of unleavened bread, when **they killed the passover**, his disciples said unto him, Where wilt thou that we go and prepare that thou mayest eat the passover?

Matthew 26:17

Now the first day of the feast of unleavened bread the disciples came to Jesus, saying unto him, Where wilt thou that we prepare for thee to **eat the passover?**

Check out another Bible version:

On the first day of sweet bread the disciples came to Jesus, saying to him, Where would you have us prepare for you to eat the **Passover lamb?**

Exodus 12:21

Then Moses called for all the elders of Israel, and said unto them, Draw out and take you a lamb according to your families, and **kill the passover.**

Job 19:23 (KJV) Oh that my words were now written! oh that they were **printed in a book**!

Was **written on a scroll**.

Note: Johannes Gutenberg was the inventor of the printing press. Indeed, the German goldsmith's 15th-century contribution to the technology was revolutionary — enabling the mass production of books and the rapid dissemination of knowledge throughout Europe.

Job was written over 3,000 years ago. There were no printed books.

1 Corinthians 15:33

Be not deceived: evil **communications** corrupt good manners.

Used to be: **company**

Song of Solomon 2:12

The flowers appear on the earth; the time of the singing of birds is come, and the **voice of the turtle** is heard in our land;

Should be: turtledove

Song of Solomon 5:8

I charge you, O daughters of Jerusalem, if ye find my beloved, that ye tell him, that **I am sick of love.**

Used to be: **lovesick**

Leviticus 12:8

And if she be not able to bring a lamb, then she shall bring **two turtles,** or two —— —young pigeons; the one for the burnt offering,and the other for a sin offering: and the priest shall make an atonement for her, and she shall be clean.

Should be: **turtledove**

2 Kings 22:14

So Hilkiah the priest, and Ahikam, and Achbor, and Shaphan, and Asahiah, went unto Huldah the prophetess, the wife of Shallum the son of Tikvah, the son of Harhas, keeper of the wardrobe; (now she dwelt in Jerusalem in the **college;**) and they communed with her.

College? Followed by a winky face emoji.

Romans 5:7

For scarcely for a righteous man will—— —- one die: yet **peradventure** for a good man some would even dare to die.

Used to be: **perhaps**

2 Corinthians 11:8

I **robbed** other churches, taking wages of them, to do you service.

Used to be: **taken from**

Genesis 32:24

And Jacob was left alone; and there wrestled a **man** with him until the breaking of the day.

(Jacob wrestled with an **angel** all night.)

Genesis 31:8

If he said thus, The speckled shall be thy wages; then all the cattle bare speckled: and if he said thus, The **ringstraked** shall be thy hire; then bare all the cattle **ringstraked.**

Used to be: **striped**

Genesis 34:12

 Ask me never so much dowry and gift, and I will give according as ye shall say unto me: but give me the **damsel to wife.**

To wife is a noun describing a woman, so the phrase "to wife" implying a noun, is a total misinterpretation of scripture, as the Hebrew says it is a noun.

Daniel 8:7

 And I saw him come close unto the ram, and he was moved with **choler** against him, and smote the ram, and brake his two horns:

Used to be: **anger**

14 And **the Lord repented of the evil** which he thought to do unto his people.

Wrong: God has no evil in Him.

Matthew 27:9

 Then was fulfilled that which was spoken by **Jeremy** the prophet, saying,

Should be: **Jeremiah**

Matthew 4:10

Then saith Jesus unto him, Get thee **hence,** Satan: for it is --------------written, Thou shalt worship the Lord thy God, and him only shalt thou serve

Used to be: **behind me**

Mark 2:22

And no man putteth new wine into old **bottles:** else the new wine doth burst the bottles, and the wine is spilled, and the bottles will be marred: but new wine must be put into new bottles.

Used to be: **wineskins**

Mark 13:10

And the gospel must first be **published** among all nations.

Used to be: **preached**

Matthew 18:20

For where **two or three** are gathered together in my name, there am I in the midst of them.

Used to be: **two or more**

Deu 12:20

When the LORD thy God shall enlarge thy border, as he hath promised ---------thee, and thou shalt say, **I will eat flesh, because thy soul longeth to eat flesh; thou mayest--------- eat flesh, whatsoever thy soul lusteth after.**

Used to be: **meat,** now it is promoting cannibalism

Exodus 7:10

And Moses and Aaron went in unto Pharaoh, and they did so as the Lord had commanded: and **Aaron** cast down his rod before Pharaoh, and before his servants, and it became a serpent.

It used to be **Moses** who cast down his staff.

Genesis 8:11

And the dove came in to him in the evening; and, lo, in her mouth was an **olive leaf plucktoff**: so Noah knew that the waters were abated from off the earth.

Plucktoff? It used to be **OLIVE BRANCH.** That's where the phrase came from, to extend an olive branch to someone.

Exodus 12-

23 For the Lord will pass through to smite the Egyptians; and when he seeth the blood upon the lintel, and on the two side posts, the **Lord** will pass over the door, and will not suffer the destroyer to come in unto your houses to smite you.

Used to say: **angel of death**

Sampson and Delilah

Sampson's name is now spelled "Samson". Samson and Delilah is one of the most well-known stories of the Bible. Now, due to the Quantum Mandela Effect, this iconic story has been changed. Many of the Bible changes appear to have no real purpose, as this one appears to be. The story used to say that **Delilah cut Sampson's hair off** while he was sleeping.

Now it reads this way, in Judges 16:

SAMSON AND DELILAH
MANDELA EFFECT

18 And when Delilah saw that he had told her all his heart, she sent and called for the lords of the Philistines, saying, Come up this once, for he hath shewed me all his heart. Then the lords of the Philistines came up unto her, and brought money in their hand.

19 And she made him sleep upon her knees; and **she called for a man, and she caused him to shave off the seven locks of his head**; and she began to afflict him, and his strength went from him.

The Golden Rule is Gone

Matthew 7:12-Therefore all things whatsoever ye would that men should do to you, do ye even so to them: for this is the law and the prophets.

golden rule

Dictionary

Search for a word

gold·en rule
/ˌgōldən ˈro͞ol/

noun

a basic principle that should always be followed to ensure success in general or in a particular activity.
"one of the golden rules in this class is punctuality"
• the biblical rule of "do unto others as you would have them do unto you" (Matt. 7:12).

Translations, word origin, and more definitions

Feedback

Luke 6:31

And as ye would that men should do to you, do ye also to them likewise.

This is the closest verse that comes to the Golden Rule in the Bible now.

Fairy Tales and Fables

The Bible is now being presented as a book of fables. As seen in this meme, words that are specific to fairy tales have been inserted into the King James Bible via the Quantum Mandela Effect changes. These words are now in the Bible, whereas they weren't, before the supernatural Bible changes:

palaces

damsel

goodly

goodliest

castle

dukes

sirs

prince

princess

royal

kings

damsel

menservants

butler

carrraige

glittering spear

magnifical

minstral

witchcraft

witch

wellfavoured

besom (witch's broom)

hemlock

mandrake

wizard

dungeon

raven

cockatrice

satyr

chamberlain

caldron

satyrs

dragons (34 times)

ravens

pheonix

unicorns

castle

Philemon 1:20

Yea, brother, let me have joy of thee in the Lord: refresh my **bowels in the Lord**.
Used to be: **heart in Christ**

Hebrews 11:34

Quenched the violence of fire, escaped the edge of the sword, out of weakness

were made strong, waxed valiant in fight, turned to flight the **armies of the aliens.**

Used to be: **foreigners**

Hebrews 12:16

Lest there be any fornicator, or profane person, as Esau, who for one morsel of meat sold his birthright.

Used to be: **food**

Daniel is now a **president:**

Daniel 6:2

And over these three **presidents; of whom Daniel was first**:

Psalm 9:4

For thou hast maintained my right and my cause; thou **satest** in the throne judging right.

Used to be: **sat**

Exodus 3 :1-2

Now Moses kept the flock of Jethro his father in law, the priest of Midian: and he led the flock to the backside of the desert, and came to the mountain of God, even to Horeb.

2 And **the angel of the Lord** appeared unto him in a flame of fire out of the midst of a bush:

Used to be: **The voice of God**

Genesis 40:3

And he put them in ward in the house of the captain of the guard, into the **prison,** the place where Joseph was bound.

Used to be: **jail**

Luke 14:26

If any man come to me, and **hate not his father, and mother, and wife, and children,** and brethren, and sisters, yea, and his own life also, he cannot be my disciple.

If any man come to me, and hate not his father, and mother, and wife, and children, and brethren, and sisters, yea, and his own life also, he cannot be my disciple.

Used to be: If any man comes after me, and loves his father, mother, wife, children, brethren, even his own life **more than me,** he cannot be my disciple.

Leviticus 19:17

Thou shalt not **hate** thy brother in thine heart: thou shalt in any wise rebuke thy neighbour, and not suffer sin upon him.

1 John 2:9

He that saith he is in the light, and **hateth** his brother, is in darkness even until now.

1 John 3:15

Whosoever **hateth** his brother is a murderer: and ye know that no murderer hath eternal life abiding in him.

1 John 4:20

If a man say, I love God, and **hateth** his brother, he is a liar: for he that loveth not his brother whom he hath seen, how can he love God whom he hath not seen?

Matthew 14:8

And she, being before instructed of her mother, said, Give me here **John Baptist's** head in a **charger**.

It should be: **John the Baptist, on a platter**

Luke 5:24

But that ye may know that the Son of man hath power upon earth to forgive sins, (he said unto the **sick of the palsy,**) I say unto thee, Arise, and take up thy **couch**, and go into thine house.

It should be: **paralytic, mat**

John 7:1

After these things Jesus walked in Galilee: for he would not walk in **Jewry**, because the Jews sought to kill him.

1 Corinthians 16:15

I beseech you, brethren, (ye know the house of Stephanas, it is the **firstfruits of Achaia,** and that they have **addicted** themselves to the ministry of the saints,)

Used to be: **first converts of Asia, devoted**

Genesis 4:21

21 And his brother's name was Jubal: he was the father of all such as handle the harp and **organ**.

Organs were not invented yet. The correct word here is:**lyre.**

Isaiah 32:8

But the **liberal** deviseth **liberal** things; and by **liberal** things shall he stand.

Was: **noble.**

Genesis 7:4

For yet seven days, and I will cause it to rain upon the earth forty days and forty nights; and every living **substance** that I have made will I destroy from off the face of the earth.

Was: **thing**.

Psalm 75:10

All the **horns** of the wicked also will I cut off; but the **horns** of the righteous shall be exalted.

Was: **power**.

Jeremiah 14:9

9 Why shouldest thou be as a man **astonied**, as a mighty man that cannot save? yet thou, O Lord, art in the midst of us, and we are called by thy name; leave us not.

We know astonied is incorrect because the correct word should be and was astonished. We will see below that they got the spelling right in many other verses all through the Bible. This is not a case of that's how they spelled astonished back then.

As usual in these corruptions there are other problems as well. The word *yet* after the question mark should be capitalized as should the words *thou* and *thy* since they are referring to God.

Mark 10:26

And they were **astonished** out of measure, saying among themselves, Who then can be saved?

Matthew 1:5

And Salmon begat **Booz** of Rachab; and Booz begat Obed of Ruth; and Obed begat Jesse;

Booz used to be **Boaz.**

Now your Bibles Now Say the Apostle Paul Had Three Sons!

We all know that the apostle Paul had no children, and was not married. The scriptures now say that he had son's. At least three by name. We will be taking a close look at perverse scriptures which now insinuate that Paul had one son while he was in prison! If you don't know in your spirit that the apostle Paul had no sons outside of marriage, then there is a problem.

Paul wrote:

1 Corinthians 7:8

I say therefore to the unmarried and widows, it is good for them if they abide even as I.

Next we will delve into the deep corruption of the following verse changes which in part claims that **Paul had a son named Marcus.**

1 Peter 5:13

The church that is at Babylon, elected together with you, saluteth you; and so doth **Marcus my son.**

This passage used to read **Marcus my brother.** We have brothers and sisters in Christ, but we do not have sons.

Let us move along to the other verses which now say that Paul had three sons. We have addressed one "son" Marcus.

1 Corinthians 4:17

17 For this cause have I sent unto you **Timotheus, who is my beloved son,** and faithful in the Lord, who shall bring you into remembrance of my ways which be in Christ, as I teach every where in every church.

As with most verse corruptions there are the tell tale signs of grammar, punctuation and spelling errors. Every where is wrong should be everywhere – one word.

Also, note how similar the wording is to:

Matthew 3:17

17 And lo a voice from heaven, saying, This is my beloved Son, in whom I am well pleased.

In the altered verse below we find that Paul and his "son" Timotheus (Timothy) were with the Bishops in Philippi.

Philippians 1:1

1 Paul and Timotheus, the servants of Jesus Christ, to all the saints in Christ Jesus which are at Philippi, with the bishops and deacons:

And now we have, Paul's son Onesimus:

Philemon 10:10

I beseech thee for **my son Onesimus,** whom I have begotten in my bonds:

He begat Onesimus while in bonds? While in prison?

Onesimus was converted into a follower of Christ by Paul while he was in prison, not begotten by Paul! **Paul originally referred to him as his brother not son.**

We do not have sons, that is unless you are a Catholic priest, or bishop, or Pope etc. There is now a very strong Catholic bent being woven into our Bibles. I will cover a few of the instances here for supporting evidence.

First, we have pastors in the Old Testament, and they are maligned in many verses.

Jeremiah 10:21

For the pastors are become brutish, and have not sought the Lord: therefore they shall not prosper, and all their flocks shall be scattered. Pastors could not have been around in Old Testament times since they are ministers of the Christian church, and came after Christ, not before. Pastors are not Catholic, but bishops are. Now we have bishops in the New Testament.

The stage is clearly being set for Christian pastors to be accused by the antichrist and false prophet (the Pope) of doing the things mentioned in the corrupted scriptures above. They will be condemned for leading the sheep astray and causing division in the new world order antichrist religion, or the religion of Mystery Babylon the great.

1 Timothy 3:1

3 This is a true saying, if a man desire the office of a bishop, he desireth a good work.

And this next verse below says that Jesus is our Bishop!

1 Peter 2:25

25 For ye were as sheep going astray; but are now returned unto the Shepherd and Bishop of your souls.

Jesus is now a Bishop – a Catholic?! That is exactly what this verse is saying.

The Catholic church under the false prophet will be the one world religion. This Pope under the guise of inclusiveness and multiculturalism welcomes and celebrates all other religions today. (except Protestantism) This is Apostasy, the great falling away is in progress.

I don't want to turn anyone off, or seem like I am attacking the Catholic church. I am only pointing out the facts as they are. The protestant denominations are likewise falling away and being seduced by the doctrines of demons.

First of all Italy did not exist at the time Paul wrote this verse, it was the Roman Empire. It does exist now, and we are to salute all who rule over us?

Remember the commands hail Caesar, and hiel Hitler? Hail is now in your Bibles!

Hail Mary

Matthew 28:8-10

And as they went to tell his disciples, behold, Jesus met them, saying, All hail. And they came and held him by the feet, and worshipped him.

This was never All hail. It was rejoice! Also, the words his and him should be capitalized since it is referring to Jesus. These punctuation errors were not in the King James before I assure You! Let's take a look at another one.

Luke 1:28

And the angel came in unto her, and said, **Hail, thou that art highly favoured, the Lord is with thee: blessed art thou among women.**

Here the angel is speaking to Mary, and said Hail. Are you familiar with the very Catholic **Hail Mary**? Here again the correct word was rejoice!

Then there is the betrayal of Judas.

Matthew 26:49

And forthwith he came to Jesus, and said, **Hail, master;** and kissed him.

Hail Master was **Greetings Rabbi!** It was never Hail, master. Note that the word *him* should be capitalized here and is not.

Acts 18:2

And found a certain Jew named Aquila, born in Pontus, lately come from **Italy,** with his wife Priscilla; (because that Claudius had commanded all Jews to depart from **Rome :**) and came unto them.

Italy here used to read Rome and is still Rome in the later part of the sentence. Note the smiley face emoticon after "depart from Rome". This is bad punctuation, and a sure sign that this verse has been altered.

Denarius Turned Into Penny

I remember the words talent and denarius used in scripture. Never was penny in my King James – EVER! But, don't take my word for it. Stick with me and I'll prove it.

The silver denarius of Augustus Caesar:

The Spanish word for money is dinero and comes from the Roman denarius. Many other nations used derivatives of the word denarius for their money as well. During the times of the Roman empire the Denarius was the empire's official currency.

Likewise the dollar is the world's official currency for international commerce. Some refer to it now as the petrodollar.

There are obviously lower denominations than the dollar. We have halves, quarters, dimes, nickles and pennies. Even with the dollar's purchasing power having been eroded through inflation by over 95 percent the penny never bought much. When I was a kid there were five and dime stores. Today they are called dollar stores and now even those items are all $1.25. A penny could get you a few pieces of bubble gum, but not much really. Please bear this in mind as we proceed.

The earliest form of anything like a penny was the Pepin of France in AD 755. Over 700 years after the crucifixion of Christ. There was no such thing as a penny in the times of Christ.

I know, the scoffers will say that the writers of the King James used a modern term that they were familiar with to describe the Denarius. That excuse doesn't hold water because the pence was the smallest denomination in England at that time, and not the penny.

Another reason the Denarius and the penny are not compatible or interchangeable is that a Denarius was worth about a day's pay in those times, a penny has never been worth a day's pay.

The authors of the King James Bible were scholars of the highest order who produced a universally recognized work of literary magnificence. They took extreme care to be accurate both historically, textually and grammatically. These were by no means backwards rubes as I have heard some suggest.

◀ VERSIONS / AUTHORIZED (KING JAMES) VERSION (AKJV)

Publisher: Cambridge University Press

Version Information

The King James Version (KJV) is the world's most widely known Bible translation, using early 17th-century English. Its powerful, majestic style has made it a literary classic, with many of its phrases and expressions embedded in the English language.

From Wikipedia: The King James Version (KJV), commonly known as the Authorized Version (AV) or King James Bible (KJB), is an English translation of the Christian Bible for the Church of England begun in 1604 and completed in 1611.

In January 1604, King James VI and I convened the Hampton Court Conference where a new English version was conceived in response to the perceived problems of the earlier translations as detected by the Puritans.

James gave the translators instructions intended to guarantee that the new version would conform to the ecclesiology and reflect the episcopal structure of the Church of England and its belief in an ordained clergy. The translation was done by 47 scholars, all of whom were members of the Church of England. In common with most other translations of the period, the New Testament was translated from Greek, the Old Testament was translated from Hebrew and Aramaic text, while the Apocrypha were translated from the Greek and Latin.

By the first half of the 18th century, the Authorized Version had become effectively unchallenged as the English translation used in Anglican and Protestant churches. Over the course of the 18th century, the Authorized Version supplanted the Latin Vulgate as the standard version of Scripture for English-speaking scholars. With the development of stereotype printing at the beginning of the 19th century, this version of the Bible became the most widely printed book in history.

I surmise that the reason the penny was introduced recently in scripture is because the United States of America is the world's superpower today just as the Roman Empire was in Jesus' day.

Let us get into the verses with the new word pennies for much more evidence that the Bible has been corrupted supernaturally.

Matthew 20:2

And when he had agreed with the labourers for a penny a day, he sent them into his vineyard.

Here a penny is not a day's wage. It was originally a denarius. This verse doesn't make sense now. I don't know any laborers who would agree to work for a penny a day, do you?

Mark 6:37

He answered and said unto them, Give ye them to eat. And they say unto him, Shall we go and buy two hundred pennyworth of bread, and give them to eat?

Pennyworth should be two words not one.

Mark 12:15

Shall we give, or shall we not give? But he, knowing their hypocrisy, said unto them, Why tempt ye me? bring me a penny, that I may see it.

The word bring after the question mark should be capitalized.

Luke 20:24

Shew me a penny. Whose image and superscription hath it? They answered and said, Caesar's.

Not only is the word penny new here, but the word superscription. The word should be, and always has been (until recently) inscription.

John 6:7

Philip answered him, Two hundred pennyworth of bread is not sufficient for them, that every one of them may take a little.

Again we have pennyworth which should be two words.

Here is the most problematic verse using the new word penny.

Revelation 6:6

And I heard a voice in the midst of the four beasts say, **A measure of wheat for a penny, and three measures of barley for a penny; and see thou hurt not the oil and the wine.**

The original message intended in this passage of prophecy was that food was going to be expensive in the later days. **It originally said a measure of wheat for a denarius and three measures of barley for a denarius. This meant that a measure of wheat (about a quart) was going to cost a day's wages. This new change will make people think that food will be extremely cheap.**

The change from denarius to penny has completely flipped the meaning of the verse from food being scarce and expensive to being cheap and plentiful. The authors and editors of the King James Bible would have seen this glaring error and corrected it.

Matthew 26: 28

For this is my blood of the **new testament,** which is————— shed for many for the remission of sins.

Used to be: **new covenant**

Exo 40:3

And thou shalt put therein the **ark of the testimony**, and cover the ark with the vail.

It should be **"ark of the covenant"**

Matthew 10:42

And whosoever shall give to drink unto one of these little ones a cup of cold water only i**n the name of a disciple,** verily I say unto you, he shall in no wise lose his reward.

It should be:

And whosoever shall give to the least of these, a drink of water in **My name**, verily I say unto you, he shall in no wise lose his reward.

Jesus Prays in the Garden of Gethsemane

Mark 14:41

And he cometh the third time, and saith unto them, **Sleep on now, and take your rest:** it is enough, the hour is come; behold, the Son of man is betrayed into the hands of sinners.

Besides the fact that it doesn't match the historical account of Jesus being frustrated with the disciples, in that they couldn't stay awake, this directly contradicts the New King James Version, and the Bible is not supposed to contradict itself:

NKJV

Then He came the third time and said to them, "**Are you still sleeping and resting? It is enough!**The hour has come; behold, the Son of Man is being betrayed into the hands of sinners.

Revelation 19:7

Let us be glad and rejoice, and give honour to him: for the marriage of the Lamb is come, and his **wife** hath made herself ready.

It should be : **bride, a wife is someone who is already married!**

Matthew 12:1

At that time Jesus went on the sabbath———— day through the **corn;** and his disciples were **an hungred**, and began to pluck the **ears of corn** and to eat.

Used to be: **grainfields, hungry, heads of grain**

Mark 6:39

And he commanded them to make all sit down by **companies** upon the **green grass.**

Used to be: **recline by groups**

Luke 1:35

And the angel answered and said unto her, The Holy Ghost shall come upon thee, and the power of the Highest shall overshadow thee: therefore also **that holy thing** which shall be born of thee shall be called the Son of God.

Should be: **Holy One**

Matthew 9:17 Neither do men put new wine into old **bottles:** else the **bottles** break, and the wine **runneth out,** and the **bottles perish:** but they put new wine into new bottles, and both are preserved.

Used to be: **wineskins, is spilled, wineskins are ruined**

Since when does putting new wine in old bottles burst the bottles?

Genesis 21:14

And Abraham rose up early in the morning, and took bread, and a bottle **of water,** and gave *it* unto Hagar, **putting** *it* **on her shoulder,**

How do you put a bottle of water on your shoulder? They put water in skins in those times.

Luke 8::33

Then went the devils out of the man, and entered into the swine: and the herd ran violently down a steep place into the lake, and were **choked.**

Should be: **drowned**

Genesis 32:24

And Jacob was left alone; and there wrestled **a man** with him until the breaking of the day.

(Jacob wrestled with an angel all night.)

Luke 12:24

Consider the **ravens:** for they neither sow nor reap; which neither have storehouse nor barn; and God feedeth them: how much more are ye better than the fowls?

Consider the **sparrows:** for they neither sow nor reap; which neither have storehouse nor barn; yet God feeds them: how much more are ye better than the birds of the air?

For me, in all my 40 years of listening to sermons and other years of directly reading the New Testament, I had never heard of the phrase "Consider the ravens..." until the Mandela Effect in 2016. The fact that ravens have replaced sparrows in a couple of places in the Bible, namely being added in the Genesis flood story, is an insertion of a bird with an evil nature. This mirrors the whole Mandela Effect, which is the addition of evil themes in the Bible. Ravens are opportunistic omnivores that prey upon and trick other animals.

Ravens, which are large crows, are the favorite bird of witchcraft. In mythology (which actually may be true) "the raven is a harbinger of death.

Witches and sorcerers were believed to have the ability to transform themselves into ravens and fly away, thus enabling them to evade capture. The Native Americans often saw the raven as a trickster, much like Coyote. There are a number of tales regarding the mischief of Raven, who is sometimes seen as a symbol of transformation. In the legends of various tribes, Raven is typically associated with everything from the creation of the world to the gift of sunlight to mankind. Some tribes knew the raven as a stealer of souls.

Luke 6:49

But he that heareth, and doeth not, is like a man that without a foundation built an house upon the **earth**; against which the stream did beat vehemently, and immediately it fell; and the ruin of that house was great.

Used to be: **sand**

Mark 16:13

And they went and told *it* unto the **residue:** neither believed they them.

John 26:8

Then cometh Simon Peter following him, and went into the sepulchre, and seeth the linen clothes lie, And the **napkin**, that was about his head, not lying with the linen clothes, but wrapped together in a place by itself.

It should be: **handkerchief**

Mark 1:32

And at even, when the sun did set, they brought unto him all that were diseased, and them that were possessed with **devils.**

Used to be: **demons**

Matthew 5:13

Ye are the salt of the earth: but if the salt have lost **his** savour, wherewith shall it be salted?

Used to be: **its**

Matthew 6: 9-13 T**he Lord's Prayer**

After this manner therefore pray ye: Our Father **which** art in heaven, Hallowed be thy name.

Thy kingdom come, Thy will be done **in** earth, as it is in heaven.

Give us this day our daily bread.

And forgive us our **debts**, as we forgive our **debtors.**

Lead us not into temptation, but deliver us from evil: For thine is the kingdom, and the power, and the glory, for ever. Amen.

Used to be: **who, on, trespasses, as we forgive those who trespass against us**

Lying Signs

Sometimes I just can't help but take things literally. Like when it says in the Bible that the antichrist will be coming with "lying signs" and wonders. I mean, like it used to say in the Bible, before it was supernaturally changed to "signs and lying wonders". Now there is not one Bible translation that uses the phrase "lying signs and wonders".

> *Even him, whose coming is after the working of Satan with all power and lying signs and wonders*
>
> *2 Thessalonians 2:9*

It is so ironic that as Christians are looking for great miracles to be wrought, like fire coming down from heaven, when in actuality the signs around them have been changed. Oh yeah, and literally no one has noticed the signs that blare them in the face when they are driving. For example:

➢ **Chic-Fil-A changed to Chick-Fil-A**
➢ **Caldwell Banker changed to Coldwell Banker**

➤ **Advanced Auto Parts changed to Advance Auto Parts**

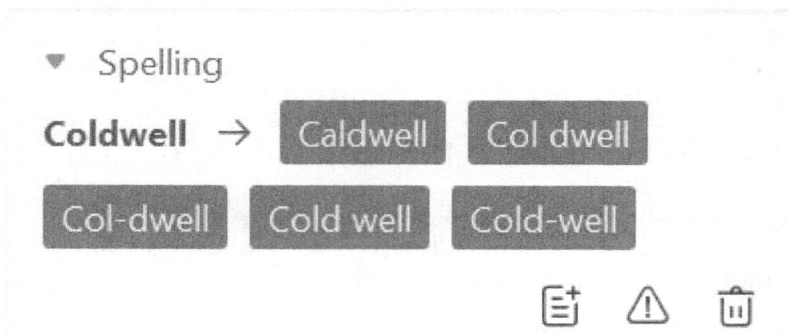

▾ Spelling

Coldwell → Caldwell   Col dwell

Col-dwell   Cold well   Cold-well

This is the Spellcheck function on my computer.
It shows that Coldwell is wrong and suggests Caldwell, as does my memory

How can it be that I so distinctly remember that Coldwell Banker used to be Caldwell Banker, and I'm not even a realtor? I just happened to be using realtors back in 2005-2009 when I was buying and selling a house and was very familiar with the company, and looked at a lot of properties that Caldwell Banker had. Where are all the people that worked for them, and why aren't they making a big deal that the name was different? I guess, like when I told a friend about the Mandela Effect, they said that if it really was a thing -it would be on the front page news.

And how can it be that the Bible has so many changes in it, and most Christians don't see it? They don't see the lying signs and wonders happening right in front of their eyes. Some people read that verse and say that the lying signs and wonders will be made by the antichrist, which will appear after the working of Satan, but I see it as Satan creating these lying signs right now. There are some who think that we will not even get a person, that the antichrist is reigning now by the general spirit of antichrist in the world.

It wasn't that long ago that preachers were shouting about how the antichrist would come with "all power and lying signs and wonders" so much that my ears were bleeding. Now, if I ask preachers about that text, they don't remember it saying that.

Yet, I can tune in to many preachers on Youtube that still use the phrase "lying signs and wonders". I have left numerous comments on how the Bible does not say that anymore, and I NEVER GET A RESPONSE. I have even written personal emails to the preacher, to no avail. They just don't want to hear it, they don't want to address it, and I don't know what is going on in their heads. Case in point: I just listened to the following preacher say that phrase at the 14 minute mark in the video below:

REMOVING
the VEIL *of*
DECEPTION

How to Recognize Lying Signs,
False Wonders and Seducing Spirits

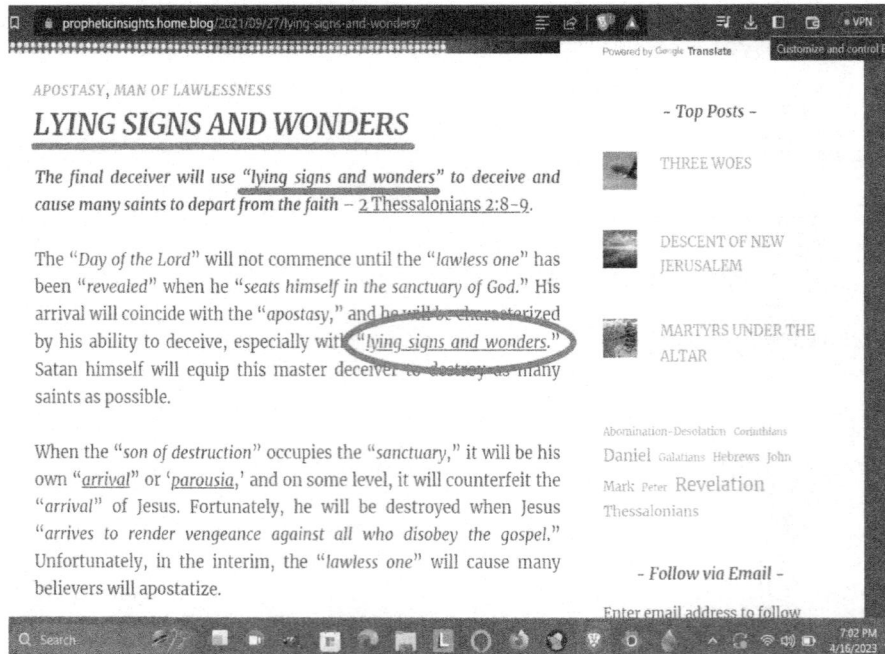

APOSTASY, MAN OF LAWLESSNESS

LYING SIGNS AND WONDERS

The final deceiver will use *"lying signs and wonders"* to deceive and cause many saints to depart from the faith – 2 Thessalonians 2:8-9.

The *"Day of the Lord"* will not commence until the *"lawless one"* has been *"revealed"* when he *"seats himself in the sanctuary of God."* His arrival will coincide with the *"apostasy,"* and he will be characterized by his ability to deceive, especially with *"lying signs and wonders."* Satan himself will equip this master deceiver to destroy as many saints as possible.

When the *"son of destruction"* occupies the *"sanctuary,"* it will be his own *"arrival"* or *'parousia,'* and on some level, it will counterfeit the *"arrival"* of Jesus. Fortunately, he will be destroyed when Jesus *"arrives to render vengeance against all who disobey the gospel."* Unfortunately, in the interim, the *"lawless one"* will cause many believers will apostatize.

– Top Posts –

THREE WOES

DESCENT OF NEW JERUSALEM

MARTYRS UNDER THE ALTAR

Abomination-Desolation Corinthians
Daniel Galatians Hebrews John
Mark Peter Revelation
Thessalonians

– Follow via Email –

Enter email address to follow

The most iconic Bible verses have been supernaturally erased from the King James Bible. Remember "he that spareth the rod spoileth the child?" Gone! How about "pride goeth before a fall and a haughty spirit before destruction?" Transposed. I had it memorized. The following residual for iconic Bible verses is found in 100 plus year old documents on this video:

https://www.youtube.com/watch?v=-7Nwf6ijdqc

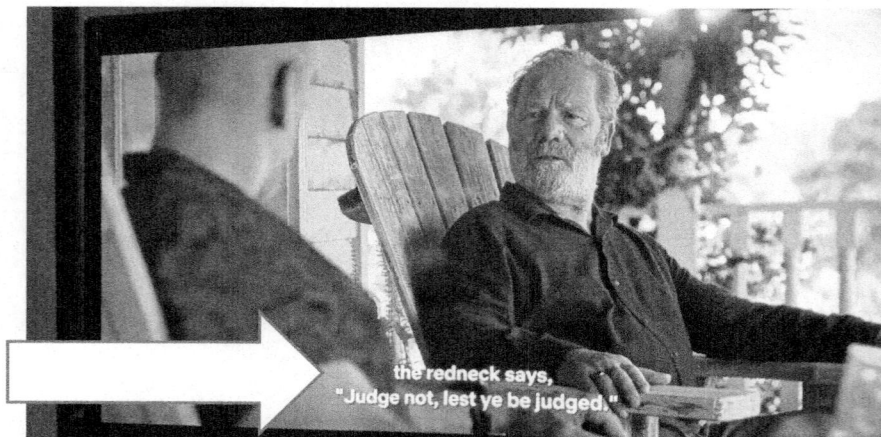

Where Did "Judge Not Lest Ye Be Judged" Go?

OZARK on Netflix: Season 1 Episode 4: 53:12 Mark on Video

I don't know about you, but there is only so much truth I can take, as none of it is ever good news. In an effort to keep myself sane, I decided to binge-watch this TV series on Netflix, called "Ozark" just to get away from the madness. Not even halfway through the first season - this hit me smack in the face : " Judge not lest ye be judged" spoken from one redneck to another.

By the way, the show is really quite good, in my opinion, and kept me distracted from the madness in this world for about 2 weeks. Of course, they had to insert the two gay couples as opposed to the only one hetero family, a typical scenario of Netflix's social engineering that Owen Shroyer of Infowars aptly describes as the New World Order "*Global Homo*".

Judge not Lest Ye Be Judged jumped right out at me on the screen caption on the TV series Ozark, seen in the previous page.

This is now how the Bible reads:

Judge not Leaſt yͤ be Judged.

Matthew 7:1

Judge not, that ye be not judged.

Here is more residual evidence that *Judge Not Lest Ye Be Judged* used to exist:

103

Judah Changed to Judas

As I was looking over an old article to republish, I noticed that a screenshot of Matthew 1:2 and 3 said the word JudaH with an H at the end,

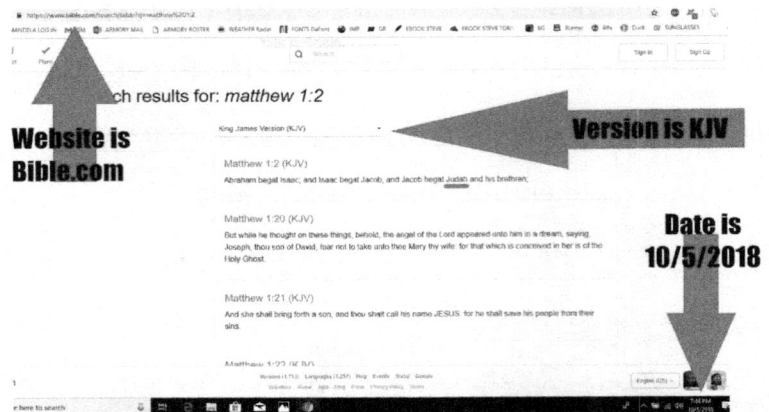

and today it has no H. A criminal lawyer would say this is a smoking gun, and I say it's proof the Bible has been changed. If any naysayers want to analyze the image to see if it's photoshopped, go for it!

Note that I am comparing apples to apples, as the website where I screenshot Matthew 1:2,3 is Bible.com. The version is KJV, as Bible.com has no variant versions of the King James.

This is the same website, Bible.com which now says JUDAS in 2022. See how it has changed? How do you explain that???"

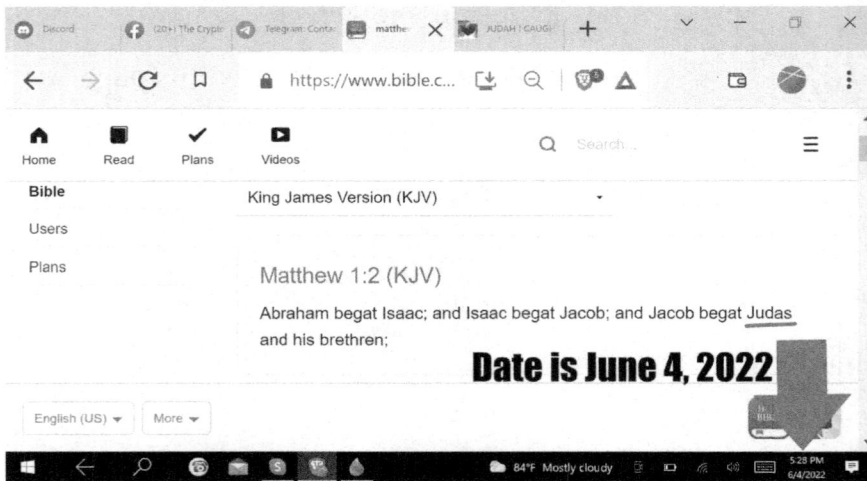

Matthew 24:33

So likewise ye, when ye shall see all these things, know that it is near, even at the **doors.**

Used to be: **door** (There is only one door to heaven - through Jesus)

All "salutes" are supposed to be "greet". There are many verses in Romans that have "salute" that I have not included here.

Used to be: **greet**

Romans 16:9

Salute Urbane, our helper in Christ, and Stachys my beloved.

Used to be: **Greet** Urbanus, co-worker

Romans 16:16

Salute one another with an holy kiss. The churches of Christ salute you.

Romans 16:21

Timotheus my workfellow, and Lucius, and Jason, and Sosipater, my kinsmen, **salute** you.

Used to be: Timothy my co-worker, **greets** you, and so do Lucius, and Jason, and Sosipater, my relatives, **greet**

Romans 16 :22

I Tertius, who **wrote this** epistle, **salute** you in the Lord.

Used to be: **wrote down, greet** (Didn't Paul write this epistle?)

Romans 16:25

Now to him that is of power to **stablish** you according to my gospel, and the preaching of Jesus Christ, according to the revelation of the mystery, which was kept secret since the world began,

Used to be: **establish**

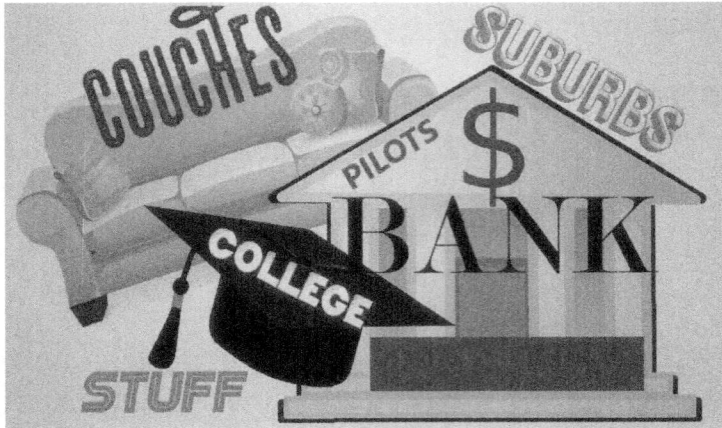

For centuries the King James Bible has been held up as one of the most majestic works of literature ever written in any language. Now it's riddled with grammatical errors.

Genesis 31:34

Now Rachel had taken the images, and put them in the **camel's furniture,** and sat upon them. And Laban searched all the tent, but found them not.

Please go confirm this change for yourselves. Furniture is the wrong word leaving the reader with a nonsensical, and awkward sentence. It used to be **saddle,** not furniture! Oh, and **images used to be idols.** Originally the issue here was about false idols, but you'd never know that from reading this passage now.

The aim of this book is to build a forensic case for the crimes committed against God and His Word. We already know the M.O. of our number one suspect Lucifer. He is the destroyer, corrupter, liar, false witness, accuser, and twister of God's Words. Let us look at more of these supernatural changes for his fingerprints.

Numbers 35:3

And the cities shall they have to dwell in; and the **suburbs** of them shall be for their cattle, and for their goods, and for all their beasts.

The words **pasture lands** was substituted with suburbs. This is very awkward since we don't raise cattle, or beasts of the field in the suburbs.

Joshua 21:19

All the cities of the children of Aaron, the priests, were thirteen cities with their **suburbs.**

Should be **pasture lands.** There are over one hundred verses polluted with the modern word suburbs now.

Ezekiel 27:28

The **suburbs** shall shake at the sound of the cry of thy **pilots.**

In this verse we have the added new word pilots as well. The word here was **seamen.** But, from a modern perspective this makes sense because pilots usually live in the suburbs.Let's move right along.

2 Kings 22:14

So Hilkiah the priest, and Ahikam, and Achbor, and Shaphan, and Asahiah, went unto Huldah the prophetess, the wife of Shallum the son of Tikvah, the son of Harhas, keeper of the wardrobe; (now she dwelt in Jerusalem in the **college ;**) and they communed with her.

Did you know there were colleges in those days? I didn't either. Both the wink emoticon after the word college and the word college are mocking us in this verse.

2 Chronicles 34:22

The scripture used to read **second quarter,** not college. So, not only is the new word college mocking us, but also the emoticons and the very bad punctuation of the emoticon itself.

Of course no suburb would be complete with out **colleges and banks.**

Luke 19:23

Wherefore then gavest not thou my money into the **bank,** that at my coming I might have required mine own with usury?

The switched word here is bank. It used to be **moneychangers.** You see everyone knows that Jesus drove out the moneychangers (Biblical banksters) who robbed the poor by usury. Moneychangers were bad, banks are "good".

Nehemiah 5:3

Some also there were that said, We have **mortgaged** our lands, vineyards, and houses, that we might buy corn, because of the dearth.

1 Timothy 6:10

"For the love of money is the root of all evil". We know who rules the moneychangers, I mean banks.

In the suburbs you need lots of stuff to keep up with the Jones'. Stuff is a modern day idol.

Virtually every Bible version now has the word **"Stuff"** supplanting the originally printed words such as: goods, belongings and possessions. There are currently, as of this writing 13 verses in both the New and Old Testaments with the modern word "stuff" inserted. Ah,but what would the suburbs be without colleges, banks and now stuff.

Gen 31:37 - Whereas thou hast searched all my **stuff,** what hast thou found of all thy household stuff? set it here before my brethren and thy brethren, that they may judge betwixt us both.

Gen 45:20 - Also regard not your **stuff;** for the good of all the land of Egypt is yours.

If a man shall deliver unto his neighbour money or **stuff** to keep, and it be stolen out of the man's house; if the thief be found, let him pay double.

Exo 36:7 - For the **stuff** they had was sufficient for all the work to make it, and too much.

Jos 7:11 - Israel hath sinned, and they have also transgressed my covenant which I commanded them: for they have even taken of the accursed thing, and have also stolen, and dissembled also, and they have put it even among their own **stuff.**

1 Samuel 10:22 - Therefore they enquired of the LORD further, if the man should yet come thither. And the LORD answered, Behold, he hath hid himself among the **stuff.**

1 Samuel 25:13 - And David said unto his men, Gird ye on every man his sword. And they girded on every man his sword; and David also girded on his sword: and there went up after David about four hundred men; and two hundred abode by the **stuff.**

COUCH

Gen 49:4 - Unstable as water, thou shalt not excel; because thou **wentest** up to thy father's bed; then defiledst thou it: he went up to my couch.

Wentest?

Job 7:13 - When I say, My bed shall comfort me, my **couch** shall ease my complaint;

Job 38:40 - When they **couch** in their dens, and abide in the covert to lie in wait?

Psa 6:6 - I am weary with my groaning; all the night make I my bed to swim; I water my **couch** with my tears.

Amo 3:12 - Thus saith the LORD; As the shepherd taketh out of the mouth of the lion two legs, or a piece of an ear; so shall the children of Israel be taken out that dwell in Samaria in the corner of a bed, and in Damascus in a **couch.**

110

In the New Testament:

Luk 5:19 - And when they could not find by what way they might bring him in because of the multitude, they went upon the housetop, and let him down through the tiling with his **couch** into the midst before Jesus.

Luk 5:24 - But that ye may know that the Son of man hath power upon earth to forgive sins, (he said unto the sick of the palsy,) I say unto thee, Arise, and take up thy **couch,** and go into thine house. This used to say **"mat"**.

Amos 6:4 - That lie upon beds of ivory, and stretch themselves upon their **couches,** and eat the lambs out of the flock, and the calves out of the midst of the stall;

Act 5:15 - Insomuch that they brought forth the sick into the streets, and laid them on beds and **couches,** that at the least the shadow of Peter passing by might overshadow some of them.

And if you are a couch potato, make sure you don't bend down, because the Bible says you'll be "couching"! I thought the word for bending down was"crouching".

Gen 49:14 - Issachar is a s**trong ass couching** down between two burdens:

In the suburbs you would expect to find couches, but not in the Bible. After all the couch wasn't even invented until 1895 by Mr. Couch himself.

Matthew 18:20

For where **two or three** are gathered together in my name, there am I in the midst of them.

We all know it used to be "where **two or more** are gathered together in my name".

Hosea 4:6

My people are **destroyed** for lack of knowledge: because thou hast rejected knowledge, I will also reject thee, that thou shalt be no priest to me: seeing thou hast forgotten the law of thy God, I will also forget thy children.

It used to be **perish.**

Moses in the Basket Among the Reeds

Exodus 2:5

And the daughter of Pharaoh came down to wash herself at the river; and her maidens walked along by the river's side; and when she saw the **ark among the flags,** she sent her maid to fetch it.

This is about Moses being in the **basket among the reeds.**

Apron

Genesis 3:7
And the eyes of them both were opened, and they knew that they were naked; and they sewed fig leaves together, and made themselves **aprons.**

Used to be: coverings

A major practice of freemasonry is wearing "aprons". Depending on their "rank" they wear different colored aprons which have different badges. Sort of like the Boy Scouts — oops — I meant to say the dual-gender Scouts.

In ancient Crete, aprons were worn by the fertility goddess, and sacred aprons were worn by Assyrian priests. Egyptian pharoahs wore jewel encrusted aprons.

ANCIENT SUN GOD OF THE MAYANS WORE **A MASONIC APRON**

Higgins' book, the Apron:

AN AMERICAN MASON OF LONG AGO

Ancient Sun-god of the Mayas. One of many such statues found by Le Plongeon in the jungle forests of Yucatan, relics of a civilization which had perished long before America was discovered by the Spaniards. Wears the symbol of "Three (times) Three" and a Masonic Apron.

THE MASONIC APRON IS DERIVED FROM EGYPTIAN SUN WORSHIP

In a 1914 book by Frank C. Higgins, the Apron, it states, "Masonic signs and symbols originated in the first separation which took place in the family of Adam."

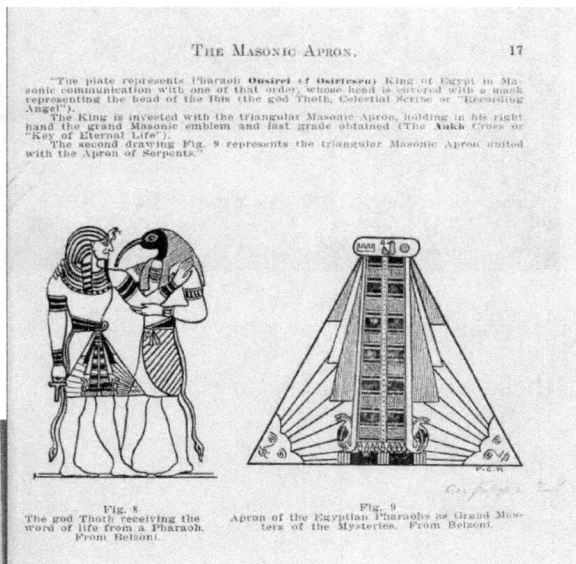

THE MASONIC APRON. 17

"The plate represents Pharaoh **Ousirei (of Osiriesu)** King of Egypt in Masonic communication with one of that order, whose head is covered with a mask representing the head of the Ibis (the god Thoth, Celestial Scribe or "Recording Angel").

The King is invested with the triangular Masonic Apron, holding in his right hand the grand Masonic emblem and last grade obtained (The **Ankh** Cross or "Key of Eternal Life").

The second drawing Fig. 9 represents the triangular Masonic Apron united with the Apron of Serpents."

Fig. 8
The god Thoth receiving the word of life from a Pharaoh. From Belzoni.

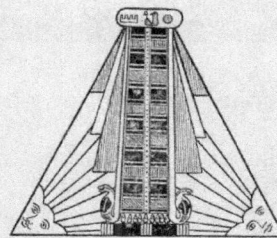

Fig. 9
Apron of the Egyptian Pharaohs as Grand Masters of the Mysteries. From Belzoni.

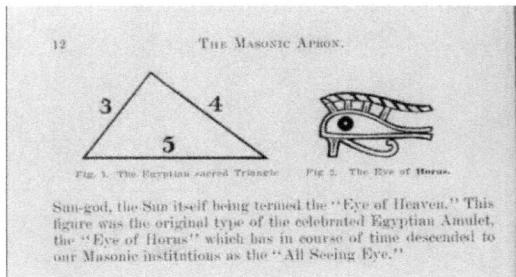

12 THE MASONIC APRON.

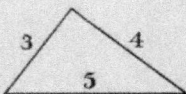

Fig. 1. The Egyptian sacred Triangle   Fig. 2. The Eye of Horus.

Sun-god, the Sun itself being termed the "Eye of Heaven." This figure was the original type of the celebrated Egyptian Amulet, the "Eye of Horus" which has in course of time descended to our Masonic institutions as the "All Seeing Eye."

The Apron is an Homage to the Sun God Represented by the One Eye of Horus

The peculiar shape of this triangle, which is composed of a right angle of three units of measure by four, the hypotheneuse of which is exactly five, was liken to the form of an eye, the symbol of the Masonic Apron…the Sun itself being termed the "Eye of Heaven."

…the "Eye of Horus" which has in course of time descended to our Masonic institutions as the "All Seeing Eye." The God that Freemasons worship is Lucifer, represented by the rebellious goat, here depicted in a hybrid form of man/goat/angel mocking the Ark of the Covenant and showing the All Seeing Eye of Lucifer above. I believe that in Noah's day, these were actual creatures.

Ebonics in the Bible

As we have seen there has been massive and ongoing changes to our Bibles in terms of spelling, punctuation, syntax and grammar errors. There are now thousands of errors that were not there before. This is proof that the scriptures have been supernaturally altered. Ebonics is one more sure manifestation of the corruption.As we have pointed out repeatedly: these errors would **not** have been tolerated by the stalwart old school English guardians. The Bible has been revered as a literary work of grandeur for centuries. This would have been considered a crime against the humanities, and certainly would not have been allowed to stand!

We will not be able to examine every example of the use of Ebonics in scripture as there are too many. Let's take a look at the first bizarre instance: (I encourage you to get your Bibles at home and verify these changes for yourselves)

Isaiah 52:5

Now therefore, what have I here, saith the Lord, that **my people is** taken away for nought? **they** that rule over them make them to howl, saith the Lord; and my name continually every day is blasphemed.

Again, we have the incorrect phrase **my people is**, and the word they after the question mark should be capitalized since it begins a new sentence.

Another:

2 Samuel 17:29 (KJV)

29 And honey, and butter, and sheep, and cheese of kine, for David, and for the people that were with him, to eat: for they said, **The people is** hungry, and weary, and thirsty, in the wilderness.

The people is should obviously be **the people are**.

This example has been highly corrupted:

Daniel 11:30 (KJV)

30 For the ships of Chittim shall come against him: therefore he shall be grieved, and return, and have indignation against the holy covenant: so shall he do; he shall even return, and **have intelligence with them** that forsake the holy covenant.

The phrase **so shall he do** is a total insert and doesn't belong there at all. The phrase **have intelligence with them** should be, **and show favor toward them**.

Another example:

John 8:33 (KJV)

33 They answered him, **We be** Abraham's seed, and were never in bondage to any man: how sayest thou, Ye shall be made free?

We be should be **we are of**.

And:

Genesis 42:32 (KJV)

We be twelve brethren, sons of our father; one is not, and the youngest is this day with our father in the land of Canaan.

Exodus 12:33 (KJV)

33 And the Egyptians were urgent upon the people, that they might send them out of the land in haste; for they said, **We be** all dead men.

Numbers 13:31 (KJV)

31 But the men that went up with him said, **We be** not able to go up against the people; for they are stronger than we.

Maybe you want to tell someone about the changes, but don't know how. A good way is to have them take the below Bible quiz and then ease into explaining to them after about the changes. Here is a good quiz you can use:

BIBLE QUIZ

Name:_____

Years You Read the King James Version Bible_____

Fill in the blanks with the most accurate memory you have of what you read in

the King James Version bible and

Is there is any wording you find to be incorrect? If so, underline the incorrect

words.

1)
Isaiah 11:6

Then the _____ shall lie down with the _____, and the bear shall
eat grass like the ox, and the child shalll play on the hole of the asp, and nothing
shall hurt nor destroy in all My Holy Mountain!

2)And now abideth faith, hope, _____, these three; but the greatest of
these is _____.

3)Genesis 1:1 In the beginning God created the _____ and the earth.
4) Matthew 6:9
After this manner therefore pray ye: Our Father which art in heaven, Hallowed be
thy name. 10 Thy kingdom come. Thy will be done _____, as it is in
heaven. 11 Give us this day our daily bread. 12 And forgive us our
_____, as we forgive
_____ 13 And lead us not into temptation, but
deliver us from evil: For thine is the _____and the glory,
for ever. Amen.

5) Matthew 10:16 King James Version (KJV)

Behold, I send you forth as sheep in the midst of wolves: be ye therefore _____ as serpents, and _____ as doves.

6)
Matthew 7 Judge not, _____ye be not judged. For with what judgment ye judge, ye shall be judged:

7)Matthew 26:40-45 King James Version (KJV)

40 And he cometh unto the disciples, and findeth them asleep, and saith unto Peter, What, could ye not watch with me one hour?

41 Watch and pray, that ye enter not into temptation: the spirit indeed is willing, but the flesh is weak.

42 He went away again the second time, and prayed, saying, O my Father, if this cup may not pass away from me, except I drink it, thy will be done.

43 And he came and found them asleep again: for their eyes were heavy.

44 And he left them, and went away again, and prayed the third time, saying the same words.

45 Then cometh he to his disciples, and saith unto them, _____: behold, the hour is at hand, and the Son of man is betrayed into the hands of sinners.

8)Luke 5:24 King James Version (KJV)

24 But that ye may know that the Son of man hath power upon earth to forgive sins, (he said unto the sick of the palsy,) I say unto thee, Arise, and take up thy _____, and go into thine house.

9)Acts 12:4 King James Version (KJV)

4 And when he had apprehended him, he put him in prison, and delivered him to four quaternions of soldiers to keep him; intending after _____(holiday) to bring him forth to the people.

10)20 The first day of the week cometh Mary Magdalene early, when it was yet dark, unto the sepulchre, and seeth the stone taken away from the sepulchre.

…3 Peter therefore went forth, and that other disciple, and came to the sepulchre.

4 So they ran both together: and the other disciple did outrun Peter, and came first to the sepulchre.

5 And he stooping down, and looking in, saw the linen clothes lying; yet went he not in.

6 Then cometh Simon Peter following him, and went into the sepulchre, and seeth the linen clothes lie,

7 And the _____, that was about his head, not lying with the linen clothes, but wrapped together in a place by itself.

PART II
Underline the word or phrases that you think are incorrect words. Then write the correct word in the blank:

11)Revelation 20:8 King James Version (KJV)
8 And shall go out to deceive the nations which are in the four quarters of the earth, Gog, and Magog, to gather them together to battle: the number of whom is as the sand of the sea. _____

12)Revelation 1:6 King James Version (KJV)
6 And hath made us kings and priests unto God and his Father; to him be glory and dominion for ever and ever. Amen._____ _____

13)Matthew 14:8 King James Version (KJV)
8 And she, being before instructed of her mother, said, Give me here John Baptist's head in a charger. _____

14)Acts 4:4-9 King James Version (KJV) (one word is incorrect)
4 Howbeit many of them which heard the word believed; and the number of the men was about five thousand.
5 And it came to pass on the morrow, that their rulers, and elders, and scribes,
6 And Annas the high priest, and Caiaphas, and John, and Alexander, and as many as were of the kindred of the high priest, were gathered together at Jerusalem.
7 And when they had set them in the midst, they asked, By what power, or by what name, have ye done this?
8 Then Peter, filled with the Holy Ghost, said unto them, Ye rulers of the people, and elders of Israel,
9 If we this day be examined of the good deed done to the impotent man, by what means he is made whole;_____

15)Luke 17:32-35 King James Version (KJV)
32 Remember Lot's wife.
33 Whosoever shall seek to save his life shall lose it; and whosoever shall lose his life shall preserve it.
34 I tell you, in that night there shall be two men in one bed; the one shall be taken, and the other shall be left.
35 Two women shall be grinding together; the one shall be taken, and the other left._____

1 Corinthians 13:13 King James Version (KJV)

16)John 3:16 For God so loved the world, that he gave His onlyl begotten son, that whomsoever believeth in Him _____but have everlasting life.

17)

Revelation 1:13 King James Version (KJV)

13 And in the midst of the seven candlesticks one like unto the Son of man, clothed with a garment down to the foot, and girt about the paps with a golden girdle. _____

18)Job 21:24 King James Version (KJV)

24 His breasts are full of milk, and his bones are moistened with marrow.

_____

19)Numbers 11:12 King James Version (KJV)

12 Have I conceived all this people? have I begotten them, that thou shouldest say unto me, Carry them in thy bosom, as a nursing father beareth the sucking child, unto the land which thou swarest unto their fathers?

_____

20)Deuteronomy 12:20 King James Version (KJV)

20 When the Lord thy God shall enlarge thy border, as he hath promised thee, and thou shalt say, I will eat flesh, because thy soul longeth to eat flesh; thou mayest eat flesh, whatsoever thy soul lusteth after.

_____

21)Luke 12:24 King James Version (KJV)

24 Consider the ravens: for they neither sow nor reap; which neither have storehouse nor barn; and God feedeth them: how much more are ye better than the fowls? _____

22)Matthew 10:12 King James Version (KJV)

12 And when ye come into an house, salute it.

_____

23)1 Samuel 16:15 King James Version (KJV)

15 And Saul's servants said unto him, Behold now, an evil spirit from God troubleth thee.

_____

24)1 Samuel 16:16 King James Version (KJV)

16 Let our lord now command thy servants, which are before thee, to seek out a man, who is a cunning player on an harp: and it shall come to pass, when the evil

spirit from God is upon thee, that he shall play with his hand, and thou shalt be well.

25)Leviticus 2:7 King James Version (KJV)

7 And if thy oblation be a meat offering baken in the fryingpan, it shall be made of fine flour with oil.

_____

26)Genesis 3:7 King James Version (KJV)

7 And the eyes of them both were opened, and they knew that they were naked; and they sewed fig leaves together, and made themselves aprons.

_____

27)Ezekiel 5:1 King James Version (KJV)

5 And thou, son of man, take thee a sharp knife, take thee a barber's razor, and cause it to pass upon thine head and upon thy beard: then take thee balances to weigh, and divide the hair.

_____

28)Acts 9:5 (KJV)

5 And he said, Who art thou, Lord? And the Lord said, I am Jesus whom thou persecutest: it is hard for thee to kick against the pricks.

29)Job 30:29 King James Version (KJV)

29 I am a brother to dragons, and a companion to owls.

_____

30) Numbers 23:22 King James Version (KJV)

22 God brought them out of Egypt; he hath as it were the strength of an unicorn.

_____

PART III

Cross out the incorrect word or phrase and write (on the blank line) what word or phrase you remember it to be :

31)Psalm 146:3 King James Version (KJV)

3 Put not your trust in princes, nor in the son of man, in whom there is no help.

_____

32)Job 25:6 King James Version (KJV)

6 How much less man, that is a worm? and the son of man, which is a worm?

_____

33)Luke 23:11 King James Version (KJV)

11 And Herod with his men of war set him at nought, and mocked him, and arrayed him in a gorgeous robe, and sent him again to Pilate.

34)James 2:3 King James Version (KJV)

3 And ye have respect to him that weareth the gay clothing, and say unto him, Sit thou here in a good place; and say to the poor, Stand thou there, or sit here under my footstool:

35)Matthew 1:1-2 King James Version (KJV)

1 The book of the generation of Jesus Christ, the son of David, the son of Abraham. 2 Abraham begat Isaac; and Isaac begat Jacob; and Jacob begat Judas and his brethren;

36)Revelation 1:13 King James Version (KJV)

13 And in the midst of the seven candlesticks one like unto the Son of man, clothed with a garment down to the foot, and girt about the paps with a golden girdle.

37)Daniel 6:2

And over these three presidents; of whom Daniel was first: that the princes might give accounts unto them, and the king should have no damage.

38)2 Thessalonians 2:9 King James Version (KJV)

9 Even him, whose coming is after the working of Satan with all power and signs and lying wonders,

39)Revelation 1:6 King James Version (KJV)

6 And hath made us kings and priests unto God and his Father; to him be glory and dominion for ever and ever. Amen. _____

40)Psalm 72:6 King James Version (KJV)

6 He shall come down like rain upon the mown grass: as showers that water the earth.

41)Psalm 129:7 King James Version (KJV)

7 Wherewith the mower filleth not his hand; nor he that bindeth sheaves his bosom….

42)Leviticus 11:35 King James Version (KJV)

35 And every thing whereupon any part of their carcase falleth shall be unclean; whether it be oven, or ranges for pots, they shall be broken down: for they are unclean and shall be unclean unto you.

_____

_____

43)34 Now Rachel had taken the images, and put them in the camel's furniture, and sat upon them. And Laban searched all the tent, but found them not._____

44) Exodus 34:19 King James Version (KJV)
19 All that openeth the matrix is mine; and every firstling among thy cattle, whether ox or sheep, that is male.

_____

45)Isaiah 32:8 King James Version (KJV)
8 But the liberal deviseth liberal things; and by liberal things shall he stand.

_____

46)Luke 17:26 King James Version (KJV)
26 And as it was in the days of Noe, so shall it be also in the days of the Son of man.

_____

47) Ezekiel 27:28
28 The suburbs shall shake at the sound of the cry of thy pilots.
48) Isaiah 23:3
3 And by great waters the seed of Shihor, the harvest of the river, is her revenue; and she is a mart of nations.

_____

49)Luke 19:23
Wherefore then gavest not thou my money into the bank, that at my coming I might have required mine own with usury?
50) Luke 12:24
Consider the ravens: for they neither sow nor reap; which neither have storehouse nor barn; and God feedeth them: how much more are ye better than the fowls?
Please put any comments or observations below (or on the reverse side):

ANSWERS:
1) wolf,lamb SHOULD BE LION, LAMB
2) charity SHOULD BE LOVE
3) heaven SHOULD BE HEAVENS

4)debts, as we forgive our debtors, kingdom and the power,

5) wise,harmless, that is correct

6) SHOULD BE LEST

7) Sleep on now SHOULD BE ARISE AND AWAKE

8) couch SHOULD BE BED or mat

9) Easter SHOULD BE PASSOVER

10) napkin SHOULD BE ??

PART II

Underline the word or phrases that you think are incorrect words. Then write the correct word in the blank:

11)

Revelation 20:8 King James Version (KJV)

8 And shall go out to deceive the nations which are in the four quarters of the earth, Gog, and Magog, to gather them together to battle: the number of whom is as the sand of the sea. It used to say CORNERS instead of QUARTERS

12)

Revelation 1:6 King James Version (KJV)

6 And hath made us kings and priests unto God and his Father; to him be glory and dominion for ever and ever. Amen. God has no father.

13)

Matthew 14:8 King James Version (KJV)

8 And she, being before instructed of her mother, said, Give me here John Baptist's head in a charger. it used to say PLATTER instead of CHARGER

14)

Acts 4:4-9 King James Version (KJV) (one word is incorrect)

4 Howbeit many of them which heard the word believed; and the number of the men was about five thousand.

5 And it came to pass on the morrow, that their rulers, and elders, and scribes,

6 And Annas the high priest, and Caiaphas, and John, and Alexander, and as many as were of the kindred of the high priest, were gathered together at Jerusalem.

7 And when they had set them in the midst, they asked, By what power, or by what name, have ye done this?

8 Then Peter, filled with the Holy Ghost, said unto them, Ye rulers of the people, and elders of Israel,

9 If we this day be examined of the good deed done to the impotent man, by what means he is made whole; IMPOTENT used to be LAME

15)

Luke 17:32-35 King James Version (KJV)

32 Remember Lot's wife.

33 Whosoever shall seek to save his life shall lose it; and whosoever shall lose his life shall preserve it.

34 I tell you, in that night there shall be two men in one bed; the one shall be taken, and the other shall be left.

35 Two women shall be grinding together; the one shall be taken, and the other left.It used to say TWO WOMEN shall be grinding together at the MILL, TWO shall be in one bed, not TWO MEN

16)

John 3:16 For God so loved the world, that he gave His only begotten son, that whomsoever believeth in Him __shall, not should__but have everlasting life.

17)

Revelation 1:13 King James Version (KJV)

13 And in the midst of the seven candlesticks one like unto the Son of man, clothed with a garment down to the foot, and girt about the paps with a golden girdle. used to say a SASH ABOUT THE CHEST

18)

Job 21:24 King James Version (KJV)

24 His breasts are full of milk, and his bones are moistened with marrow.
used to say PAILS are full of milk

19)

Numbers 11:12 King James Version (KJV)

12 Have I conceived all this people? have I begotten them, that thou shouldest say unto me, Carry them in thy bosom, as a nursing father beareth the sucking child, unto the land which thou swarest unto their fathers?
fathers do not nurse!!

20)

Deuteronomy 12:20 King James Version (KJV)

20 When the Lord thy God shall enlarge thy border, as he hath promised thee, and thou shalt say, I will eat flesh, because thy soul longeth to eat flesh; thou mayest eat flesh, whatsoever thy soul lusteth after. TOTALLY AGAINST GOD'S WORD not to EAT FLESH..or to LUSTETH AFTER WHATSOEVER YOU WANT!

21)

Luke 12:24 King James Version (KJV)

24 Consider the ravens: for they neither sow nor reap; which neither have storehouse nor barn; and God feedeth them: how much more are ye better than the fowls? USED to say SPARROWS

22)

Matthew 10:12 King James Version (KJV)

12 And when ye come into an house, salute it.

instead of salute, GREET

23)

1 Samuel 16:15 King James Version (KJV)

15 And Saul's servants said unto him, Behold now, an evil spirit from God troubleth thee.

God is not an evil spirit

24)

1 Samuel 16:16 King James Version (KJV)

16 Let our lord now command thy servants, which are before thee, to seek out a man, who is a cunning player on an harp: and it shall come to pass, when the evil spirit from God is upon thee, that he shall play with his hand, and thou shalt be well. God is not an evil spirit

25)

Leviticus 2:7 King James Version (KJV)

7 And if thy oblation be a meat offering baken in the fryingpan, it shall be made of fine flour with oil.

baken is not proper English, which would be BAKING, no FYRINGPAN in those times, and the word wouldn't be together as one

26)

Genesis 3:7 King James Version (KJV)

7 And the eyes of them both were opened, and they knew that they were naked; and they sewed fig leaves together, and made themselves aprons.

aprons used to be COVERINGS

27)

Ezekiel 5:1 King James Version (KJV)

5 And thou, son of man, take thee a sharp knife, take thee a barber's razor, and cause it to pass upon thine head and upon thy beard: then take thee balances to weigh, and divide the hair.

no barbers or razors in those times

28)

Acts 9:5 (KJV)

5 And he said, Who art thou, Lord? And the Lord said, I am Jesus whom thou persecutest: it is hard for thee to kick against the pricks.

Kick against the pricks wasn't there before

29)

Job 30:29 King James Version (KJV)

29 I am a brother to dragons, and a companion to owls.

ridiculous..dragons

Numbers 23:22 King James Version (KJV)

22 God brought them out of Egypt; he hath as it were the strength of an unicorn.

used to be OX. That's where the saying STRONG AS AN OX comes from

PART III

Cross out the incorrect word or phrase and write (on the blank line) what word or phrase you remember it to be :

31)

Psalm 146:3 King James Version (KJV)

3 Put not your trust in princes, nor in the son of man, in whom there is no help.

no trust in the Son of Man?..which should be capitalized

32)

Job 25:6 King James Version (KJV)

6 How much less man, that is a worm? and the son of man, which is a worm?

the Son of Man is a worm? Again not capitalized

33)

Luke 23:11 King James Version (KJV)

11 And Herod with his men of war set him at nought, and mocked him, and arrayed him in a gorgeous robe, and sent him again to Pilate.

GORGEOUS used to be Scarlet

34)

James 2:3 King James Version (KJV)

3 And ye have respect to him that weareth the gay clothing, and say unto him, Sit thou here in a good place; and say to the poor, Stand thou there, or sit here under my footstool:

GAY CLOTHING ..don't know what it used to say

35)

Matthew 1:1-2 King James Version (KJV)

1 The book of the generation of Jesus Christ, the son of David, the son of Abraham.

2 Abraham begat Isaac; and Isaac begat Jacob; and Jacob begat Judas and his brethren;

JUDAS USED TO BE JUDAH…Judas is not in the lineage of Jesus

36)

Revelation 1:13 King James Version (KJV)

13 And in the midst of the seven candlesticks one like unto the Son of man, clothed with a garment down to the foot, and girt about the paps with a golden girdle.

Paps are female breasts

37)

Daniel 6:2

And over these three presidents; of whom Daniel was first: that the princes might give accounts unto them, and the king should have no damage.

There were no presidents in Biblical times

38)

2 Thessalonians 2:9 King James Version (KJV)

9 Even him, whose coming is after the working of Satan with all power and signs and lying wonders,

Used to say LYING SIGNS and WONDERS

39)

Revelation 1:6 King James Version (KJV)

6 And hath made us kings and priests unto God and his Father; to him be glory and dominion for ever and ever. Amen. God has no father

40)

Psalm 72:6 King James Version (KJV)

6 He shall come down like rain upon the mown grass: as showers that water the earth.

No lawn mowers in Biblical times

41)

Psalm 129:7 King James Version (KJV)

7 Wherewith the mower filleth not his hand; nor he that bindeth sheaves his bosom….

no mowers

42)

Leviticus 11:35 King James Version (KJV)

35 And every thing whereupon any part of their carcase falleth shall be unclean; whether it be oven, or ranges for pots, they shall be broken down: for they are unclean and shall be unclean unto you.

no ovens, ranges in Biblical times

43)34 Now Rachel had taken the images, and put them in the camel's furniture, and sat upon them. And Laban searched all the tent, but found them not.

Camels' furniture???

Exodus 34:19 King James Version (KJV)

19 All that openeth the matrix is mine; and every firstling among thy cattle, whether ox or sheep, that is male.

MATRIX used to WOMB

45)Isaiah 32:8 King James Version (KJV)

8 But the liberal deviseth liberal things; and by liberal things shall he stand.

Is this promoting LIBERALISM, you think? Not sure what it used to say

46)

Luke 17:26 King James Version (KJV)

26 And as it was in the days of Noe, so shall it be also in the days of the Son of man.

NOAH

47)

Ezekiel 27:28 King James Version (KJV)

28 The suburbs shall shake at the sound of the cry of thy pilots. SUBURBS in Biblical times?

48)

Isaiah 23:3

3 And by great waters the seed of Shihor, the harvest of the river, is her revenue; and she is a mart of nations.

Mart....like WALMART???

49)Luke 19:23

Wherefore then gavest not thou my money into the bank, that at my coming I might have required mine own with usury?

Bank never used to be in the Bible

50) Luke 12:24

Consider the ravens: for they neither sow nor reap; which neither have storehouse nor barn; and God feedeth them: how much more are ye better than the fowls?

It used to say SPARROWS, not ravens.

Chapter 6

Mandela Effects to the Human Body and Music

❖

"What I thought was unreal now, for me, seems in some ways to be more real than what I think to be real, which seems now to be unreal." — *Fred Alan Wolf*

One of the most astounding supernatural changes has occurred to the human body. There have been changes in the rib structure, position of kidneys and the heart. Growing up, we always put our hand over our left chest and said the Pledge of Allegiance in school. Many still do that today, not realizing that our hearts are now actually in the middle.

If our heart was in the center, then why does everyone use their RIGHT HAND to put over their heart? The flag is even Mandela Effected, with the stripe below the blue now being white, whereas it used to be red.

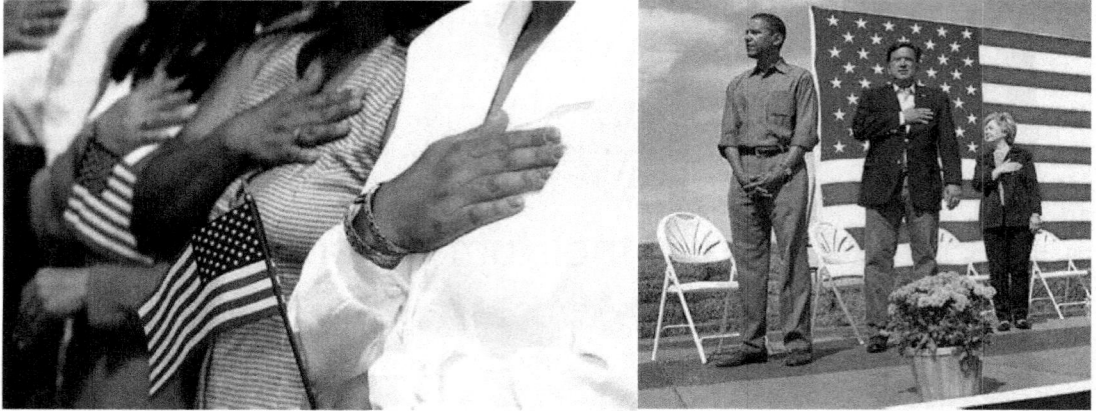

Notice the Muslim traitor didn't put his hand on his heart.

Just in case you didn't know, this is where they say our heart is located now:

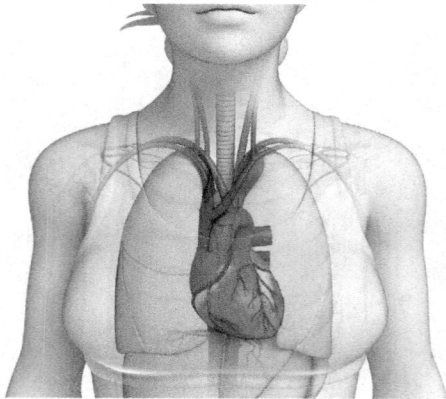

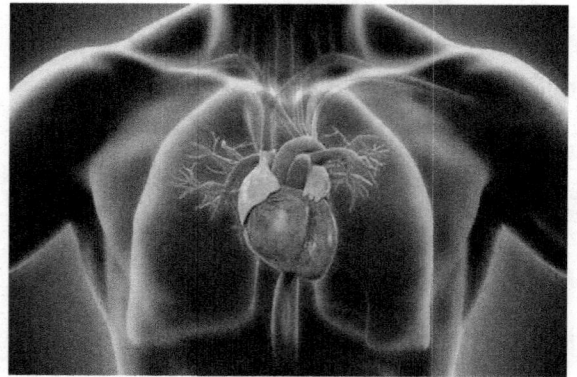

Kidneys Have Moved

Once located just above the beltine, the kidneys were vulnerable to boxing punches, hence the term "kidney punch".

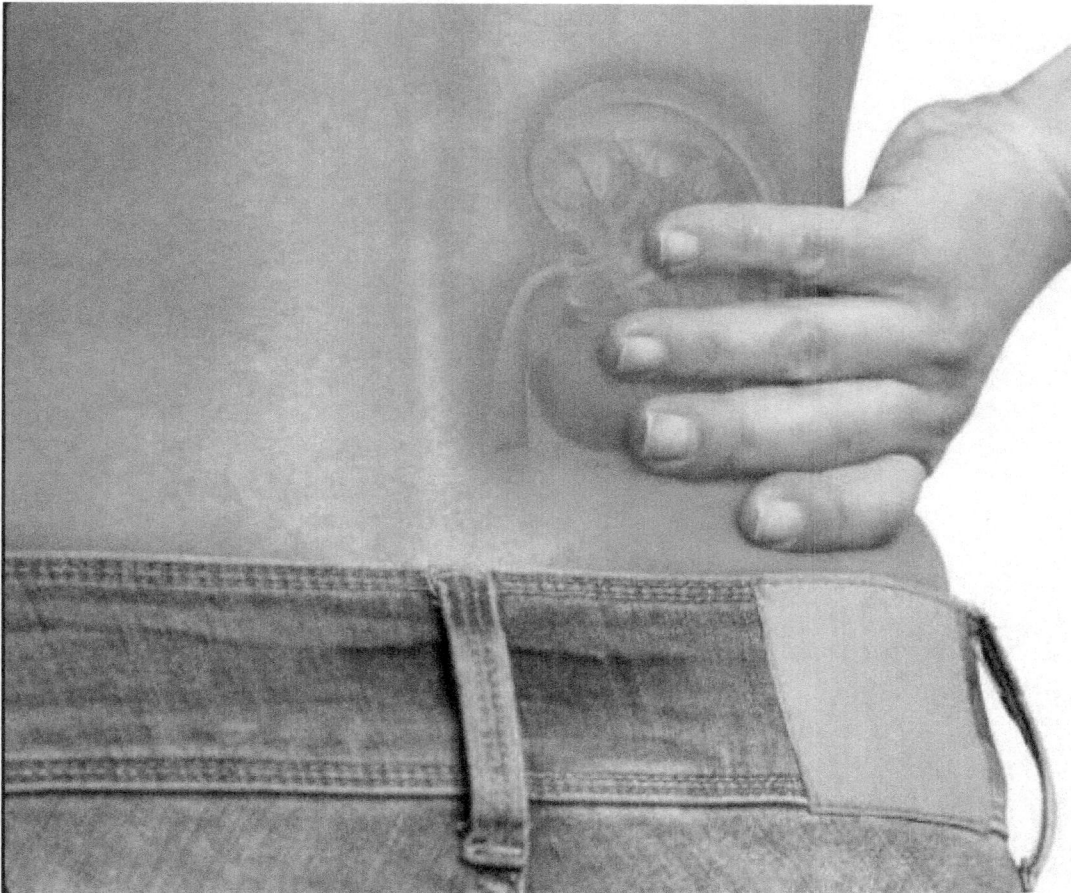

Now they are much higher up the body and The illustration above shows the kidneys where we were formerly told and on the next page it shows where the kidneys are now:

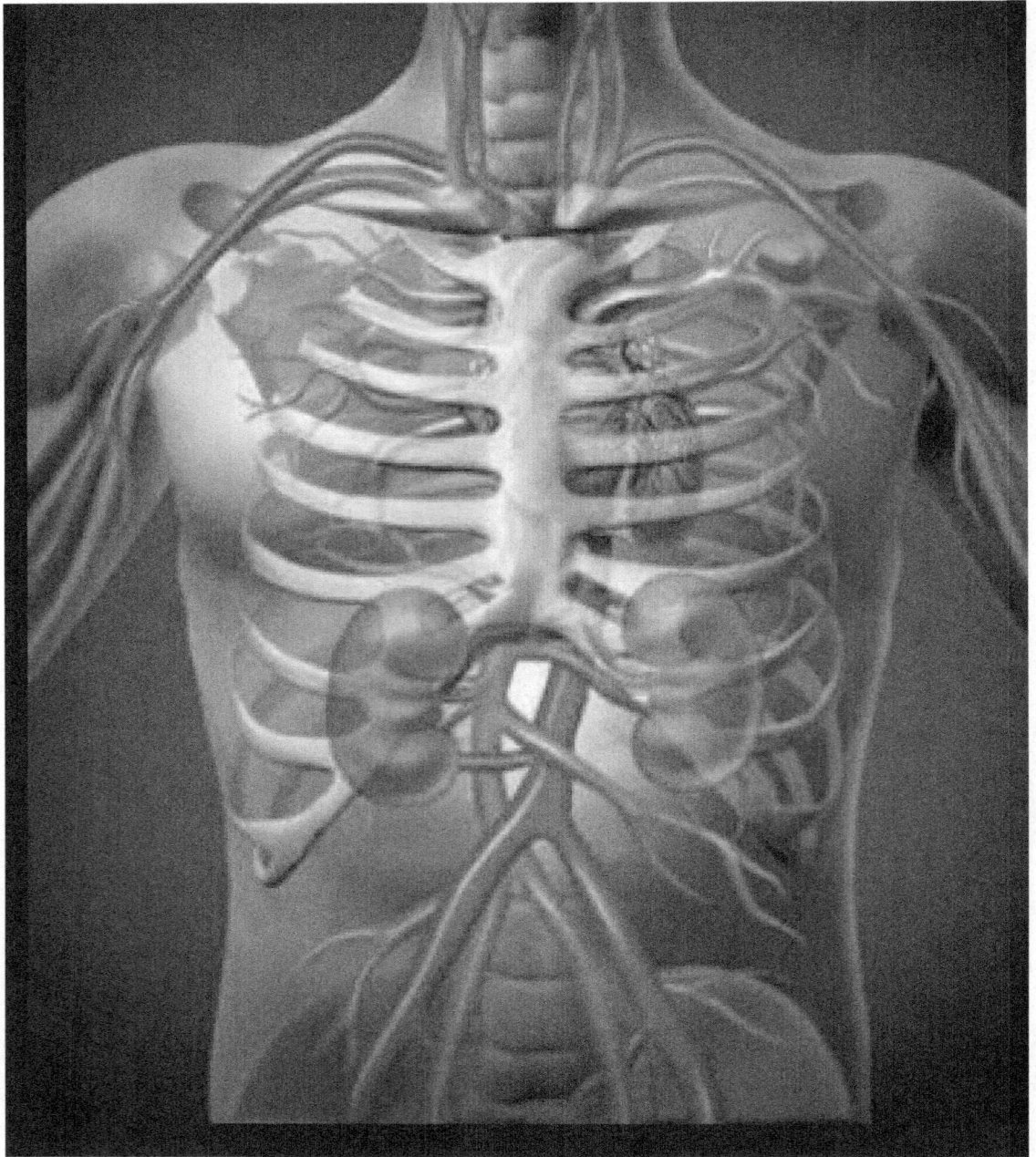

MUSIC

Take my short quiz and I think you'll be SHOCKED at how songs we all know have been slightly changed!

Take the Musical Mandela Effect Quiz

I will give you the Mandela Effect questions first. Answer it if you know it before you read on, watch the videos or get on a search engine. Send this to your friends to see how they do. Don't read ahead until you answer the questions so you're not influenced by anything I say.

Take the Quiz!

Fill in the missing word labeled BLANK

#1 Joan Jett – I love rock n roll.
In her famous song "I Love Rock n Roll" fill in the blank to the first line.
"I saw him there (BLANK) there by the record machine."

#2) Mamas and Papas – California Dreamin

In the middle of the song, there is a verse talking about going to a church. Fill in the blank word.
Stopped into a church
I passed along the way
Well, I got down on my knees (got down on my knees)
And I (BLANK) to pray

#3) Queen – We Are The Champions

This is a different one – in this one choose the correct ending of the song.
Does the very last line of song end with
"No Time for losers
Cause we are the champions"
or does it end with

"No Time for losers
Cause we are the champions…of the world

Choose the correct ending of the song.

#4) Bee Gees – How Deep Is Your Love

In the Bee Gees song, "How Deep is your Love" which is the correct lyric

How Deep is your Love?

I really mean to learn

or was it

How Deep is your Love?

I really need to know

ANSWER ALL FOUR QUESTIONS BEFORE READING FURTHER!

Okay now let's check in on what our reality says are the correct answers and compare it to your own memories.Okay those of you old enough to have a good memory of those songs should have already answered the quiz and now it's time to see how your memory compared to mine and share some videos talking about these Mandela Effects.

MUSIC QUIZ

#1) Joan Jett – I Love Rock n Roll

It was always "I saw him standing there by the record machine" to me! But in this reality it's "I saw him dancing there by the record machine." Sorry not buying it! Not my reality! Straight guys don't dance by themselves by the record machine.

Here's the official song in our reality now where she says "dancing by the record machine"

2) Mamas and Papas – California Dreamin

This is another one I would literally bet anything on! Why? Because I love the song and like to sing it karaoke after a couple of beers!

Here's how the song goes in my reality and every time I sang it.

Stopped into a church
I passed along the way
Well, I got down on my knees (got down on my knees)
And I BEGAN to pray

but in this reality now it's

Stopped into a church
I passed along the way
Well, I got down on my knees (got down on my knees)
And I PRETEND to pray

Sorry but I never sang about "pretending to pray". The only people who "pretend" to pray are people who don't believe in God. I have more proof somebody on youtube found a "residual" of the correct song in the movie **Artemis** and it's clearly saying BEGAN to pray! I also heard "BEGAN to pray" in the movie, "Once Upon a Time in Hollywood".

#3) Queen – We Are The Champions

I remember this song very vividly because my high school swim team in Alaska sang this song on the way back home on the bus from our swim meets if we won. We had a very good team and we won almost every single week for 4 years so we sang it a lot!

For me, in my reality as a teenager, the song always ended with

"No Time for losers

Cause we are the champions...of the world!

but now our reality says it just ends with

"No Time for losers

Cause we are the champions"

This ending is very unsatisfying and lame. This is the same version as was produced in the studio and the official lyrics. Our reality says it never ended with "....of the World!" Liars!

There is one live version online where the song ends in "Of the World". Interesting I've been told in the recent Queen movie "Bohemian Rhapsody" they sang it with "Of the World" at the very end but this is NOT the song according to the lyrics and all the official sources.

#4) In the song, "How Deep is your Love" the correct lyric in my time line has always and WILL always be

How Deep is your Love?

I really need to know

Not the insanely stupid lyric they say it's always been which is

How Deep is your Love?

I really mean to learn

"I really mean to learn" is so ridiculously lame! It doesn't fit at all with my memories at all.

 Here's a video with the Bee Gees singing it the current version in our reality – "I really need to learn".   Not buying it!

 But if I'm just "crazy" and remembering it all wrong then why did somebody find Andy Gibb singing it the right way and saying "I really need to know" in (2) live concerts and a tribute to his brother! This is the way the song was always to me. What is going on here? Is Andy Gibb remembering it the way I always knew it here?

What's Up or What's Going On?

https://youtu.be/-BoTx70RRe0

Videos

Original Title

New Title of Same Song

4 Non Blondes - Whats Going on — 4:58 — 14M views

P!nk - What's Up (from Live from Wembley Arena, London, England) — 5:50 — 27M views

Lady Gaga - "What's Up" 4 Non Blondes Live Cover at #artRaveVienna — 6:59 — 10M views

→ More Videos

Are these links helpful? Yes No

Whats Going On
4 Non Blondes

Twenty-five years and my life is still
Trying to get up that great big hill of hope
For a destination
And I realized quickly when I knew I should
That the world was made up of this brotherhood of man
For whatever that means.

More at MetroLyrics

4 Non Blondes - What's Up? Lyrics | Genius Lyrics
https://genius.com/4-non-blondes-whats-up-lyrics
"What's Up" was the second single from the 1992 album Bigger, Better, Faster, More by 4 Non Blondes. It shot the band into international stardom, topping the charts in seven countries ...

Send Feedback

The new Mandela title of the song *What's Going On?* is "*What's Up?*" Those words aren't even in the song…then or now. The song is sung with alot of emotion with the singer crying out" What's Going On?" So, it doesn't even sound right to call the song *What's Up?*

Pink and Lady Gaga, both wonderful castrato singers, remake the song and it is now titled, "What's Up?" Yet, Pink announces that the song she is singing is "What's Going On?" at the beginning of the following video:

And we continue to ask, *What's going on?*

This musician attributes the changing of his lyrics to the Mandela Effect:

Video: Brendon Urie Blames the Mandela Effect for his lyrics changing in recent interview

https://youtu.be/uLneNYW66as

140

Chapter 7

List of Supernatural Bible Changes

in the New Testament

❖

"To the timid and hesitating everything is impossible because it seems so." – Sir Walter Scott

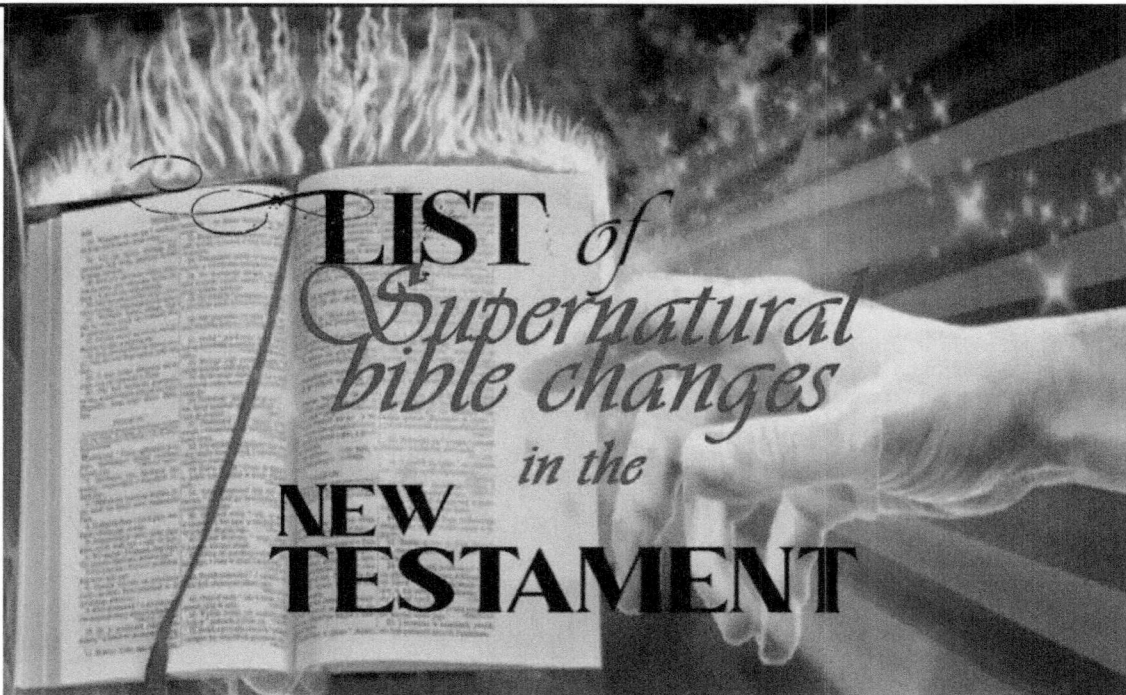

The Bible has been supernaturally changing since about 2016. Nevertheless, this chart is what I consider to be a very authentic first edition, along with the memories of what it used to be.

List of Changes in the New Testament

Scripture	Discrepancies in KJV Scripture	Memories of the 1611 KJV	Notes:
Matt 1:1	The book of the generation of Jesus Christ, the son of David, the son of Abraham.	This is the record of the genealogy of Jesus Christ, the son of David, the son of Abraham.	generation! account
Matt 1:2	Abraham begat Isaac; and Isaac begat Jacob; and Jacob begat Judas and his brethren;	Abraham begat Isaac; and Isaac begat Jacob; and Jacob begat Judah and his brethren;	
Matt 1:3	And Judas begat Phares and Zara of Thamar; and Phares begat Esrom; and Esrom begat Aram;	And Judah begat Perez and Zerah of Tamar; and Perez begat Hezron; and Hezron begat Ram;	
Matt 1:4	And Aram begat Aminadab; and Aminadab begat Naasson; and Naasson begat Salmon;	And Ram begat Aminadab; and Aminadab begat Nahshon; and Nahshon begat Salmon;	
Matt 1:5	And Salmon begat Booz of Rachab; and Booz begat Obed of Ruth; and Obed begat Jesse;	And Salmon begat Boaz of Rahab; and Boaz begat Obed of Ruth; and Obed begat Jesse;	
Matt 1:6	And Jesse begat David the king; and David the king begat Solomon of her that had been the wife of Urias;	And Jesse begat David the king; and David the king begat Solomon of her that had been the wife of Uriah;	
Matt 1:7	And Solomon begat Roboam; and Roboam begat Abia; and Abia begat Asa;	And Solomon begat Rehoboam; and Rehoboam begat Abijah; and Abijah begat Asa;	
Matt 1:8	And Asa begat Josaphat; and Josaphat begat Joram; and Joram begat Ozias;	And Asa begat Jehoshaphat; and Jehoshaphat begat Joram; and Joram begat Uzziah;	
Matt 1:9	And Ozias begat Joatham; and Joatham begat Achaz; and Achaz begat Ezekias;	And Uzziah begat Jotham; and Jotham begat Ahaz; and Ahaz begat Hezekiah;	
Matt 1:10	And Ezekias begat Manasses; and Manasses begat Amon; and Amon begat Josias;	And Hezekiah begat Manasseh; and Manasseh begat Amon; and Amon begat Josiah;	
Matt 1:11	And Josias begat Jechonias and his brethren, about the time they were carried away to Babylon:	And Josiah begat Jechoniah and his brethren, about the time they were carried away to Babylon:	
Matt 1:12	And after they were brought to Babylon, Jechonias begat Salathiel; and Salathiel begat Zorobabel;	And after they were brought to Babylon, Jechoniah begat Salathiel; and Salathiel begat Zerubbabel;	
Matt 1:13	And Zorobabel begat Abiud; and Abiud begat Eliakim; and Eliakim	And Zerubbabel begat Abiud; and Abiud begat Eliakim; and Eliakim	

Scripture	Discrepancies in KJV Scripture	Memories of the 1611 KJV	Notes:
	begat Azor;	begat Azor;	
Matt 1:14	And Azor begat Sadoc; and Sadoc begat Achim; and Achim begat Eliud;	And Azor begat Zadok; and Zadok begat Achim; and Achim begat Eliud;	
Matt 1:17	So all the generations from Abraham to David are fourteen generations; and from David until the carrying away into Babylon are fourteen generations; and from the carrying away into Babylon unto Christ are fourteen generations.	So all the generations from Abraham to David are fourteen generations; and from David until the captivity in Babylon are fourteen generations; and from the captivity in Babylon unto Christ are fourteen generations.	
Matt 1:23	Behold, a virgin shall be with child, and shall bring forth a son, and they shall call his name Emmanuel, which being interpreted is, God with us.	Behold, a virgin shall be with child, and shall bring forth a son, and they shall call his name Emmanuel, which being interpreted, God with us.	sounds like a question!

1

Scripture	Discrepancies in KJV Scripture	Memories of the 1611 KJV	Notes:
Matt 2:6	And thou Bethlehem, in the land of Juda, art not the least among the princes of Juda: for out of thee shall come a Governor, that shall rule my people Israel.	And thou Bethlehem, in the land of Judah, art not the least among the rulers of Judah: for out of thee shall come a governor, that shall shepherd my people Israel.	Juda!
Matt 3:4	And the same John had his raiment of camel's hair, and a leathern girdle about his loins; and his meat was locusts and wild honey.	Now John himself had his raiment of camel's hair, and a leather girdle about his waist; and his food was locusts and wild honey.	leathern!
Matt 3:8	Bring forth therefore fruits meet for repentance:	Bring forth therefore fruits worthy of repentance:	befitting
Matt 3:11	I indeed baptize you with water unto repentance: but he that cometh after me is mightier than I, whose shoes I am not worthy to bear: he shall baptize you with the Holy Ghost, and with fire:	I indeed baptize you with water unto repentance: but he who cometh after me is mightier than I, whose sandals I am not worthy to loose: he shall baptize you with the Holy Ghost, and with fire:	Shoes! (KJV generally used Ghost for Spirit)
Matt 3:12	Whose fan is in his hand, and he will throughly purge his floor, and gather his wheat into the garner; but he will burn up the chaff with unquenchable fire.	Whose winnowing fork is in his hand, and he will throughly cleanse his threshing-floor, and gather his wheat into the barn; but the chaff he will burn with unquenchable fire.	garner! storehouse
Matt	Then saith Jesus unto him, Get thee	Then saith Jesus unto him, Get thee	hence!

Scripture	Discrepancies in KJV Scripture	Memories of the 1611 KJV	Notes:
4:10	hence, Satan: for it is written, Thou shalt worship the Lord thy God, and him only shalt thou serve.	behind me, Satan: for it is written, "Thou shalt worship the Lord thy God, and him only shalt thou serve."	
Matt 4:16	The people which sat in darkness saw great light; and to them which sat in the region and shadow of death light is sprung up.	The people which sat in darkness saw a great light; and to them which sat in the land and shadow of death, light has dawned.	GK:ANS
Matt 4:24	And his fame went throughout all Syria: and they brought unto him all sick people that were taken with divers diseases and torments, and those which were possessed with devils, and those which were lunatick, and those that had the palsy; and he healed them.	And his fame went throughout all Syria: and they brought unto him all the sick that were taken with divers diseases and torments, and those which were possessed with devils, and those which were epileptic, and those that had the palsy; and he healed them.	lunatick! various
Matt 5:9	Blessed are the peacemakers: for they shall be called the children of God.	Blessed are the peacemakers: for they shall be called the sons of God.	
Matt 5:12	Rejoice, and be exceeding glad: for great is your reward in heaven: for so persecuted they the prophets which were before you.	Rejoice, and be exceedingly glad: for great is your reward in heaven: for so persecuted they the prophets which were before you.	
Matt 5:14	Ye are the light of the world. A city that is set on an hill cannot be hid.	Ye are the light of the world. A city that is set on a hill cannot be hid.	GK:GNS
Matt 5:20	For I say unto you, That except your righteousness shall exceed the righteousness of the Scribes and Pharisees, ye shall in no case enter into the kingdom of heaven.	For I say unto you, That except your righteousness exceed the righteousness of the Scribes and Pharisees, ye shall in no wise enter into the kingdom of heaven.	
Matt 5:21	Ye have heard that it was said by them of old time, Thou shalt not kill; and whosoever shall kill shall be in danger of the judgment:	Ye have heard that it was said to them of old, Thou shalt not kill; and whosoever shall kill shall be in danger of the judgment:	
Matt 5:22	But I say unto you, That whosoever is angry with his brother without a cause shall be in danger of the judgment: and whosoever shall say to his brother, Raca, shall be in danger of the council: but whosoever shall say, Thou fool, shall be in danger of hell fire.	But I say unto you, That whosoever is angry with his brother without a cause shall be in danger of the judgment: and whosoever shall say to his brother, Raka, shall be subject before the Sanhedrin: but whosoever says, Thou fool, shall be in danger of hell fire.	
Matt	Agree with thine adversary quickly,	Agree with thine adversary quickly,	whiles!

Scripture	Discrepancies in KJV Scripture	Memories of the 1611 KJV	Notes:
5:25	whiles thou	whilst thou art	

2

Scripture	Discrepancies in KJV Scripture	Memories of the 1611 KJV	Notes:

	art in the way with him; lest at any time the adversary deliver thee to the judge, and the judge deliver thee to the officer, and thou be cast into prison.	in the way with him; lest at any time thine adversary deliver thee to the judge, and the judge deliver thee to the officer, and thou be cast into prison.	
Matt 5:28	But I say unto you, That whosoever looketh on a woman to lust after her hath committed adultery with her already in his heart.	But I say unto you, That whosoever looketh at a woman to lust after her hath already committed adultery with her in his heart.	
Matt 5:32	But I say unto you, That whosoever shall put away his wife, saving for the cause of fornication, causeth her to commit adultery: and whosoever shall marry her that is divorced committeth adultery.	But I say unto you, That whosoever shall put away his wife, save for the cause of fornication, causeth her to commit adultery: and whosoever shall marry her that is put away commits adultery.	committeth!
Matt 5:37	But let your communication be, Yea, yea; Nay, nay: for whatsoever is more than these cometh of evil.	But let your speech be, Yea, yea; Nay, nay: for whatsoever is more than this is from the wicked one.	Ref. James 5:12
Matt 5:39	But I say unto you, That ye resist not evil: but whosoever shall smite thee on thy right cheek, turn to him the other also.	But I say unto you, resist not him that is evil: but whosoever shall smite thee on thy right cheek, turn to him the other also.	
Matt 6:9	After this manner therefore pray ye: Our Father which art in heaven, Hallowed be thy name.	After this manner therefore pray ye: Our Father Who art in heaven, Hallowed be thy name.	
Matt 6:10	Thy kingdom come. Thy will be done in earth, as it is in heaven.	Thy kingdom come. Thy will be done on earth, as it is in heaven.	GK:epi,on
Matt 6:12	And forgive us our debts, as we forgive our debtors.	And forgive us our trespasses, as we forgive those who trespasses against us.	debts! debtors
Matt 6:22	The light of the body is the eye: if therefore thine eye be single, thy whole body shall be full of light.	The lamp of the body is the eye: if therefore thine eye is sound, thy whole body shall be full of light.	be single! healthy
Matt 6:26	Behold the fowls of the air: for they sow not, neither do they reap, nor gather into barns; yet your heavenly	Behold the birds of the air: for they sow not, neither do they reap, nor gather into barns; yet your	fowls!

Scripture	Discrepancies in KJV Scripture	Memories of the 1611 KJV	Notes:
	Father feedeth them. Are ye not much better than they?	heavenly Father feedeth them. Are ye not worth more than they?	
Matt 6:30	Wherefore, if God so clothe the grass of the field, which to day is, and to morrow is cast into the oven, shall he not much more clothe you, O ye of little faith?	Wherefore, if God so clothe the grass of the field, which today is, and tomorrow is cast into the furnace, shall he not much more clothe you, Oh ye of little faith?	to day! to morrow!
Matt 7:1	Judge not, that ye be not judged.	Judge not, lest ye be judged.	(TS-lest)
Matt 7:13	Enter ye in at the strait gate: for wide is the gate, and broad is the way, that leadeth to destruction, and many there be which go in thereat:	Enter ye in at the narrow gate: for wide is the gate, and broad is the road, which leads to destruction, and many enter through it.	strait! threat!
Matt 7:14	Because strait is the gate, and narrow is the way, which leadeth unto life, and few there be that find it.	Because small is the gate, and narrow is the road, that leads unto life, and only few find it.	
Matt 7:15	Beware of false prophets, which come to you in sheep's clothing, but inwardly they are ravening wolves.	Beware of false prophets, which come to you in sheep's clothing, but inwardly they are ravenous wolves.	ravening!
Matt 7:22	Many will say to me in that day, Lord, Lord, have we not prophesied in thy name? and in thy name have cast out devils? and in thy name done many wonderful works?	Many will say to me in that day, Lord, Lord, have we not prophesied in thy name? and by thy name have cast out demons? and by thy name done many mighty works?	

3

Scripture	Discrepancies in KJV Scripture	Memories of the 1611 KJV	Notes:
Matt 8:20	And Jesus saith unto him, The foxes have holes, and the birds of the air have nests; but the Son of man hath not where to lay his head.	And Jesus saith unto him, The foxes have holes, and the birds of the air have nests; but the Son of Man hath nowhere to lay his head.	not where!
Matt 8:24	And, behold, there arose a great tempest in the sea, insomuch that the ship was covered with the waves: but he was asleep.	And, behold, there arose a great tempest in the sea, insomuch that the boat was covered with the waves: but he was asleep.	Many verses now say "ship" but should be "boat"
Matt 9:9	And as Jesus passed forth from thence, he saw a man, named Matthew, sitting at the receipt of custom: and he saith unto him,	And as Jesus passed on from there, he saw a man, named Matthew, sitting at the tax booth: and he saith unto him, Follow	receipt of custom! place of toll customhouse

Scripture	Discrepancies in KJV Scripture	Memories of the 1611 KJV	Notes:
	Follow me. And he arose, and followed him.	me. And he arose, and followed him.	
Matt 9:10	And it came to pass, as Jesus sat at meat in the house, behold, many publicans and sinners came and sat down with him and his disciples.	And it came to pass, as Jesus reclined in the house, behold, many publicans and sinners came and reclined with him and his disciples.	sat at meat!
Matt. 9:17	Neither do men put new wine into old bottles: else the bottles break, and the wine runneth out, and the bottles perish: but they put new wine into new bottles, and both are preserved.	Neither do men put new wine into old wineskins: else the wineskins burst, and the wine is spilled, and the wineskins are ruined: but they put new wine into new wineskins, and both are preserved.	wineskins tear and bottles break! (In 1881 KJV wine-skins)
Matt 9:22	But Jesus turned him about, and when he saw her, he said, Daughter, be of good comfort; thy faith hath made thee whole. And the woman was made whole from that hour.	But Jesus turned and seeing her said, Daughter, be of good cheer; thy faith hath made thee whole. And the woman was made whole from that hour.	
Matt 9:23	And when Jesus came into the ruler's house, and saw the minstrels and the people making a noise,	And when Jesus came into the ruler's house, and saw the flute-players and the crowd making a tumult,	minstrels! TMB bringing in casseroles!
Matt 9:24	He said unto them, Give place: for the maid is not dead, but sleepeth. And they laughed him to scorn.	He said unto them, go away: for the girl is not dead, but only sleepeth. And they laughed him to scorn.	stop crying maid! damsel
Matt 9:26	And the fame hereof went abroad into all that land.	And this report went forth into all the land.	region,whole area report
Matt 10:10	Nor scrip for your journey, neither two coats, neither shoes, nor yet staves: for the workman is worthy of his meat.	Nor bag for your journey, neither two coats, neither sandals, nor yet a staff: for the workman is worthy of his hire.	food also Mk 6:8 & Luke 9:3
Matt 10:42	And whosoever shall give to drink unto one of these little ones a cup of cold water only in the name of a disciple, verily I say unto you, he shall in no wise lose his reward.	And whosoever shall give to the least of these, a drink of water in My name, verily I say unto you, he shall in no wise lose his reward.	name of a disciple!
Matt 12:1	At that time Jesus went on the sabbath day through the corn; and	At that time Jesus went on the sabbath day through the grain	corn! hungred!

Scripture	Discrepancies in KJV Scripture	Memories of the 1611 KJV	Notes:
	his disciples were an hungred, and began to pluck the ears of corn, and to eat.	fields; and his disciples hungered, and began to pluck the heads of grain, and to eat.	
Matt 12:32	And whosoever speaketh a word against the Son of man, it shall be forgiven him: but whosoever speaketh against the Holy Ghost, it shall not be forgiven him, neither in this world, neither in the world to come.	And whosoever speaketh a word against the Son of man, it shall be forgiven him: but whosoever speaketh against the Holy Ghost, it shall not be forgiven him, neither in this age, nor in the age to come.	(KJV used 'Ghost' instead of 'Spirit' many times)

4

Scripture	Discrepancies in KJV Scripture	Memories of the 1611 KJV	Notes:
Matt 12:33	Either make the tree good, and his fruit good; or else make the tree corrupt, and his fruit corrupt: for the tree is known by his fruit.	Either make the tree good, and its fruit good; or else make the tree corrupt, and its fruit corrupt: for the tree is known by its fruit.	GK:GN3S
Matt 12:50	For whosoever shall do the will of my Father which is in heaven, the same is my brother, and sister, and mother.	For whosoever does the will of my Father which is in heaven, the same is my brother, and sister, and mother.	
Matt 13:5	Some fell upon stony places, where they had not much earth: and forthwith they sprung up, because they had no deepness of earth:	Some fell on rocky places, where they did not have much soil, and immediately they sprang up, because they had no depth of soil.	
Matt 13:15	For this people's heart is waxed gross, and their ears are dull of hearing, and their eyes they have closed; lest at any time they should see with their eyes, and hear with their ears, and should understand with their heart, and should be converted, and I should heal them.	For this people's hearts are waxed cold, and their ears are dull of hearing, and their eyes they have closed; lest at any time they should see with their eyes, and hear with their ears, and should understand with their heart, and are converted, and I will heal them.	
Matt 13:20	But he that received the seed into stony places, the same is he that heareth the word, and anon with joy receiveth it;	But he that received the seed into stony places, the same is he that heareth the word, and immediately with joy receiveth it;	anon!
Matt	Yet hath he not root in himself, but dureth	Yet hath he not root in himself,	dureth!

Scripture	Discrepancies in KJV Scripture	Memories of the 1611 KJV	Notes:
13:21	for a while: for when tribulation or persecution ariseth because of the word, by and by he is offended.	but endureth for awhile: for when tribulation or persecution ariseth because of the word, immediately he is offended.	by and by!
Matt 13:22	He also that received seed among the thorns is he that heareth the word; and the care of this world, and the deceitfulness of riches, choke the word, and he becometh unfruitful.	He also that planted seed among the thorns is he that heareth the word; and the cares of this world, and the deceitfulness of riches, choke the word, and it becomes unfruitful.	
Matt 13:49	So shall it be at the end of the world: the angels shall come forth, and sever the wicked from among the just,	So shall it be at the end of the age: the angels shall come forth, and separate the wicked from among the righteous,	
Matt 14:15	And when it was evening, his disciples came to him, saying, This is a desert place, and the time is now past; send the multitude away, that they may go into the villages, and buy themselves victuals.	And when it was evening, his disciples came to him, saying, This is a deserted place, and the hour is late; send the multitude away, that they may go into the villages, and buy themselves food.	victuals!
Matt 14:23	And when he had sent the multitudes away, he went up into a mountain apart to pray: and when the evening was come, he was there alone.	And when he had sent the multitudes away, he went up unto a mountain apart to pray: and when the evening was come, he was there alone.	
Matt 15:4	For God commanded, saying, thy father and mother: and, He that curseth father or mother, let him die the death.	For God commanded, saying, Honour thy father and mother: and, He that curseth father or mother, let him surely die.	die the death! see Exo 21:17
Matt 16:13	When Jesus came into the coasts of Caesarea Philippi, he asked his disciples, saying, Whom do men say that I the Son of man am?	When Jesus came into the borders of Caesarea Philippi, he asked his disciples, saying, Whom do men say that I am?	coasts!
Matt 16:14	And they said, Some say that thou art John the Baptist: some, Elias; and others, Jeremias, or one of the prophets.	And they said, Some say that thou art John the Baptist: some, Elijah; and others, Jeremiah, or one of the prophets.	Elias! Jeremias!
Matt 16:26	For what is a man profited, if he shall gain the whole world, and lose his own soul? or what shall a man give in exchange for	For what profits a man, if he shall gain the whole world, and lose his own soul? or what shall	

Scripture	Discrepancies in KJV Scripture	Memories of the 1611 KJV	Notes:
	his soul?	a man give in exchange for his soul?	
Matt 17:15	Lord, have mercy on my son: for he is lunatick,	Lord, have mercy on my son: for he is epileptic and	lunatick!

5

Scripture	Discrepancies in KJV Scripture	Memories of the 1611 KJV	Notes:
	and sore vexed: for ofttimes he falleth into the fire, and oft into the water.	sore vexed: for often he falleth into the fire, and often into the water.	
Matt 17:17	Then Jesus answered and said, O faithless and perverse generation, how long shall I be with you? how long shall I suffer you? bring him hither to me.	Then Jesus answered and said, Oh faithless and perverse generation, how long shall I be with you? how long shall I put up with you? bring him hither to me.	bear
Matt 17:22	And while they abode in Galilee, Jesus said unto them, The Son of man shall be betrayed into the hands of men:	And while they abode in Galilee, Jesus said unto them, The Son of man is about to be delivered into the hands of men:	see Luke 24:7
Matt 17:23	And they shall kill him, and the third day he shall be raised again. And they were exceeding sorry.	And they shall kill him, and the third day he shall be raised up. And they were exceedingly sad.	sorry!
Matt 17:27	Notwithstanding, lest we should offend them, go thou to the sea, and cast an hook, and take up the fish that first cometh up; and when thou hast opened his mouth, thou shalt find a piece of money: that take, and give unto them for me and thee.	Notwithstanding, lest we cause them to stumble, go thou to the sea, and cast a hook, and take up the fish that comes up first; and when thou hast opened its mouth, thou shalt find a shekel: take that, and give unto them for me and thee.	piece of money! drachma
Matt 18:19	Again I say unto you, That if two of you shall agree on earth as touching any thing that they shall ask, it shall be done for them of my Father which is in heaven.	Again I say unto you, That if two of you shall agree on earth concerning any thing that they shall ask, it shall be done for them of my Father who is in heaven.	touching!
Matt 19:14	But Jesus said, Suffer little children, and forbid them not, to come unto me: for of such is the kingdom of heaven.	But Jesus said, Suffer the little children to come unto me, and forbid them not, for such is the kingdom of heaven.	GK:ta, the
Matt 19:18	He saith unto him, Which? Jesus said, Thou shalt do no murder, Thou shalt not commit adultery,	He saith unto him, Which? Jesus said, Thou shalt not murder, Thou shalt not commit adultery, Thou	

Scripture	Discrepancies in KJV Scripture	Memories of the 1611 KJV	Notes:
	Thou shalt not steal, Thou shalt not bear false witness,	shalt not steal, Thou shalt not bear false witness,	
Matt 20:11	And when they had received it, they murmured against the goodman of the house,	And when they had received it, they murmured against the master of the house,	goodman!
Matt 20:25	But Jesus called them unto him, and said, Ye know that the princes of the Gentiles exercise dominion over them, and they that are great exercise authority upon them.	But Jesus called them unto him, and said, Ye know that the rulers of the Gentiles lord it over them, and they that are great exercise authority over them.	
Matt 21:7-8	7 And brought the ass, and the colt, and put on them their clothes, and they set him thereon. 8 And a great multitude spread their garments in the way; others cut down branches from the trees, and strawed them in the way.	7 They brought the donkey and the colt, and put their garments on them, and he sat thereon. 8 And the crowd spread their garments in the way; and others cut down branches from the trees, and strewed them in the way.	strawed!
Matt 21:19	And when he saw a fig tree in the way, he came to it, and found nothing thereon, but leaves only, and said unto it, Let no fruit grow on thee henceforward for ever. And presently the fig tree withered away.	And when he saw a fig tree by the wayside, he came to it, and found nothing thereon, but leaves only, and said unto it, Let no fruit grow on thee henceforth forever. And immediately the fig tree withered away.	henceforward ! road
Matt 21:31	Whether of them twain did the will of his father? They say unto him, The first. Jesus saith unto them, Verily I say unto you, That the publicans and the harlots go into the kingdom of God before you.	Whether of them did the will of his father? They say unto him, The first. Jesus saith unto them, Verily I say unto you, That the publicans and the sinners go into the kingdom of God before you.	twain!

6

Scripture	Discrepancies in KJV Scripture	Memories of the 1611 KJV	Notes:
Matt 21:42	Jesus saith unto them, Did ye never read in the scriptures, The stone which the builders rejected, the same is become the head of the corner: this is the Lord's doing, and it is marvellous in our eyes?	Jesus saith unto them, Did ye never read in the scriptures, "The stone which the builders rejected, the same is become the chief cornerstone: this is the Lord's doing, and it is marvelous in our eyes?"	head of the corner!
Matt 22:5	But they made light of it, and went their ways, one to his farm, another	But they made light of it, and went their way, one to his	

Scripture	Discrepancies in KJV Scripture	Memories of the 1611 KJV	Notes:
	to his merchandise:	field, another to his business:	
Matt 22:6,7	6 And the remnant took his servants, and entreated them spitefully, and slew them. 7 But when the king heard thereof, he was wroth: and he sent forth his armies, and destroyed those murderers, and burned up their city.	6 And the rest took his servants, and entreated them spitefully, and killed them. 7 But when the king heard thereof, he became angry: and he sent forth his soldiers, and destroyed those murderers, and burned up their city.	(I don't remember the king having such vengeance?)
Matt 22:9,10	9 Go ye therefore into the highways, and as many as ye shall find, bid to the marriage. 10 So those servants went out into the highways, and gathered together all as many as they found, both bad and good: and the wedding was furnished with guests.	9 Go ye therefore into the highways and byways, and as many as ye shall find, bid to the wedding feast. 10 So those servants went out into the highways and byways, and gathered together all as many as they found, and the wedding was filled with guests. And the door was shut.	
Matt 22:19	Shew me the tribute money. And they brought unto him a penny.	Shew me the tribute money. And they brought unto him a denarius.	coin also in Mark 12:15
Matt 22:36	Master, which is the great commandment in the law?	Teacher, which is the greatest commandment in the law?	Also Matt 22:38
Matt 23:12	And whosoever shall exalt himself shall be humbled; and he that shall humble himself shall be exalted.	And whosoever shall exalt himself shall be abased; and he that shall humble himself shall be exalted.	abased! also Luke 14:11,18:14
Matt 23:16	Woe unto you, ye blind guides, which say, Whosoever shall swear by the temple, it is nothing; but whosoever shall swear by the gold of the temple, he is a debtor!	Woe unto you, blind guides, which say, Whosoever shall swear by the temple, it is nothing; but whosoever shall swear by the gold of the temple, he is bound by his oath!	
Matt 24:22	And except those days should be shortened, there should no flesh be saved: but for the elect's sake those days shall be shortened.	And except those days should be shortened, no flesh would be saved: but for the elect's sake those days shall be shortened.	
Matt	For wheresoever the carcase is,	For wheresoever the carcass	ref. Luke

Scripture	Discrepancies in KJV Scripture	Memories of the 1611 KJV	Notes:
24:28	there will the eagles be gathered together.	is, there will the vultures be gathered together.	17:37
Matthew 24:33	So likewise ye, when ye shall see all these things, know that it is near, even at the doors.	So likewise ye, when ye shall see all these things, know that it is near, even at the door.	Used to be: door (There is only one door to heaven - through Jesus)
Matt 24:43	But know this, that if the goodman of the house had known in what watch the thief would come, he would have watched, and would not have suffered his house to be broken up.	But know this, that if the master of the house had known in what watch the thief would come, he would have watched, and would not have suffered his house to be broken up.	goodman! also Luke 12:39
Matt 24:49	And shall begin to smite his fellowservants, and to eat and drink with the drunken;	And shall begin to smite his fellow servants, and to eat and drink with the drunkards;	
Matt 25:15	And unto one he gave five talents, to another two, and to another one; to every man according to his several ability; and straightway took his journey.	And unto one he gave five talents, to another two, and to another one; to every man according to his particular ability; and straightway took his journey.	several! own
Matt 25:26	His lord answered and said unto him, Thou wicked and slothful servant, thou knewest that I reap where I sowed not, and gather where I have	His lord answered and said unto him, Thou wicked and slothful servant, thou knewest that I reap where I sowed not, and gather where I did not scatter:	strawed!

7

Scripture	Discrepancies in KJV Scripture	Memories of the 1611 KJV	Notes:
	not strawed:		
Matt 25:27	Thou oughtest therefore to have put my money to the exchangers, and then at my coming I should have received mine own with usury.	Thou ought therefore to have put my money to the exchangers, and then at my coming I should have received mine own with interest.	oughtest!
Matt 25:36	Naked, and ye clothed me: I was sick, and ye visited me: I was in prison, and ye visited me.	I was naked, and ye clothed me: I was sick, and ye visited me: I was in prison, and ye came unto me.	came unto!

Scripture	Discrepancies in KJV Scripture	Memories of the 1611 KJV	Notes:
Matt 26:24	The Son of man goeth as it is written of him: but woe unto that man by whom the Son of man is betrayed! it had been good for that man if he had not been born.	The Son of man goeth as it is written of him: but woe unto that man by whom the Son of man is betrayed! it had been better for that man if he had not been born.	
Matt 26:64	Jesus saith unto him, Thou hast said: nevertheless I say unto you, Hereafter shall ye see the Son of man sitting on the right hand of power, and coming in the clouds of heaven.	Jesus saith unto him, Thou hast said: nevertheless I say unto you, Hereafter shall ye see the Son of man sitting at the right hand of the Father and coming in the clouds of heaven.	also Mk 14:62
Matt 26:69	Now Peter sat without in the palace: and a damsel came unto him, saying, Thou also wast with Jesus of Galilee.	Now Peter sat without in the courtyard: and a servant girl came unto him, saying, Thou also wast with Jesus the Galilaean.	courtyard! damsel!
Matt 26:73	And after a while came unto him they that stood by, and said to Peter, Surely thou also art one of them; for thy speech bewrayeth thee.	And after a while came unto him they that stood by, and said to Peter, Surely thou also art one of them; for thy speech betrayeth thee.	bewrayeth!
Matt 27:3	Then Judas, which had betrayed him, when he saw that he was condemned, repented himself, and brought again the thirty pieces of silver to the chief priests and elders,	Then Judas, which had betrayed him, when he saw that he was condemned, repented himself, and brought back the thirty pieces of silver to the chief priests and elders,	again!
Matt 27:29	And when they had platted a crown of thorns, they put it upon his head, and a reed in his right hand: and they bowed the knee before him, and mocked him, saying, Hail, King of the Jews!	And when they had wove a crown of thorns, they put it upon his head, and put a staff in his right hand: and they bowed the knee before him, and mocked him, saying, Hail, King of the Jews!	platted! reed! also Mk 15:17 & Jn 19:2
Matt 27:32	And as they came out, they found a man of Cyrene, Simon by name: him they compelled to bear his cross.	And as they came out,(tradition says; Jesus carried his cross until he could bear it no longer) they found a man of Cyrene, Simon by name: him they compelled to bear his cross.	Contradicts Jn 19:17
Matt 27:39	And they that passed by reviled him, wagging their heads,	And they that passed by reviled him, shaking their heads,	wagging!

Scripture	Discrepancies in KJV Scripture	Memories of the 1611 KJV	Notes:
			Doc. Error both thieves did not curse him only one did.
Matt 27:44	The thieves also, which were crucified with him, cast the same in his teeth.	The thieves also, which were crucified with him, reviled him the same way.	cast the same in his teeth!
Matt 28:9	And as they went to tell his disciples, behold, Jesus met them, saying, All hail. And they came and held him by the feet, and worshipped him.	And as they went to tell his disciples, behold, Jesus met them, saying, greetings! and they took hold of his feet and worshipped him.	All hail!
Matt 28:12	And when they were assembled with the elders, and had taken counsel, they gave large money unto the soldiers,	And when they were assembled with the elders, and had taken counsel, they gave much silver unto the soldiers,	large money!
Matt 28:19	Go ye therefore, and teach all nations, baptizing them in the name of the Father, and of the Son,	Go ye therefore, and make disciples of all nations, baptizing them in the name of the Father, and of the	

8

Scripture	Discrepancies in KJV Scripture	Memories of the 1611 KJV	Notes:
	and of the Holy Ghost:	Son, and of the Holy Ghost:	
Matt 28:20	Teaching them to observe all things whatsoever I have commanded you: and, lo, I am with you alway, even unto the end of the world. Amen.	Teaching them to observe all things whatsoever I have commanded you: and, lo, I am with you always, even unto the end of the age. Amen.	
Mark 1:7	And preached, saying, There cometh one mightier than I after me, the latchet of whose shoes I am not worthy to stoop down and unloose.	And preached, saying, There cometh one mightier than I after me, the latchet of whose sandals I am not worthy to loose.	stoop!
Mrk 1:8	I baptized you in water; But he shall baptize you in the Holy Spirit.	I indeed have baptized you in water; But he shall baptize you in the Holy Ghost.	
Mrk 1:26	And the unclean spirit, tearing him and crying with a loud voice, came out of him.	And the unclean spirit, tearing him and crying with a loud voice, came out of him.	
Mrk 1:30	But Simon's wife's mother lay sick of a fever, and anon they tell him of	But Simon's wife's mother lay sick of a fever, and straightway they tell	anon!

Scripture	Discrepancies in KJV Scripture	Memories of the 1611 KJV	Notes:
	her.	him of her.	
Mrk 1:32	And at even, when the sun did set, they brought unto him all that were diseased, and them that were possessed with devils.	And at even, when the sun did set, they brought unto him all that were diseased, and them that were possessed with demons.	
Mrk 1:34	And he healed many that were sick of divers diseases, and cast out many devils; and suffered not the devils to speak, because they knew him.	And he healed many that were sick of diverse diseases, and cast out many demons; and permitted not the demons to speak, because they knew him.	
Mrk 1:45	But he went out, and began to publish it much, and to blaze abroad the matter, insomuch that Jesus could no more openly enter into the city, but was without in desert places: and they came to him from every quarter.	But he went out, and began to proclaim it freely, and to spread the matter abroad, insomuch that Jesus could no more openly enter into the city, but stayed in deserted places: and they came to him from every quarter.	
Mrk 2:18	And the disciples of John and of the Pharisees used to fast: and they come and say unto him, Why do the disciples of John and of the Pharisees fast, but thy disciples fast not?	And they came and said unto him, Why do the disciples of John fast, but thy disciples fast not?	used to fast!? Matt 9:14 says they are D of John?
Mrk 2:22	And no man putteth new wine into old bottles: else the new wine doth burst the bottles, and the wine is spilled, and the bottles will be marred: but new wine must be put into new bottles.	And no man putteth new wine into old wineskins: else the new wine doth burst the skins, and the wine is spilled, and the wineskins will be ruined: but new wine must be put into new wineskins.	bottles!
Mrk 3:17	And James the son of Zebedee, and John the brother of James; and he surnamed them Boanerges, which is, The sons of thunder:	And James the son of Zebedee, and John the brother of James; and he surnamed them Barrjonas, which is, The sons of thunder:	Boanerges!
Mrk 3:18	And Andrew, and Philip, and Bartholomew, and Matthew, and Thomas, and James the son of Alphaeus, and Thaddaeus, and Simon the Canaanite,	And Andrew, and Philip, and Bartholomew, and Matthew, and Thomas, and James the son of Alphaeus, and Thaddaeus, and Simon the Zealot,	Canaanite!
Mrk 3:35	For whosoever shall do the will of God, the same is my brother, and my sister, and mother.	For whosoever doeth the will of God, the same is my brother, and my sister, and mother.	

Scripture	Discrepancies in KJV Scripture	Memories of the 1611 KJV	Notes:
Mrk 4:19	And the cares of this world, and the deceitfulness of riches, and the lusts of other things entering in, choke the word, and it becometh unfruitful.	And the cares of this world, and the deceitfulness of riches, and the lust of the flesh, choke the word, and it becomes unfruitful.	
Mrk 4:21	And he said unto them, Is a candle brought to be put under a bushel, or under a bed? and not to be set on a candlestick?	And he said unto them, Is a lamp brought to be put under a bushel, or under a bed? and not to be set on a lampstand?	candle! candlestick!

9

Scripture	Discrepancies in KJV Scripture	Memories of the 1611 KJV	Notes:
Mrk 4:22	For there is nothing hid, which shall not be manifested; neither was any thing kept secret, but that it should come abroad.	For there is nothing hid, which shall not be manifested; neither was any thing kept secret, except that it should come to light.	
Mrk 4:32	But when it is sown, it groweth up, and becometh greater than all herbs, and shooteth out great branches; so that the fowls of the air may lodge under the shadow of it.	But when it is sown, it groweth up, and becometh greater than all herbs, and shooteth out great branches; so that the birds of heaven may lodge under the shadow thereof.	
Mrk 5:30	And Jesus, immediately knowing in himself that virtue had gone out of him, turned him about in the press, and said, Who touched my clothes?	And Jesus, immediately knowing in himself that virtue had gone out of him, turned himself around in the crowd, and said, Who touched me?	Press! also Luke 19:3
Mrk 5:41	And he took the damsel by the hand, and said unto her, Talitha cumi; which is, being interpreted, Damsel, I say unto thee, arise.	And he took the child's hand, and said unto her, Talitha cumi; which is, being interpreted, little girl, I say unto thee, arise.	damsel!
Mrk 6:4	But Jesus said unto them, A prophet is not without honour, but in his own country, and among his own kin, and in his own house.	But Jesus said unto them, A prophet is not without honour, save in his own country, and among his own relatives, and in his own house.	kin!
Mrk 6:7	And he called unto him the twelve, and began to send them forth by two and two; and gave them power over unclean spirits;	And he called unto him the twelve, and began to send them forth two by two; and gave them authority over unclean spirits;	
Mrk 6:8	And commanded them that they should take nothing for their journey, save a staff only; no scrip, no bread, no money in their purse:	And commanded them that they should take nothing for their journey, except a staff only; no bag, no bread, no money in their purse:	scrip!

Scripture	Discrepancies in KJV Scripture	Memories of the 1611 KJV	Notes:
Mrk 6:25	And she came in straightway with haste unto the king, and asked, saying, I will that thou give me by and by in a charger the head of John the Baptist.	And she came in straightway with haste unto the king, and asked, saying, I will that thou give me immediately on a dish the head of John the Baptist.	by and by!
Mrk 6:32	And they departed into a desert place by ship privately.	And they departed into a deserted place by boat privately.	desert/ship!
Mrk 6:33	And the people saw them departing, and many knew him, and ran afoot thither out of all cities, and outwent them, and came together unto him.	And the people saw them departing, and many knew them, and ran together on foot out of the cities, and went before them,	outwent!
Mrk 6:35	And when the day was now far spent, his disciples came unto him, and said, This is a desert place, and now the time is far passed:	And when the day was now far spent, his disciples came unto him, and said, This is a desolate place, and now the time is far passed:	deserted
Mrk 6:39	And he commanded them to make all sit down by companies upon the green grass.	And he commanded them to make all recline by groups upon the green grass.	
Mrk 7:2	And when they saw some of his disciples eat bread with defiled, that is to say, with unwashen, hands, they found fault.	And when they saw some of his disciples eat bread with unclean, hands, they found fault.	unwashen!
Mrk 7:11	But ye say, If a man shall say to his father or mother, It is Corban, that is to say, a gift, by whatsoever thou mightest be profited by me; he shall be free.	But ye say, If a man shall say to his father or mother, It is Korban, that is to say, a gift, by whatsoever thou mightest be profited by me; he shall be free.	Corban!
Mrk 7:35	And straightway his ears were opened, and the string of his tongue was loosed, and he spake plain.	And straightway his ears were opened, and the impediment of his tongue was loosed, and he spake plain.	string!
Mrk 7:36	And he charged them that they should tell no man: but the more he charged them, so much the more a great deal they published it;	And he charged them that they should tell no man: but the more he charged them, so much more they widely proclaimed it;	exceedingly

10

Scripture	Discrepancies in KJV Scripture	Memories of the 1611 KJV	Notes:
Mrk 8:3	And if I send them away fasting to their own houses, they will faint by the way: for divers of them came from far.	And if I send them away fasting to their own houses, they will faint by the way: for some of have come from afar.	

Scripture	Discrepancies in KJV Scripture	Memories of the 1611 KJV	Notes:
Mrk 8:12	And he sighed deeply in his spirit, and saith, Why doth this generation seek after a sign? verily I say unto you, There shall no sign be given unto this generation.	And he sighed deeply in his spirit, and saith, Why doth this generation seek after a sign? verily I say unto you, none will be given it except the sign of the prophet Jonah.	
Mrk 9:20	And they brought him unto him: and when he saw him, straightway the spirit tare him; and he fell on the ground, and wallowed foaming.	And they brought him unto the child: and when he saw him, immediately the foul spirit tore him; and he fell on the ground foaming at the mouth.	
Mrk 9:28	And when he was come into the house, his disciples asked him privately, Why could not we cast him out?	And when he had come into the house, his disciples asked him privately, Why could we not cast it out?	
Mrk 10:40	But to sit on my right hand and on my left hand is not mine to give; but it shall be given to them for whom it is prepared.	But to sit at my right hand and at my left hand is not mine to give; but it shall be given to them for whom it is prepared.	Also Matt 20:23 GK:ek,out of
Mrk 10:46	And they came to Jericho: and as he went out of Jericho with his disciples and a great number of people, blind Bartimaeus, the son of Timaeus, sat by the highway side begging.	And they came to Jericho: and as he went out of Jericho with his disciples and a great number of people, blind Bartimaeus, the son of Timaeus, sat by the roadside begging.	
Mrk 13:10	And the gospel must first be published among all nations.	And the gospel must first be proclaimed to all the nations.	
Mrk 13:22	For false Christs and false prophets shall rise, and shall shew signs and wonders, to seduce, if it were possible, even the elect.	For false Christs and false prophets shall rise, and shall shew signs and wonders, to deceive, if it were possible, even the elect.	seduce!
Mrk 14:3	And being in Bethany in the house of Simon the leper, as he sat at meat, there came a woman having an alabaster box of ointment of spikenard very precious; and she brake the box, and poured it on his head.	And being in Bethany in the house of Simon the leper, as he sat at supper, there came a woman having an alabaster jar of ointment of spikenard very precious; and she broke the jar, and poured it on his head.	also Matt 26:7 (see Luke 7:38 and Jn 12:3)
Mrk 14:30	And Jesus saith unto him, Verily I say unto thee, That this day, even in this night, before the cock crow twice, thou shalt deny me thrice.	And Jesus saith unto him, Verily I say unto thee, That this day, even in this night, before the cock crows twice, thou shalt deny me three times.	thrice! rooster

Scripture	Discrepancies in KJV Scripture	Memories of the 1611 KJV	Notes:
Mrk 14:44	And he that betrayed him had given them a token, saying, Whomsoever I shall kiss, that same is he; take him, and lead him away safely.	And he that betrayed him had given them a sign, saying, Whomsoever I shall kiss, that same is he; take him, and lead him away.	token!
Mrk 14:51	51) And there followed him a certain young man, having a linen cloth cast about his naked body; and the young men laid hold on him: 52) And he left the linen cloth, and fled from them naked.	51) And there followed him (Jesus) a certain young man, and some men laid hold of him: 52) And he was afraid and he left his linen garment, and fled from them naked. (I reconstructed this the best way I remembered it.)	Yes this was Mark but it didn't say it this way at all
Mrk 14:61	But he held his peace, and answered nothing. Again the high priest asked him, and said unto him, Art thou the Christ, the Son of the Blessed?	But he held his peace, and answered nothing. Again the high priest asked him, and said unto him, Art thou the Christ, the Son of the living God?	
Mrk 14:68	But he denied, saying, I know not, neither understand I what thou sayest. And he went out into the porch; and the cock crew.	But he denied, saying, I know not, neither understand I what thou sayest. And he went out into the courtyard; and the cock crowed.	
Mrk 14:72	And the second time the cock crew. And Peter called to mind the word that Jesus said unto him, Before the cock crow twice, thou shalt deny me	And the second time the cock crowed. And Peter called to mind the word that Jesus said unto him, Before the cock crows twice, thou shalt deny me	see Mt. 26:75 & Lk. 22:61

11

Scripture	Discrepancies in KJV Scripture	Memories of the 1611 KJV	Notes:
	thrice. And when he thought thereon, he wept.	three times. And when he thought thereon, he wept.	
Mrk 15:21	And they compel one Simon a Cyrenian, who passed by, coming out of the country, the father of Alexander and Rufus, to bear his cross.	And they compel one Simon a Cyrenian, who passed by, (tradition says; Jesus carried his cross until he could bear it no longer) to bear his cross.	Contradicts Jn 19:17
Mrk 15:31	Likewise also the chief priests mocking said among themselves with the scribes, He saved others; himself he cannot save.	Likewise also the chief priests mocking said among themselves with the scribes, He saved others; yet himself he cannot save.	but
Mrk 15:37	And Jesus cried with a loud voice, and gave up the ghost.	And Jesus cried with a loud voice, and breathed his last.	expired
Mrk	And when the centurion, which stood	And when the centurion,	expired

Scripture	Discrepancies in KJV Scripture	Memories of the 1611 KJV	Notes:
15:39	over against him, saw that he so cried out, and gave up the ghost, he said, Truly this man was the Son of God.	which stood over against him, saw that he so cried out so, and breathed his last, he said, Truly this man was the Son of God.	
Mrk 15:43	Joseph of Arimathaea, a honourable counsellor, which also waited for the kingdom of God, came, and went in boldly unto Pilate, and craved the body of Jesus.	Joseph of Arimathaea, a member of the Sanhedrin which also waited for the kingdom of God, came, and went in boldly unto Pilate, and asked for Jesus' body.	
Mrk 15:46	And he bought fine linen, and took him down, and wrapped him in the linen, and laid him in a sepulchre which was hewn out of a rock, and rolled a stone unto the door of the sepulchre.	And he bought fine linen, and took him down, and wrapped him in the linen, and laid him in a tomb which was hewn out of a rock, and rolled a stone unto the door of the tomb.	
Mrk 15:47	And Mary Magdalene and Mary the mother of Joses beheld where he was laid.	And Mary Magdalene and Mary the mother of Joseph beheld where he was laid.	Joses mentioned other verses is Jesus
Mrk 16:5,6	5 And entering into the sepulchre, they saw a young man sitting on the right side, clothed in a long white garment; and they were affrighted. 6 And he saith unto them, Be not affrighted: Ye seek Jesus of Nazareth, which was crucified: he is risen; he is not here: behold the place where they laid him.	5 And entering into the tomb, they saw a young man sitting on the right side, clothed in a long white garment; and they were afraid. 6 And he saith unto them, Be not afraid: Ye seek Jesus of Nazareth, which was crucified: he is risen; he is not here: behold the place where they laid him.	affrighted!
Mrk 16:13	And they went and told it unto the residue: neither believed they them.	And they went and told it unto the rest: but they didn't believe them.	residue!
Mrk 16:14	Afterward he appeared unto the eleven as they sat at meat, and upbraided them with their unbelief and hardness of heart, because they believed not them which had seen him after he was risen.	Afterward he appeared unto the eleven as they reclined at the table, and upbraided them with their unbelief and hardness of heart, because they believed not them which had seen him after he was	sat at meat!

Scripture	Discrepancies in KJV Scripture	Memories of the 1611 KJV	Notes:
		risen.	
Mrk 16:15	And he said unto them, Go ye into all the world, and preach the gospel to every creature.	And he said unto them, Go ye into all the world, and proclaim the gospel to all creation.	
Mrk 16:16	He that believeth and is baptized shall be saved; but he that believeth not shall be damned.	He that believeth and is baptized shall be saved; but he that believeth not shall be condemned.	damned!
Luk 1:1	Forasmuch as many have taken in hand to set forth in order a declaration of those things which are most surely believed among us,	Forasmuch as many have taken in hand to draw up a narrative of these matters which have been accomplished among us,	declaration! fulfilled
Luk 1:28	And the angel came in unto her, and said, Hail, thou that art highly favoured, the Lord is with thee: blessed art thou among women.	And the angel came unto her, and said, Hail, thou that art highly favoured, the Lord is with thee: blessed art thou among women.	(Scripture verse twisted to perverse)

12

Scripture	Discrepancies in KJV Scripture	Memories of the 1611 KJV	Notes:
Luk 1:35	And the angel answered and said unto her, The Holy Ghost shall come upon thee, and the power of the Highest shall overshadow thee: therefore also that holy thing which shall be born of thee shall be called the Son of God.	And the angel answered and said unto her, The Holy Ghost shall come upon thee, and the power of the Most High shall overshadow thee: wherefore also that which is to be born shall be called Holy, the Son of God.	Jesus called a thing! And Luke 2:15
Luk 1:37	For with God nothing shall be impossible.	For with God nothing is impossible.	shall be!
Luk 2:26	And it was revealed unto him by the Holy Ghost, that he should not see death, before he had seen the Lord's Christ.	And it was revealed unto him by the Holy Ghost, that he should not see death, before he had seen the Messiah.	
Luk 2:36	And there was one Anna, a prophetess, the daughter of Phanuel, of the tribe of Aser: she was of a great age, and had lived with an husband seven years from her virginity;	And there was one Anna, a prophetess, the daughter of Phanuel, of the tribe of Aser: she was of a great age, and had lived with a husband seven years until his death;	
Luk 2:44	But they, supposing him to have	But they, supposing him to have	

Scripture	Discrepancies in KJV Scripture	Memories of the 1611 KJV	Notes:
	been in the company, went a day's journey; and they sought him among their kinsfolk and acquaintance.	been in the company, went a day's journey; and they sought him among their relatives and acquaintances.	
Luk 2:46	And it came to pass, that after three days they found him in the temple, sitting in the midst of the doctors, both hearing them, and asking them questions.	And it came to pass, that after three days they found him in the temple, sitting in the midst of the teachers, both hearing them, and asking them questions.	rabbis
Luk 2:48	And when they saw him, they were amazed: and his mother said unto him, Son, why hast thou thus dealt with us? behold, thy father and I have sought thee sorrowing.	And when they saw him, they were amazed: and his mother said unto him, Son, why hast thou thus dealt with us? behold, thy father and I have been looking for thee everywhere.	
Luk 2:49	And he said unto them, How is it that ye sought me? wist ye not that I must be about my Father's business?	And he said unto them, How is it that ye sought me? Do you not know that I must be about my Father's business?	wist ye!
Luk 3:5	Every valley shall be filled, and every mountain and hill shall be brought low; and the crooked shall be made straight, and the rough ways shall be made smooth;	Every valley shall be exalted, and every mountain and hill shall be brought low; and the crooked shall be made straight, and the rough ways shall be made smooth;	filled!
Luk 3:22	And the Holy Ghost descended in a bodily shape like a dove upon him, and a voice came from heaven, which said, Thou art my beloved Son; in thee I am well pleased.	And the Holy Ghost descended like a dove upon him, and a voice came from heaven, which said, Thou art my beloved Son; in Whom I am well pleased.	in a bodily shape!
Luk 3:32	Which was the son of Jesse, which was the son of Obed, which was the son of Booz, which was the son of Salmon, which was the son of Naasson,	Which was the son of Jesse, which was the son of Obed, which was the son of Boaz, which was the son of Sala, which was the son of Nahshon,	booz! salmon!
Luk 4:18-19	18 The Spirit of the Lord is upon me, because he hath anointed me to preach the gospel to the poor; he hath sent me to heal the brokenhearted, to preach deliverance to the captives, and recovering of sight to the blind, to set at liberty	18 The Spirit of the Lord is upon me, because he hath anointed me to preach the gospel to the poor; he hath sent me to heal the brokenhearted, to proclaim liberty to the captives, and recovering of sight to the blind, to set at liberty	deliverance!

Scripture	Discrepancies in KJV Scripture	Memories of the 1611 KJV	Notes:
	them that are bruised, 19 To preach the acceptable year of the Lord.	them that are oppressed: 19 To proclaim the acceptable year of the Lord.	
Luk 5:17	And it came to pass on a certain day, as he was teaching, that there were Pharisees and doctors of the law sitting by, which were come out of every town of Galilee, and Judaea, and Jerusalem: and the power of the Lord was	And it came to pass on a certain day, as he was teaching, that there were Pharisees and teachers of the law sitting by, which were come out of every village of Galilee, and Judaea, and Jerusalem: and the power of the Lord was present to heal them.	doctors!

13

Scripture	Discrepancies in KJV Scripture	Memories of the 1611 KJV	Notes:
	present to heal them.		
Luk 5:19	And when they could not find by what way they might bring him in because of the multitude, they went upon the housetop, and let him down through the tiling with his couch into the midst before Jesus.	And when they could not find by what way they might bring him in because of the multitude, they went upon the housetop, and let him down through the roof with his mat into the midst before Jesus.	couch! pallet, mat, stretcher, cot
Luk 5:24	But that ye may know that the Son of man hath power upon earth to forgive sins, (he said unto the sick of the palsy,) I say unto thee, Arise, and take up thy couch, and go into thine house.	But that ye may know that the Son of man hath authority upon earth to forgive sins, (he said unto the paralytic,) I say unto thee, Arise, and take up thy mat, and go into thine house.	bed
Luk 5:26	And they were all amazed, and they glorified God, and were filled with fear, saying, We have seen strange things to day.	And they were all amazed, and they glorified God, and were filled with fear, saying, We have seen remarkable things today.	wonderful
Luk 5:27	And after these things he went forth, and saw a publican, named Levi, sitting at the receipt of custom: and he said unto him, Follow me.	And after these things he went forth, and saw a tax collector, named Levi, sitting at the tax booth: and he said unto him, Follow me.	Also Matt 10:3
Luk 5:33	And they said unto him, Why do the disciples of John fast often, and make prayers, and likewise the disciples of the Pharisees; but thine eat and drink?	And they said unto him, Why do the disciples of John pray and fast often, but thy disciples fast not?	
Luk 5:37	And no man putteth new wine into old bottles; else the new wine will	And no man putteth new wine into old wineskins; else the new	poured

Scripture	Discrepancies in KJV Scripture	Memories of the 1611 KJV	Notes:
	burst the bottles, and be spilled, and the bottles shall perish.	wine will burst the skins, and be spilled out, and the wineskins shall perish.	
Luk 5:38	But new wine must be put into new bottles; and both are preserved.	But new wine must be put into new wineskins; and both are preserved.	bottles!
Luk 6:32	For if ye love them which love you, what thank have ye? for sinners also love those that love them.	For if ye love them which love you, what credit have ye? for sinners also love those that love them.	also v33,34
Luk 6:35	But love ye your enemies, and do good, and lend, hoping for nothing again; and your reward shall be great, and ye shall be the children of the Highest: for he is kind unto the unthankful and to the evil.	But love ye your enemies, and do good, and lend, expecting nothing in return; and your reward shall be great, and ye shall be the Sons of the Most High: for he is kind to the ungrateful and to the wicked.	
Luk 6:38	Give, and it shall be given unto you; good measure, pressed down, and shaken together, and running over, shall men give into your bosom. For with the same measure that ye mete withal it shall be measured to you again.	Give, and it shall be given unto you; good measure, pressed down, and shaken together, and running over, shall men give into your bosom. For with the same measure that ye met it shall be measured to you again.	mete withal!
Luk 6:40	The disciple is not above his master: but every one that is perfect shall be as his master.	The disciple is not above his teacher: but every one that is fully trained shall be as his teacher.	master!
Luk 6:44	For every tree is known by his own fruit. For of thorns men do not gather figs, nor of a bramble bush gather they grapes.	For every tree is known by it's own fruit. For of thorns men do not gather figs, nor of a bramble bush gather they grapes.	
Luk 6:48	He is like a man which built an house, and digged deep, and laid the foundation on a rock: and when the flood arose, the stream beat vehemently upon that house, and could not shake it: for it was founded upon a rock.	He is like a man which built a house on the rock. And the rain fell, and the floods came, and the winds blew and beat upon that house, but it had been founded on the rock.	vehemently!
Luk 6:49	But he that heareth, and doeth not, is like a man that without a foundation built an house upon	But he that heareth my words, and doeth not, is like a man who built a house on the sand, and the rain	

14

Scripture	Discrepancies in KJV Scripture	Memories of the 1611 KJV	Notes:
	the earth; against which the stream did beat vehemently, and immediately it fell; and the ruin of that house was great.	fell, and the floods came, and the winds blew and beat upon that house, and immediately it fell; and great was the fall of it.	
Luk 7:1	Now when he had ended all his sayings in the audience of the people, he entered into Capernaum.	Now when he had ended all his sayings in the hearing of the people, he entered into Capernaum.	audience!
Luk 7:4	And when they came to Jesus, they besought him instantly, saying, That he was worthy for whom he should do this:	And when they came to Jesus, they besought him diligently saying, That he was worthy for whom he should do this:	instantly!
Luk 7:25	But what went ye out for to see? A man clothed in soft raiment? Behold, they which are gorgeously apparelled, and live delicately, are in kings' courts.	But what went ye out for to see? A man clothed in soft raiment? Behold, they which are costly apparel, and live delicately, are in houses of kings.	king's courts
Luk 7:42	And when they had nothing to pay, he frankly forgave them both. Tell me therefore, which of them will love him most?	And when they had nothing to pay, he freely forgave them both. Tell me therefore, which of them will love him most?	frankly!
Luk 8:1	And it came to pass afterward, that he went throughout every city and village, preaching and shewing the glad tidings of the kingdom of God: and the twelve were with him,	And it came to pass soon afterwards, that he went through cities and villages, preaching and proclaiming the good news of the kingdom of God: and the twelve were with him,	
Luk 8:14	And that which fell among thorns are they, which, when they have heard, go forth, and are choked with cares and riches and pleasures of this life, and bring no fruit to perfection.	That morever, they are those which fell among the thorns, which, when they have heard, go forth, and are choked with cares of this life, and bring forth no fruit to maturity.	
Luk 8:17	For nothing is secret, that shall not be made manifest; neither any thing hid, that shall not be known and come abroad.	For nothing is hidden, that shall not be revealed; neither any thing secret, that shall not be made known.	
Luk 8:33	Then went the devils out of the man, and entered into the swine: and the herd ran violently down a steep place into the lake, and were choked.	Then went the demons out of the man, and entered into the pigs: and the herd ran violently down a steep slope into the lake, and were drowned.	bank
Luk 8:39	Return to thine own house, and	Return to thine own house, and	

166

Scripture	Discrepancies in KJV Scripture	Memories of the 1611 KJV	Notes:
	shew how great things God hath done unto thee. And he went his way, and published throughout the whole city how great things Jesus had done unto him.	shew how great things God hath done unto thee. And he went his way, and proclaimed throughout the whole city how great things Jesus had done unto him.	
Luk 8:44	Came behind him, and touched the border of his garment: and immediately her issue of blood stanched.	Came behind him, and touched the hem of his garment: and immediately her issue of blood stopped.	stanched! ceased
Luk 8:55	And her spirit came again, and she arose straightway: and he commanded to give her meat.	And her spirit came again, and she arose straightway: and he commanded to give her something to eat.	
Luk 9:12	And when the day began to wear away, then came the twelve, and said unto him, Send the multitude away, that they may go into the towns and country round about, and lodge, and get victuals: for we are here in a desert place.	And when the day began to wear away, then came the twelve, and said unto him, Send the multitude away, that they may go into the surrounding villages and farms, and lodge, and get food: for we are here in a deserted place.	desolate
Luk 9:20	He said unto them, But whom say ye that I am? Peter answering said, The Christ of God.	He said unto them, But whom say ye that I am? Peter answering said, You are Christ the Son of the living God.	Christ of God!
Luk 9:25	For what is a man advantaged, if he gain the whole world, and lose himself, or be cast away?	For what profits a man, if he gain the whole world, and lose his own soul?	advantaged! cast away!

15

Scripture	Discrepancies in KJV Scripture	Memories of the 1611 KJV	Notes:
Luk 9:26	For whosoever shall be ashamed of me and of my words, of him shall the Son of man be ashamed, when he shall come in his own glory, and in his Father's, and of the holy angels.	For whosoever shall be ashamed of me and of my words, of him shall the Son of man be ashamed, when he shall come in his glory, and in his Father's glory, and of the holy angels.	see John 8:50
Luk 9:29	And as he prayed, the fashion of his countenance was altered, and his raiment was white and glistering.	And as he prayed, the appearance of his countenance changed,	face glistering!

Scripture	Discrepancies in KJV Scripture	Memories of the 1611 KJV	Notes:
		and his raiment became dazzling white.	
Luk 9:31	Who appeared in glory, and spake of his decease which he should accomplish at Jerusalem.	Who appeared in glory, and spake of his departure which he should accomplish at Jerusalem.	
Luk 9:35	And there came a voice out of the cloud, saying, This is my beloved Son: hear him.	And there came a voice out of the cloud, saying, This is my beloved Son: hear ye him.	
Luk 9:57	And it came to pass, that, as they went in the way, a certain man said unto him, Lord, I will follow thee whithersoever thou goest.	And it came to pass, that, as they went in the way, a certain man said unto him, Lord, I will follow thee wheresoever thou goest.	whithersoever!
Luk 9:58	And Jesus said unto him, Foxes have holes, and birds of the air have nests; but the Son of man hath not where to lay his head.	And Jesus said unto him, Foxes have holes, and birds of the air have nests; but the Son of Man hath nowhere to lay his head.	not where!
Luk 11:2	And he said unto them, When ye pray, say, Our Father which art in heaven, Hallowed be thy name. Thy kingdom come. Thy will be done, as in heaven, so in earth.	And he said unto them, When ye pray, say, Our Father Who art in heaven, Hallowed be Thy name. Thy kingdom come, Thy will be done, as in heaven so on earth.	GK:epi,on
Luk 11:8	I say unto you, Though he will not rise and give him, because he is his friend, yet because of his importunity he will rise and give him as many as he needeth.	I say unto you, Though he will not rise and give him, because he is his friend, yet because of his persistence he will rise and give him as many as he needeth.	importunity!
Luk 11:32	The men of Nineve shall rise up in the judgment with this generation, and shall condemn it: for they repented at the preaching	The men of Nineveh shall rise up in the judgment with this	Johas! Luke 11:8,29 also Matt

Scripture	Discrepancies in KJV Scripture	Memories of the 1611 KJV	Notes:
	of Jonas; and, behold, a greater than Jonas is here.	generation, and shall condemn it: for they repented at the preaching of Jonah; and, behold, a greater than Jonah is here.	12:39,40,41
Luk 11:48	Truly ye bear witness that ye allow the deeds of your fathers: for they indeed killed them, and ye build their sepulchres.	Truly ye bear witness that ye approve the deeds of your fathers: for they indeed killed them, and ye build their sepulchres.	
Luk 11:52	Woe unto you lawyers! for ye took away the key of knowledge: ye entered not in yourselves, and them that were entering in ye hindered.	Woe unto you scribes! for ye took away the key of knowledge: ye entered not in yourselves, and them that were entering in ye hindered.	lawyers!
Luk 12:1	In the mean time, when there were gathered together an innumerable multitude of people, insomuch that they trode one upon another, he began to say unto his disciples first of all, Beware ye of the leaven of the Pharisees, which is hypocrisy.	Meanwhile, when the crowd gathered by the myriads, insomuch that they trampled upon one another, he bagan to speak first to his disciples, Beware ye of the leaven of the Pharisees, which is hypocrisy.	trode! thousands
Luk 12:24	Consider the ravens: for they neither sow nor reap; which neither have storehouse nor barn; and God feedeth them: how much more are ye better than the fowls?	Consider the birds of the air: for they neither sow nor reap; which neither have storehouse nor barn; yet God feeds them: how much more are ye better than the birds?	ravens!
Luk 12:45	But and if that servant say in his heart, My lord delayeth his coming; and shall begin to beat the menservants and maidens, and to eat and drink, and to be drunken;	But and if that servant say in his heart, my lord delayeth his coming; and shall begin to beat the menservants and maidservants, and to eat and drink, and to be drunken;	maidens!

Scripture	Discrepancies in KJV Scripture	Memories of the 1611 KJV	Notes:
Luk 12:50	But I have a baptism to be baptized with; and	But I have a baptism to be baptized with; and how	pressed,

Scripture	Discrepancies in KJV Scripture	Memories of the 1611 KJV	Notes:
	how am I straitened till it be accomplished!	am I distressed until it be accomplished!	constrained, aguished
Luk 12:54	And he said also to the people, When ye see a cloud rise out of the west, straightway ye say, There cometh a shower; and so it is.	And he said also to the people, When ye see a cloud rise out of the west, straightway ye say, There cometh a storm; and so it is.	
Luk 13:32	And he said unto them, Go ye, and tell that fox, Behold, I cast out devils, and I do cures to day and to morrow, and the third day I shall be perfected.	And he said unto them, Go ye, and tell that fox, Behold, I cast out devils, and I perform cures today and tomorrow, and the third day I shall be perfected.	to day! to morrow!
Luk 13:33	Nevertheless I must walk to day, and to morrow, and the day following: for it cannot be that a prophet perish out of Jerusalem.	Nevertheless I must walk today, and tomorrow, and the day following: for it cannot be that a prophet perish out of Jerusalem.	
Luk 14:7-10	7 And he put forth a parable to those which were bidden, when he marked how they chose out the chief rooms; saying unto them, 8 When thou art bidden of any man to a marriage feast, sit not down in the chief seat; lest haply a more honorable man than thou be bidden of him, 9 And he that bade thee and him come and say to thee, Give this man place; and thou begin with shame to take the lowest room. 10 But when thou art bidden, go and sit down in the lowest room; that when he that bade thee cometh, he may say unto thee, Friend, go up higher: then shalt	7 And he put forth a parable to those which were invited, when he noticed how they chose out the first seats; saying unto them, 8 When thou art invited of any man to a marriage feast, recline not in the first seat; lest haply a more honourable man than thou be invited of him, 9 And he that invited thee and him come and say to thee, Give this man your seat; and thou begin with disgrace to take the second seat. 10 But when thou art invited, go and recline in the second seat; that when he that invited thee cometh, he may say unto thee, Friend, go up higher: then shalt thou have glory in the presence of them that recline at table with thee.	bidden!

Scripture	Discrepancies in KJV Scripture	Memories of the 1611 KJV	Notes:
	thou have worship in the presence of them that sit at meat with thee.		
Luk 14:26	If any man come to me, and hate not his father, and mother, and wife, and children, and brethren, and sisters, yea, and his own life also, he cannot be my disciple.	If any man come after me, and loves his father, mother, wife, children, brethren, even, his own life more than me, he cannot be my disciple.	Doc error hate your self? see Matt 10:37
Luk 14:32	Or else, while the other is yet a great way off, he sendeth an ambassage, and desireth conditions of peace.	Or else, while the other is still a great way off, he will send a delegation and ask for terms of peace.	ambassage! deligation
Luk 14:34	Salt is good: but if the salt have lost his savour, wherewith shall it be seasoned?	Salt is good: but if the salt has lost its savour, wherewith shall it be seasoned?	his and its in one sentence?
Luk 15:13	And he would fain have filled his belly with the husks that the swine did eat: and no man gave unto him.	And he would have earnestly desired to fill his belly with the husks that the swine ate: and no man gave him anything.	
Luk 17:4	And if he trespass against thee seven times in a day, and seven times in a day turn again to thee, saying, I repent; thou shalt forgive him.	And if he trespass against thee seven times in a day, and seven times in a day turn again to thee, saying, I repent; thou shalt forgive him.	contradicts Matt. 18:22
Luk 17:6	And the Lord said, If ye had faith as a grain of mustard seed, ye might say unto this sycamine tree, Be thou plucked up by the root, and be thou planted in the sea; and it should obey you.	And the Lord said, If ye had faith as a grain of mustard seed, ye might say unto this mulberry tree, Be thou plucked up by the root, and be thou planted in the sea; and it should obey you.	
Luk 17:7-10	7 But which of you, having a servant plowing or feeding cattle, will say unto him by and by, when he is come from the field, Go and sit down to meat?	7 But which of you, having a servant plowing or feeding sheep, will say unto him by and by, when he is come from the field, Go and recline? 8 And will not rather say unto him, Make ready	Not sure these verses were in the Bible at all.

17

Scripture	Discrepancies in KJV Scripture	Memories of the 1611 KJV	Notes:
	8 And will not rather say unto him, Make ready wherewith I may sup, and gird thyself, and serve me, till I	wherewith I may sup, and gird thyself, and serve me, till I have eaten and drunken; and afterward thou	

Scripture	Discrepancies in KJV Scripture	Memories of the 1611 KJV	Notes:
	have eaten and drunken; and afterward thou shalt eat and drink? 9 Doth he thank that servant because he did the things that were commanded him? I trow not. 10 So likewise ye, when ye shall have done all those things which are commanded you, say, We are unprofitable servants: we have done that which was our duty to do.	shalt eat and drink? 9 Doth he thank that servant because he did the things that were commanded him? I think not. 10 So likewise ye, when ye shall have done all those things which are commanded you, say, We are unprofitable servants: we have done that which was our duty to do.	
Luk 17:22	And he said unto the disciples, The days will come, when ye shall desire to see one of the days of the Son of man, and ye shall not see it.	And he said unto the disciples, The days will come, when ye shall desire to see the days of the Son of man, and ye shall not see it.	
Luk 17:31	In that day, he which shall be upon the housetop, and his stuff in the house, let him not come down to take it away: and he that is in the field, let him likewise not return back.	In that day, he which shall be upon the housetop, and his goods in the house, let him not come down to take it away: and he that is in the field, let him likewise not return back.	stuff! possessions
Luk 17:34-35	34 I tell you, in that night there shall be two men in one bed; the one shall be taken, and the other shall be left. 35 Two women shall be grinding together; the one shall be taken, and the other left.	34 I tell you, in that night there shall be two in one bed; the one shall be taken, and the other shall be left. 35 Two women shall be grinding at the mill together; the one shall be taken, and the other left.	Greek says two people does not say men.
Luk 17:37	"And they answered and said unto him, Where, Lord? And he said unto them, Wheresoever the body is, thither will the eagles be gathered together."	"And they answered and said unto him, Where, Lord? And he said unto them, Wheresoever the corpse is, there will the vultures be gathered together."	carcass ref. Matt 24:28
Luk 18:10	Two men went up into the temple to pray; the one a Pharisee, and the other a publican.	Two men went up into the temple to pray; the one a Pharisee, and the other a tax-collector.	also Luke 18:11
Luk 18:15	And they brought unto him also infants, that he would touch them: but when his disciples saw it, they rebuked them.	And they brought unto him also little children, that he would bless them: but when his disciples saw it, they rebuked them.	infants! touch! Also Matt 19:13 & Mk 10:13
Luk	Who shall not receive manifold	Who shall not receive many times	manifold!

Scripture	Discrepancies in KJV Scripture	Memories of the 1611 KJV	Notes:
18:30	more in this present time, and in the world to come life everlasting.	more in this present time, and in the world to come life everlasting.	
Luk 18:42	And Jesus said unto him, Receive thy sight: thy faith hath saved thee.	And Jesus said unto him, Receive thy sight: thy faith hath made thee whole.	
Luk 19:13	And he called his ten servants, and delivered them ten pounds, and said unto them, Occupy till I come.	And he called his ten servants, and delivered them ten minas, and said unto them, Occupy till I come.	
Luk 19:14	But his citizens hated him, and sent a message after him, saying, We will not have this man to reign over us.	But his citizens hated him, and sent a message after him, saying, We will not have this man to reign over us.	This verse sets up verse 27
Luk 19:20	And another came, saying, Lord, behold, here is thy pound, which I have kept laid up in a napkin:	And another came, saying, Lord, behold, here is thy minas, which I have kept laid up in a handkerchief:	napkin!
Luk 19:23	Wherefore then gavest not thou my money into the bank, that at my coming I might have required mine own with usury?	Wherefore then gavest not thou my money to the moneychangers, that at my coming I might have required mine own with interest?	Ref.Matt. 25:27 bank! exchangers

18

Scripture	Discrepancies in KJV Scripture	Memories of the 1611 KJV	Notes:
Luk 19:27	But those mine enemies, which would not that I should reign over them, bring hither, and slay them before me.	But those mine enemies, which would not that I should reign over them, bring hither, and shew them before me.	(not sure if Jesus ever said v.14 or 27?)
Luk 19:38	Saying, Blessed be the King that cometh in the name of the Lord: peace in heaven, and glory in the highest.	Saying, Blessed be the King that cometh in the name of the Lord: Hosanna in the highest.	See Luke 2:14
Luk 19:46	Saying unto them, It is written, My house is the house of prayer: but ye have made it a den of thieves.	Saying unto them, It is written, My house is a house of prayer: but ye have made it a den of thieves.	GK:NMS
Luk 20:17	And he beheld them, and said, What is this then that is written, The stone which the builders rejected, the same is become the head of the corner?	But Jesus looked at them, and said, What then is this that is written, "The stone which the builders rejected, this became the chief cornerstone?"	Also mark 12:10
Luk 20:24	Shew me a penny. Whose image and superscription hath it? They answered and said, Caesar's.	Shew me a denarius. Whose image and inscription hath it? They answered and said, Caesar's.	superscription!

Scripture	Discrepancies in KJV Scripture	Memories of the 1611 KJV	Notes:
Luk 20:36	Neither can they die any more: for they are equal unto the angels; and are the children of God, being the children of the resurrection.	For they are equal unto the angels.	
Luk 21:2	And he saw also a certain poor widow casting in thither two mites.	And he saw also a certain poor widow casting in her two mites.	
Luk 21:4	For all these have of their abundance cast in unto the offerings of God: but she of her penury hath cast in all the living that she had.	For all these have of their abundance cast in unto the offerings of God: but she of her poverty hath cast in all the living that she had.	penury!
Luk 21:9	But when ye shall hear of wars and commotions, be not terrified: for these things must first come to pass; but the end is not by and by.	But when ye shall hear of wars and commotions, be not terrified: for these things must first come to pass; but the end is not yet.	at once
Luk 21:16	And ye shall be betrayed both by parents, and brethren, and kinsfolks, and friends; and some of you shall they cause to be put to death.	And ye shall be betrayed both by parents, and brethren, and relatives, and friends; and some of you shall they cause to be put to death.	
Luk 21:21	Then let them which are in Judaea flee to the mountains; and let them which are in the midst of it depart out; and let not them that are in the countries enter thereinto.	Then let them which are in Judaea flee to the mountains; and let them which are in the city depart; and let not them that are in the country enter therein.	open spaces
Luk 21:26	Men's hearts failing them for fear, and for looking after those things which are coming on the earth: for the powers of heaven shall be shaken.	Men's hearts failing them for fear, and for looking after those things which are coming on the earth: for the powers of heavens shall be shaken.	GK:GMP
Luk 21:32	Verily I say unto you, This generation shall not pass away, till all be fulfilled.	"Verily I say unto you, This generation shall not pass away, till all these things be fulfilled."	
Luk 21:34	And take heed to yourselves, lest at any time your hearts be overcharged with surfeiting, and drunkenness, and cares of this life, and so that day come upon you unawares.	And take heed to yourselves, lest at any time your hearts be weighted down with carousing, and drunkenness, and cares of this life, and so that day come upon you unawares.	surfeiting!
Luk 22:7	Then came the day of unleavened bread, when the passover must be killed.	Then came the day of unleavened bread, when the passover had to be sacrificed.	
Luk	Likewise also the cup after supper,	Likewise also he took the cup after	Testament!

174

Scripture	Discrepancies in KJV Scripture	Memories of the 1611 KJV	Notes:
22:20	saying, This cup is the new testament in my blood, which is	supper, saying, This is the cup of the new covenant through my	And Matt

19

Scripture	Discrepancies in KJV Scripture	Memories of the 1611 KJV	Notes:
	shed for you.	blood, which is shed for you.	26:28
Luk 22:23	(As it is written in the law of the Lord, Every male that openeth the womb shall be called holy to the Lord;)	(As it is written in the law of the Lord, Every male that opens the womb shall be called holy to the Lord;)	Ref. Exo 13:2
Luk 22:53	When I was daily with you in the temple, ye stretched forth no hands against me: but this is your hour, and the power of darkness.	When I was daily with you in the temple, ye stretched forth no hands against me: but this is your hour, and the authority of the darkness.	
Luke 22:8	And when Herod saw Jesus, he was exceeding glad: for he was desirous to see him of a long season, because he had heard many things of him; and he hoped to have seen some miracle done by him.	And when Herod saw Jesus, he was exceedingly glad: for he desired to see him for a long time, because he had heard many things about him; and he hoped to have seen some miracle done by him.	
Luk 23:11	And Herod with his men of war set him at nought, and mocked him, and arrayed him in a gorgeous robe, and sent him again to Pilate.	And Herod with his soldiers treated him with contempt and mocked him, and arrayed him in a splendid robe, and sent him again to Pilate.	gorgeous!
Luk 23:14	Said unto them, Ye have brought this man unto me, as one that perverteth the people: and, behold, I, having examined him before you, have found no fault in this man touching those things whereof ye accuse him:	Said unto them, Ye have brought this man unto me, as one that perverteth the people: and, behold, I, having examined him before you, have found no fault in this man concerning those things whereof ye accuse him:	
Luk 23:26	And as they led him away, they laid hold upon one Simon, a Cyrenian, coming out of the country, and on him they laid the cross, that he might bear it after Jesus.	And as they led him away,(tradition says; Jesus carried his cross until he could bear it no longer) they laid hold upon one Simon, a Cyrenian, and on him they laid the cross, that he might bear it after Jesus.	Contradicts Jn 19:17
Luk 23:33	And when they were come to the place, which is called Calvary, there they crucified him, and the malefactors, one on the right hand, and the other on the left.	And when they were come to the place, which is called The Skull, there they crucified him, and the malefactors, one on the right hand, and the other on the left.	Calvary! Place of the skull Golgotha criminals

Scripture	Discrepancies in KJV Scripture	Memories of the 1611 KJV	Notes:
Luk 23:46	And when Jesus had cried with a loud voice, he said, Father, into thy hands I commend my spirit: and having said thus, he gave up the ghost.	And when Jesus had cried with a loud voice, he said, Father, into thy hands I commend my spirit: and having said thus, he breathed his last.	
Luk 23:53	And he took it down, and wrapped it in linen, and laid it in a sepulchre that was hewn in stone, wherein never man before was laid.	And he took him down, and wrapped him in linen, and laid him in a tomb that was hewn in stone, wherein never man before was laid.	Jesus an it! sepulchure! GK:NMS
Jhn 1:12	But as many as received him, to them gave he power to become the sons of God, even to them that believe on his name:	But as many as received him, to them gave he authority to become the sons of God, even to them that believe on his name:	
Jhn 1:21	And they asked him, What then? Art thou Elias? And he saith, I am not. Art thou that prophet? And he answered, No.	And they asked him, What then? Art thou Elijah? And he saith, I am not. Art thou that prophet? And he answered, No.	
Jhn 1:23	He said, I am the voice of one crying in the wilderness, Make straight the way of the Lord, as said the prophet Esaias.	He said, I am the voice crying in the wilderness, Make straight the way of the Lord, as said the prophet Isaiah.	Esaias! Also Luke 3:4 and Matt 13:14
Jhn 1:28	These things were done in Bethabara beyond Jordan, where John was baptizing.	These things were done in Bethany beyond Jordan, where John was baptizing.	Bethabara!

20

Scripture	Discrepancies in KJV Scripture	Memories of the 1611 KJV	Notes:
Jhn 1:29	The next day John seeth Jesus coming unto him, and saith, Behold the Lamb of God, which taketh away the sin of the world.	The next day John seeth Jesus coming unto him, and saith, Behold the Lamb of God, which taketh away the sins of the world.	
Jhn 1:41	He first findeth his own brother Simon, and saith unto him, We have found the Messias, which is, being interpreted, the Christ.	He first findeth his own brother Simon, and saith unto him, We have found the Messiah, (which is, being interpreted, the Christ.)	Messias!
Jhn 1:42	And he brought him to Jesus. And when Jesus beheld him, he said, Thou art Simon the son of Jona: thou shalt be called Cephas, which is by interpretation, A stone.	And he brought him to Jesus. And when Jesus beheld him, he said, Thou art Simon the son of Jonah: thou shalt be called Cephas, which is by interpretation, Peter.	Jona!
Jhn 2:16	And said unto them that sold doves,	He said unto those who sold doves,	of trade,

Scripture	Discrepancies in KJV Scripture	Memories of the 1611 KJV	Notes:
	Take these things hence; make not my Father's house an house of merchandise.	Take these things hence; make not my Father's house a den of thieves.	of merchandise
Jhn 2:17	And his disciples remembered that it was written, The zeal of thine house hath eaten me up.	And his disciples remembered that it was written, The zeal of thine house hath consumed me up.	
Jhn 3:8	The wind bloweth where it listeth, and thou hearest the sound thereof, but canst not tell whence it cometh, and whither it goeth: so is every one that is born of the Spirit.	The wind blows where it wills, and thou hearest the sound thereof, but cannot tell from whence it comes, and whither it goes: so is every one that is born of the Spirit.	listeth!
Jhn 3:10	Jesus answered and said unto him, Art thou a master of Israel, and knowest not these things?	Jesus answered and said unto him, Art thou a teacher of Israel, and knowest not these things?	
Jhn 3:13	And no man hath ascended up to heaven, but he that came down from heaven, even the Son of man which is in heaven.	And no man hath ascended up to heaven, but he that came down from heaven, even the Son of Man who is in heaven.	
Jhn 3:15	That whosoever believeth in him should not perish, but have eternal life.	That everyone who believes in him may have eternal life.	verse is a duplicate of v.16.
Jhn 3:16	For God so loved the world, that he gave his only begotten Son, that whosoever believeth in him should not perish, but have everlasting life.	For God so loved the world, that he gave his only begotten Son, that whosoever believeth in him shall not perish, but have everlasting life.	
Jhn 4:24	God is a Spirit: and they that worship him must worship him in spirit and in truth.	God is Spirit: and they that worship him must worship him in spirit and in truth.	
Jhn 4:25	The woman saith unto him, I know that Messias cometh, which is called Christ: when he is come, he will tell us all things.	The woman saith unto him, I know that Messiah cometh, which is called Christ: when he is come, he will tell us all things.	Messias!
Jhn 4:46	So Jesus came again into Cana of Galilee, where he made the water wine. And there was a certain nobleman, whose son was sick at Capernaum.	So Jesus came again into Cana of Galilee, where he made the water into wine. And there was a certain nobleman, whose son was sick at Capernaum.	
Jhn 5:7	The impotent man answered him, Sir, I have no man, when the water is troubled, to put me into the pool: but while I am coming, another	The sick man answered him, Sir, I have no one, to put me into the pool when the water is stirred, but while I am going, another steps down	lame

Scripture	Discrepancies in KJV Scripture	Memories of the 1611 KJV	Notes:
	steppeth down before me.	before me.	
Jhn 5:13	And he that was healed wist not who it was: for Jesus had conveyed himself away, a multitude being in that place.	And he that was healed knew not who it was: for Jesus had passed through the crowd, a multitude being in that place.	conveyed himself away!
Jhn 6:7	Philip answered him, Two hundred pennyworth of bread is not sufficient for them, that every one of them may take a little.	Philip answered him, Two hundred denarius worth of bread is not sufficient for them, that every one of them may take a little.	also in Mark 6:37

21

Scripture	Discrepancies in KJV Scripture	Memories of the 1611 KJV	Notes:
Jhn 6:24	When the people therefore saw that Jesus was not there, neither his disciples, they also took shipping, and came to Capernaum, seeking for Jesus.	When the people therefore saw that Jesus was not there, neither his disciples, they also took entered into small boats, and came to Capernaum, seeking for Jesus.	took shipping!
Jhn 6:51	I am the living bread which came down from heaven: if any man eat of this bread, he shall live for ever: and the bread that I will give is my flesh, which I will give for the life of the world.	I am the living bread which came down from heaven: if any man eat of this bread, he shall live for ever: for the bread that I will give is my body, which I will give for the sins of the world.	
Jhn 6:53	Then Jesus said unto them, Verily, verily, I say unto you, Except ye eat the flesh of the Son of man, and drink his blood, ye have no life in you.	Then Jesus said unto them, Verily, verily, I say unto you, Except ye eat the body of the Son of man, and drink his blood, ye have no part in me.	(This verse is repeated in 4 verses, with little variation?)
Jhn 6:54	Whoso eateth my flesh, and drinketh my blood, hath eternal life; and I will raise him up at the last day.	Whosoever eateth my body, and drinketh my blood, hath eternal life; and I will raise him up at the last day.	2.
Jhn 6:55	For my flesh is meat indeed, and my blood is drink indeed.	For my body is food indeed, and my blood is drink indeed.	3.
Jhn 6:56	He that eateth my flesh, and drinketh my blood, dwelleth in me, and I in him.	He that eateth my body, and drinketh my blood, dwelleth in me, and I in him.	4.
Jhn 6:70	Jesus answered them, Have not I chosen you twelve, and one of you is a devil?	Jesus answered them, Have I not chosen you twelve, and one of you is a devil.	

Scripture	Discrepancies in KJV Scripture	Memories of the 1611 KJV	Notes:
Jhn 7:1	After these things Jesus walked in Galilee: for he would not walk in Jewry, because the Jews sought to kill him.	After these things Jesus walked in Galilee: for he would not walk in Judea because the Jews sought to kill him.	Jewry!
Jhn 7:6	Then Jesus said unto them, My time is not yet come: but your time is alway ready.	Then Jesus said unto them, My time is not yet come: but your time is always ready.	
Jhn 7:7	The world cannot hate you; but me it hateth, because I testify of it, that the works thereof are evil.	The world cannot hate you; but me it hateth, because I testify of it, that the works thereof are evil.	3rd doc error Contradicts John 15:18 but agrees with 15:19
Jhn 7:26	But, lo, he speaketh boldly, and they say nothing unto him. Do the rulers know indeed that this is the very Christ?	But, lo, he speaketh boldly, and they say nothing unto him. Do the rulers know indeed that this is indeed the Christ?	also Acts 9:22
Jhn 7:34	Ye shall seek me, and shall not find me: and where I am, thither ye cannot come.	Ye shall seek me, and shall not find me: and where I am, ye cannot come.	
Jhn 8:7	So when they continued asking him, he lifted up himself, and said unto them, He that is without sin among you, let him first cast a stone at her.	So when they continued asking him, he lifted up himself, and said unto them, He that is without sin among you, let him cast the first stone.	
Jhn 8:14	Jesus answered and said unto them, Though I bear record of myself, yet my record is true: for I know whence I came, and whither I go; but ye cannot tell whence I come, and whither I go.	Jesus answered and said unto them, Though I bear witness of myself, yet my witness is true: for I know whence I come, and whither I go; but ye cannot tell whence I come, and whither I go.	record!
Jhn 8:32	And ye shall know the truth, and the truth shall make you free.	And ye shall know the truth, and the truth shall set you free.	
Jhn 8:36	If the Son therefore shall make you free, ye shall be free indeed.	He whom the Son sets free, is free indeed.	
Jhn 10:3	To him the porter openeth; and the sheep hear	To him the shepherd openeth; and the sheep hear his	porter!

22

Scripture	Discrepancies in KJV Scripture	Memories of the 1611 KJV	Notes:
	his voice: and he calleth his own	voice: and he calleth his own sheep	doorkeeper

Scripture	Discrepancies in KJV Scripture	Memories of the 1611 KJV	Notes:
	sheep by name, and leadeth them out.	by name, and leadeth them out.	
Jhn 11:44	And he that was dead came forth, bound hand and foot with graveclothes: and his face was bound about with a napkin. Jesus saith unto them, Loose him, and let him go.	And he that was dead came forth, bound hand and foot with linen strips: and his face was bound about with a handkerchief. Jesus saith unto them, Loose him, and let him go.	graveclothes
Jhn 12:15	Fear not, daughter of Sion: behold, thy King cometh, sitting on an ass's colt.	Fear not, daughter of Zion: behold, thy King cometh, sitting on an donkey's colt.	Sion!
Jhn 12:24	Verily, verily, I say unto you, Except a corn of wheat fall into the ground and die, it abideth alone: but if it die, it bringeth forth much fruit.	Verily, verily, I say unto you, Except a grain of wheat fall into the ground and die, it abideth alone: but if it die, it bringeth forth much fruit.	corn of wheat!
Jhn 12:25	He that loveth his life shall lose it; and he that hateth his life in this world shall keep it unto life eternal.	He that loveth his life shall lose it; and he that looses his life in this world shall keep it unto life eternal.	see Luke 9:24
Jhn 13:5	After that he poureth water into a bason, and began to wash the disciples' feet, and to wipe them with the towel wherewith he was girded.	After that he poureth water into a basin, and began to wash the disciples' feet, and to wipe them with the towel wherewith he was girded.	bason!
Jhn 13:17	If ye know these things, happy are ye if ye do them.	If ye know these things, blessed are ye if ye do them.	
Jhn 14:18	I will not leave you comfortless: I will come to you.	I will not leave you orphans: I will come to you.	comfortless!
Jhn 15:2	Every branch in me that beareth not fruit he taketh away: and every branch that beareth fruit, he purgeth it, that it may bring forth more fruit.	Every branch in me that bares not fruit he taketh away: and every branch that bares fruit, he prunes it, that it may bring forth more fruit.	purgeth!
Jhn 15:19	If ye were of the world, the world would love his own: but because ye are not of the world, but I have chosen you out of the world, therefore the world hateth you.	If ye were of the world, the world would love you as its own: but because ye are not of the world, but I have chosen you out of the world, therefore the world hateth you.	his!
Jhn 16:25	These things have I spoken unto you in proverbs: but the time cometh, when I shall no more speak unto you in proverbs, but I shall shew you plainly of the Father.	These things have I spoken unto you in parables: but the time cometh, when I shall no more speak unto you in parables, but I shall shew you plainly of the Father.	proverbs!

Scripture	Discrepancies in KJV Scripture	Memories of the 1611 KJV	Notes:
Jhn 17:15	I pray not that thou shouldest take them out of the world, but that thou shouldest keep them from the evil.	I pray not that thou shouldest take them out of the world, but that thou shouldest keep them from the evil one.	
Jhn 18:2	And Judas also, which betrayed him, knew the place: for Jesus ofttimes resorted thither with his disciples.	And Judas also, which betrayed him, knew the place: for Jesus often resorted there with his disciples.	
Jhn 20:11	But Mary stood without at the sepulchre weeping: and as she wept, she stooped down, and looked into the sepulchre,	But Mary stood without at the tomb weeping: and as she wept, she bowed down, and looked into the tomb,	stooped! knelt
Jhn 20:23	whose soever sins ye forgive, they are forgiven unto them; whose soever sins ye retain, they are retained.	whosoever sins ye forgive, they are forgiven unto them; whosoever sins ye retain, they are retained.	
Jhn 20:25	The other disciples therefore said unto him, We have seen the Lord. But he said unto them, Except I shall see in his hands the print of the nails, and put my finger into the print of the nails, and thrust my hand into his side, I will not	The other disciples therefore said unto him, We have seen the Lord. But he said unto them, Except I shall see, in his hands, the mark of the nails, and put my finger into the mark of the nails, and put my hand into his side, I will not believe.	GWT says Thomas

23

Scripture	Discrepancies in KJV Scripture	Memories of the 1611 KJV	Notes:
	believe.		
Jhn 21:3	Simon Peter saith unto them, I go a fishing. They say unto him, We also go with thee. They went forth, and entered into a ship immediately; and that night they caught nothing.	Simon Peter saith unto them, I am going fishing. They say unto him, We also go with thee. They went forth, and entered into a boat immediately; and that night they caught nothing.	
Jhn 21:7	Therefore that disciple whom Jesus loved saith unto Peter, It is the Lord. Now when Simon Peter heard that it was the Lord, he girt his fisher's coat unto him, (for he was naked,) and did cast himself into the sea.	Therefore that disciple whom Jesus loved saith unto Peter, It is the Lord. Now when Simon Peter heard that it was the Lord, he put on his outer garment, (for he was naked,) and did cast himself into the sea.	fisher's coat
Acts 1:12	Then returned they unto Jerusalem from the mount called Olivet, which	Then returned they unto Jerusalem from the mount called Olivet,	½ mile

Scripture	Discrepancies in KJV Scripture	Memories of the 1611 KJV	Notes:
	is from Jerusalem a sabbath day's journey.	which is nigh to Jerusalem a sabbath day's journey.	
Acts 1:19	And it was known unto all the dwellers at Jerusalem; insomuch as that field is called in their proper tongue, Aceldama, that is to say, The field of blood.	And it was known unto all the dwellers at Jerusalem; insomuch as that field is called in their own tongue, Aceldama, that is to say, The field of blood.	proper!
Acts 1:20	For it is written in the book of Psalms, Let his habitation be desolate, and let no man dwell therein: and his bishoprick let another take.	For it is written in the book of Psalms, "Let his habitation be desolate, and let no man dwell therein" and his office let another take.	bishoprick! Psalms 69:25
Acts 2:12	And they were all amazed, and were in doubt, saying one to another, What meaneth this?	And they were all amazed, and were perplexed, saying one to another, What meaneth this?	Doc. error; those at upper room did not doubt.
Acts 2:24	Whom God hath raised up, having loosed the pains of death: because it was not possible that he should be holden of it.	Whom God hath raised up, having loosed the pangs of death: because it was not possible that he should be holden of it.	also Acts 2:34
Acts 2:25	For David speaketh concerning him, I foresaw the Lord always before my face, for he is on my right hand, that I should not be moved:	For David speaketh concerning him, I foresaw the Lord always before my face, for he is at my right hand, that I should not be moved:	Gk:ek,at,out of
Acts 2:34	For David is not ascended into the heavens: but he saith himself, The LORD said unto my Lord, Sit thou on my right hand,	For David is not ascended into the heavens: but he saith himself, The LORD said unto my Lord, Sit thou at my right hand,	GK: ek,at, out of
Acts 2:35	Until I make thy foes thy footstool.	Until I make mine enemies thy footstool.	
Acts 2:40	And with many other words did he testify and exhort, saying, Save yourselves from this untoward generation.	And with many other words did he testify and exhort, saying, "Save yourselves from this crooked generation."	untoward! perverse
Acts 3:19	Repent ye therefore, and be converted, that your sins may be blotted out, when the times of refreshing shall come from the presence of the Lord;	Repent ye therefore, and be converted, that your sins may be blotted out,	
Acts 3:21	Whom the heaven must receive until the times of restitution of all things,	Whom the heaven must receive until the times of restoration of all	restitution!

Scripture	Discrepancies in KJV Scripture	Memories of the 1611 KJV	Notes:
	which God hath spoken by the mouth of all his holy prophets since the world began.	things, which God hath spoken by the mouth of all his holy prophets since the world began.	
Acts 4:9	If we this day be examined of the good deed done to the impotent man, by what means he is made whole;	If we this day be examined of the good deed done to the crippled man, by what means he is made whole;	impotent!
Acts 4:11	This is the stone which was set at nought of you	This is the stone which was set at nought of you	

24

Scripture	Discrepancies in KJV Scripture	Memories of the 1611 KJV	Notes:
	builders, which is become the head of the corner.	builders, which is become the chief cornerstone.	
Acts 4:27,28	27 For of a truth against thy holy child Jesus, whom thou hast anointed, both Herod, and Pontius Pilate, with the Gentiles, and the people of Israel, were gathered together, 28 For to do whatsoever thy hand and thy counsel determined before to be done.	27 For there were truly assembled in this city against thy holy Son Jesus, whom thou hast anointed, Herod, and Pontius Pilate, with the Gentiles and the people of Israel, 28 to do whatsoever thy hand and thy council foreordained to come to pass.	
Acts 4:30	By stretching forth thine hand to heal; and that signs and wonders may be done by the name of thy holy child Jesus.	By stretching forth thine hand to heal; and that signs and wonders may be done by the name of thy holy servant Jesus.	
Acts 5:21	And when they heard that, they entered into the temple early in the morning, and taught. But the high priest came, and they that were with him,and they that were with him, and called the council together, and all the senate of the children of Israel, and sent to the prison to have them brought.	And when they heard that, they entered into the temple early in the morning, and taught. But the high priest came, and they that were with him, and called the Sanhedrin together, and all the elders of the children of Israel, and sent to the prison to have them brought.	senate! Sanhedrin
Acts 5:29	Then Peter and the other apostles answered and said, We ought to obey God rather than men.	Then Peter and the apostles answered and said, We must obey God rather than men.	
Acts 5:34	Then stood there up one in the council, a Pharisee, named Gamaliel, a doctor of the law, had in reputation	Then stood up one of the members of the Sanhedrin, a Pharisee, named Gamaliel, a	Sanhedrin

Scripture	Discrepancies in KJV Scripture	Memories of the 1611 KJV	Notes:
	among all the people, and commanded to put the apostles forth a little space;	teacher of the law, had in reputation among all the people, and commanded to put the apostles outside a short while;	
Acts 7:19	The same dealt subtilly with our kindred, and evil entreated our fathers, so that they cast out their young children, to the end they might not live.	The same dealt subtly with our kindred, and evil entreated our fathers, so that they cast out their young children, to the end they might not live.	
Acts 7:30	And when forty years were expired, there appeared to him in the wilderness of mount Sina an angel of the Lord in a flame of fire in a bush.	And when forty years were expired, there appeared to him in the wilderness of Mount Sinai an angel of the Lord in a flame of fire in a bush.	Sina!
Acts 7:38	This is he, that was in the church in the wilderness with the angel which spake to him in the mount Sina, and with our fathers: who received the lively oracles to give unto us:	This is he, that was in the assembly in the wilderness with the angel which spake to him on Mount Sinai, and with our fathers: who received the living oracles to give unto us:	Mount Sina! congregation
Acts 7:45	Which also our fathers that came after brought in with Jesus into the possession of the Gentiles, whom God drave out before the face of our fathers, unto the days of David;	Which also our fathers that came after brought in with Jesus into the possession of the Gentiles, whom God drove out before the face of our fathers, unto the days of David;	
Acts 7:49	Heaven is my throne, and earth is my footstool: what house will ye build me? saith the Lord: or what is the place of my rest?	Heaven is my throne, and earth is my footstool: what house will ye build for me? saith the Lord:	
Acts 8:3	As for Saul, he made havock of the church, entering into every house, and haling men and women committed them to prison.	As for Saul, havoc on the church, entering into every house, and haling men and women committed them to prison.	havock!
Acts 8:9	But there was a certain man, called Simon, which beforetime in the same city used sorcery, and bewitched the people of Samaria, giving out that himself was some great one:	But there was a certain man, called Simon, which beforetime in the same city used sorcery, and amazed the people of Samaria, giving out that himself was some great one:	bewitched!

25

Scripture	Discrepancies in KJV Scripture	Memories of the 1611 KJV	Notes:
Acts 8:31	And he said, How can I, except some man should guide me? And he desired Philip that he would come up and sit with him.	And he said, How can I, except some man should guide me? And he besought Philip that he would come up and sit with him.	desired!
Acts 8:40	But Philip was found at Azotus: and passing through he preached in all the cities, till he came to Caesarea.	But Philip was found at Antioch: and passing through he preached in all the cities, till he came to Caesarea.	
Acts 9:2	And desired of him letters to Damascus to the synagogues, that if he found any of this way, whether they were men or women, he might bring them bound unto Jerusalem.	And desired of him letters to Damascus to the synagogues, that if he found any of 'the way', whether they were men or women, he might bring them bound unto Jerusalem.	this way!
Acts 9:26	And when Saul was come to Jerusalem, he assayed to join himself to the disciples: but they were all afraid of him, and believed not that he was a disciple.	And when Saul was come to Jerusalem, he attempt to join himself to the disciples: but they were all afraid of him, and believed not that he was a disciple.	assayed! Also Acts 16:7
Acts 10:1	There was a certain man in Caesarea called Cornelius, a centurion of the band called the Italian band,	There was a certain man in Caesarea called Cornelius, a centurion of the band called the Italian regiment,	Acts 27:1 cohort
Acts 10:11	And saw heaven opened, and a certain vessel descending unto him, as it had been a great sheet knit at the four corners, and let down to the earth:	And saw heaven opened, and a jar descending, as it had been a great sheet knit at the four corners, and let down to the earth:	vessel!
Acts 10:37	That word, I say, ye know, which was published throughout all Judaea, and began from Galilee, after the baptism which John preached;	That word, I say, ye know, which was proclaimed throughout all Judaea, and began from Galilee, after the baptism which John preached;	
Acts 11:5	I was in the city of Joppa praying: and in a trance I saw a vision, A certain vessel descend, as it had been a great sheet, let down from heaven by four corners; and it came even to me:	I was in the city of Joppa praying: and in a trance I saw a vision, a certain jar something like a great sheet descending, let down from heaven by four corners; and it came even to me:	vessel!
Acts	Now they which were scattered	Now they which were scattered	Another

Scripture	Discrepancies in KJV Scripture	Memories of the 1611 KJV	Notes:
11:19	abroad upon the persecution that arose about Stephen travelled as far as Phenice, and Cyprus, and Antioch, preaching the word to none but unto the Jews only.	abroad upon the persecution that arose about Stephen travelled as far as Phoenicia, and Cyprus, and Antioch, preaching the word to none but unto the Jews only.	name for 'Phoenix', and sounds like 'penis'
Acts 12:4	And when he had apprehended him, he put him in prison, and delivered him to four quaternions of soldiers to keep him; intending after Easter to bring him forth to the people.	And when he had seized him, he put him in prison, and delivered him to four squads of four soldiers to keep him; intending after Passover to bring him forth to the people.	apprehended! quaternions! Easter! arrested
Acts 12:20	And Herod was highly displeased with them of Tyre and Sidon: but they came with one accord to him, and, having made Blastus the king's chamberlain their friend, desired peace; because their country was nourished by the king's country.	(I don't remember this verse)	
Acts 13:1	Now there were at Antioch, in the church that was there, prophets and teachers, Barnabas, and Symeon that was called Niger, and Lucius of Cyrene, and Manaen the foster-brother of Herod the tetrarch, and Saul.	Now there were at Antioch, in the church that was there, prophets and teachers, Barnabas, and Simeon that was called Niger, and Lucius of Cyrene, and Manaen who had been brought up with Herod the tetrarch, and Saul.	
Acts 13:8	But Elymas the sorcerer (for so is his name by interpretation) withstood them, seeking to turn away the deputy from the faith.	But Elymas the sorcerer (for so is his name by interpretation) withstood them, seeking to turn away the proconsul from the faith.	deputy!

26

Scripture	Discrepancies in KJV Scripture	Memories of the 1611 KJV	Notes:
Acts 13:49	And the word of the Lord was published throughout all the region.	And the word of the Lord was preached throughout all the region.	published! also in Mark 13:10
Acts 14:12	And they called Barnabas, Jupiter; and Paul, Mercurius, because he was the chief speaker.	And they called Barnabas, Zeus; and Paul, Hermes, because he was the chief speaker.	Jupiter! Mercurius!
Acts 15:20	But that we write unto them, that they abstain from pollutions of idols, and from fornication, and from things strangled, and from blood.	But that we write unto them, that they abstain from defilements of idols, and from fornication, and from things strangled, and from	contaminations

Scripture	Discrepancies in KJV Scripture	Memories of the 1611 KJV	Notes:
		blood.	
Acts 15:33	And after they had tarried there a space, they were let go in peace from the brethren unto the apostles.	And after they had tarried there awhile, they were let go in peace from the brethren unto the apostles.	space!
Acts 16:13	And on the sabbath we went out of the city by a river side, where prayer was wont to be made; and we sat down, and spake unto the women which resorted thither.	And on the sabbath day we went out of the city by the river side, where prayer was supposed to be made; and we sat down, and spake unto the women which gathered there.	resorted!
Acts 16:31	And they said, Believe on the Lord Jesus Christ, and thou shalt be saved, and thy house.	And they said, Believe on the Lord Jesus Christ, and thou shalt be saved, thee and thy household.	
Acts 16:38	And the serjeants told these words unto the magistrates: and they feared, when they heard that they were Romans.	And the floggers told these words unto the judges: and they feared, when they heard that they were Roman citizens.	serjents!
Acts 17:3	Opening and alleging, that Christ must needs have suffered, and risen again from the dead; and that this Jesus, whom I preach unto you, is Christ.	Opening and proving, that Christ must needs have suffered, and risen again from the dead; and that this Jesus, whom I preach unto you, is Christ.	alleging!
Acts 17:5	But the Jews which believed not, moved with envy, took unto them certain lewd fellows of the baser sort, and gathered a company, and set all the city on an uproar, and assaulted the house of Jason, and sought to bring them out to the people.	But the Jews which believed not, moved with envy, took unto them certain wicked men of the baser sort, and gathered a company, and set all the city in an uproar, and attacking the house of Joshua, and sought to bring them out to the people.	agatitor
Acts 17:6	And when they found them not, they drew Jason and certain brethren unto the rulers of the city, crying, These that have turned the world upside down are come hither also;	And when they found them not, they drew Joshua and certain brethren unto the rulers of the city, crying, These that have turned the world upside down are come hither also;	Jason!
Acts 17:7	Whom Jason hath received: and these all do contrary to the decrees of Caesar, saying that there is another king, one Jesus.	Whom Joshua hath received: and these all do contrary to the decrees of Caesar, saying that there is another king, this Jesus.	
Acts	Then Paul stood in the midst of	Then Paul stood in the midst of	superstitious!

Scripture	Discrepancies in KJV Scripture	Memories of the 1611 KJV	Notes:
17:22	Mars' hill, and said, Ye men of Athens, I perceive that in all things ye are too superstitious.	Mars' hill, and said, Ye men of Athens, I perceive that in all things ye are very religious.	
Acts 17:30	And the times of this ignorance God winked at; but now commandeth all men every where to repent:	And the times of this ignorance God overlooked; but now commandeth all men every where to repent:	
Acts 19:9	But when divers were hardened, and believed not, but spake evil of that way before the multitude, he departed from them, and separated the disciples, disputing daily in the school of one Tyrannus.	But when some were hardened, and believed not, but spake evil of that way before the multitude, he departed from them, and separated the disciples, disputing daily in the hall of one Tyrannus.	school!
Acts 19:13	Then certain of the vagabond Jews, exorcists, took upon them to call over them which had evil	Then certain of the wandering Jews, exorcists, took upon them to call over them which had evil spirits	Vagabond! itinerant

27

Scripture	Discrepancies in KJV Scripture	Memories of the 1611 KJV	Notes:
	spirits the name of the Lord Jesus, saying, We adjure you by Jesus whom Paul preacheth.	the name of the Lord Jesus, saying, We adjure you by Jesus whom Paul preacheth.	
Acts 19:24	For a certain man named Demetrius, a silversmith, which made silver shrines for Diana, brought no small gain unto the craftsmen;	For a certain one, Demetrius by name, a worker in silver sanctuaries, of Artemis, was bringing to the artificers gain not a little,	Diana is a Roman god
Acts 19:27	So that not only this our craft is in danger to be set at nought; but also that the temple of the great goddess Diana should be despised, and her magnificence should be destroyed, whom all Asia and the world worshippeth.	So that not only this our craft is in danger to be set at nought; but also that the temple of the great goddess Artemis is reputed as nothing, in whom all Asia and the world worships.	
Acts 19:31	And certain of the chief of Asia, which were his friends, sent unto him, desiring him that he would not adventure himself into the theatre.	And certain also of the chief men of Asia, being his friends, having sent unto him, were entreating him not venture himself into the theatre.	adventure!
Acts 19:32	Some therefore cried one thing, and some another: for the assembly was confused; and the more part knew not wherefore they were come together.	Some therefore cried one thing, and some another: for the crowd was confused; the greater part knew not wherefore they were come together.	

Scripture	Discrepancies in KJV Scripture	Memories of the 1611 KJV	Notes:
Acts 19:33	And they drew Alexander out of the multitude, the Jews putting him forward. And Alexander beckoned with the hand, and would have made his defence unto the people.	(I don't remember this verse)	
Acts 19:35	And when the townclerk had appeased the people, he said, Ye men of Ephesus, what man is there that knoweth not how that the city of the Ephesians is a worshipper of the great goddess Diana, and of the image which fell down from Jupiter?	And when the town scribe had appeased the people, he said, Ye men of Ephesus, what man is there that knoweth not how that the city of the Ephesians is a worshipper of the great goddess Artemis, and of the image which fell down from the sky?	townclerk! heaven Jupiter!
Acts 19:37	For ye have brought hither these men, which are neither robbers of churches, nor yet blasphemers of your goddess.	For ye have brought hither these men, which are neither robbers of temples, nor blasphemers of our goddess.	
Acts 19:38	Wherefore if Demetrius, and the craftsmen which are with him, have a matter against any man, the law is open, and there are deputies: let them implead one another.	Wherefore if Demetrius, and the artisans who are with him, have a matter against any man, courts are being held, and there are proconsuls: let them accuse one another.	
Acts 19:39	But if ye enquire any thing concerning other matters, it shall be determined in a lawful assembly.	But if ye enquire anything concerning other matters, it shall be brought before the city council.	any thing!
Acts 19:40	For we are in danger to be called in question for this day's uproar, there being no cause whereby we may give an account of this concourse.	For we are in danger to be called in question for this day's events, there being no cause whereby we may give an account of this gathering.	concourse!
Acts 20:13	And we went before to ship, and sailed unto Assos, there intending to take in Paul: for so had he appointed, minding himself to go afoot.	And we went before by ship, and sailed unto Assos, there intending to take in Paul: for so had he appointed, minding himself to go by foot.	
Acts 20:23	Save that the Holy Ghost witnesseth in every city, saying that bonds and afflictions abide me.	Save that the Holy Ghost witnesseth in every city, saying that bonds and afflictions await me.	abide!
Acts 21:1	And it came to pass, that after we were gotten from them, and had launched, we came with a straight course unto Coos, and the day following unto Rhodes, and from thence unto Patara:	And it came to pass, that after we were parted from them, and had set sail, we came with a straight course unto Cos, and the day following unto Rhodus, and from thence unto Patara:	

28

Scripture	Discrepancies in KJV Scripture	Memories of the 1611 KJV	Notes:
Acts 21:15	And after those days we took up our carriages, and went up to Jerusalem.	And after those days we made ready, and went up to Jerusalem.	carriages! baggage
Acts 21:16	There went with us also certain of the disciples of Caesarea, and brought with them one Mnason of Cyprus, an old disciple, with whom we should lodge.	(I don't remember this verse)	
Acts 21:18	And the day following Paul went in with us unto James; and all the elders were present.	(I don't remember this verse)	
Acts 21:28	Crying out, Men of Israel, help: This is the man, that teacheth all men every where against the people, and the law, and this place: and further brought Greeks also into the temple, and hath polluted this holy place.	Crying out, Men of Israel, help: This is the man, that teaches all men every where against the people, and the law, and this place: and further brought Greeks also into the temple, and hath defiled this holy place.	polluted!
Acts 21:34	And some cried one thing, some another, among the multitude: and when he could not know the certainty for the tumult, he commanded him to be carried into the castle.	And some cried one thing, some another, among the multitude: and when he could not know the certainty for the uproar, he commanded him to be carried into the barracks.	castle! (There were never castles in Israel)
Acts 22:4	And I persecuted this way unto the death, binding and delivering into prisons both men and women.	And I persecuted the way unto the death, binding and delivering into prisons both men and women.	this way!
Acts 22:24	The chief captain commanded him to be brought into the castle, and bade that he should be examined by scourging; that he might know wherefore they cried so against him.	The tribune commanded him to be brought into the barracks, and bade that he should be examined by flogging; that he might know wherefore they cried so against him.	castle!
Acts 22:25	And as they bound him with thongs, Paul said unto the centurion that stood by, Is it lawful for you to scourge a man that is a Roman, and uncondemned?	And as they bound him with straps, Paul said unto the centurion that stood by, Is it lawful for you to scourge a man that is a Roman Citizen?	
Acts 23:1	And Paul, earnestly beholding the council, said, Men and brethren, I have lived in all good conscience	And Paul, steadfastly beholding the council, said, Men and brethren, I have lived in all good conscience	earnestly!

Scripture	Discrepancies in KJV Scripture	Memories of the 1611 KJV	Notes:
	before God until this day.	before God until this day.	
Acts 23:10	And when there arose a great dissension, the chief captain, fearing lest Paul should have been pulled in pieces of them, commanded the soldiers to go down, and to take him by force from among them, and to bring him into the castle.	And when there arose a great dissension, the tribunal fearing lest Paul should have been torn into pieces of them, commanded the soldiers to go down, and to take him by force from among them, and to bring him into the barracks.	tribune, fortress castle!
Acts 23:15	Now therefore ye with the council signify to the chief captain that he bring him down unto you to morrow, as though ye would enquire something more perfectly concerning him: and we, or ever he come near, are ready to kill him.	Now therefore ye with the council signify to the chief captain that he bring him down unto you tomorrow, as though ye would enquire something more perfectly concerning him: and we, or before he come near, are ready to kill him.	to morrow! ever!
Acts 23:16	And when Paul's sister's son heard of their lying in wait, he went and entered into the castle, and told Paul.	And when Paul's sister's son heard of their lying in wait, he came and entered the barracks and told Paul.	castle!
Acts 23:24	And provide them beasts, that they may set Paul on, and bring him safe unto Felix the governor.	And provide them mounts, that they may set Paul on, and bring him safe unto Felix the governor.	beasts! horses
Acts 23:27	This man was taken of the Jews, and should have been killed of them: then came I with an	This man was taken of the Jews, and would have been killed of them: then came I with troops, and	soldiers

29

Scripture	Discrepancies in KJV Scripture	Memories of the 1611 KJV	Notes:
	army, and rescued him, having understood that he was a Roman.	rescued him, having understood that he was a Roman.	
Acts 23:32	On the morrow they left the horsemen to go with him, and returned to the castle:	On the morrow they left the horsemen to go with him, and returned to the barracks:	
Acts 24:1	And after five days Ananias the high priest descended with the elders, and with a certain orator named Tertullus, who informed the governor against Paul.	And after five days Ananias the high priest came down with the elders, and with a certain orator named Tertullus, who informed the governor against Paul.	
Acts 24:4	Notwithstanding, that I be not further tedious unto thee, I pray thee that thou wouldest hear us of thy clemency a few words.	Notwithstanding, that I be not further burden unto thee, I pray thee that thou wouldest hear us of thy kindness a few words.	tedious! clemency!

Scripture	Discrepancies in KJV Scripture	Memories of the 1611 KJV	Notes:
Acts 24:5	For we have found this man a pestilent fellow, and a mover of sedition among all the Jews throughout the world, and a ringleader of the sect of the Nazarenes:	For we have found this man a persistent fellow, and a mover of sedition among all the Jews throughout the world, and a leader of the sect of the Nazarenes:	troublemaker
Acts 24:14	But this I confess unto thee, that after the way which they call heresy, so worship I the God of my fathers, believing all things which are written in the law and in the prophets:	But this I confess unto thee, that according to the Way, which they call a sect, so serve I the God of my fathers, believing all things which are written in the law and the prophets:	
Acts 24:15	And have hope toward God, which they themselves also allow, that there shall be a resurrection of the dead, both of the just and unjust.	And have hope toward God, which they themselves also accept, that there shall be a resurrection of the dead, both of the just and unjust.	allow!
Acts 24:27	But after two years Porcius Festus came into Felix' room: and Felix, willing to shew the Jews a pleasure, left Paul bound.	But after two years Festus came unto Felix , and willing to shew favour among the Jews, he left Paul in prison.	Porcius!
Acts 25:19	But had certain questions against him of their own superstition, and of one Jesus, which was dead, whom Paul affirmed to be alive.	But had certain questions against him of their own religion a certain Jesus, who had died, whom Paul affirmed to be alive.	supersitition!
Acts 26:16	But rise, and stand upon thy feet: for I have appeared unto thee for this purpose, to make thee a minister and a witness both of these things which thou hast seen, and of those things in the which I will appear unto thee;	But rise, and stand upon thy feet: for I have appeared unto thee for this purpose, to make thee a minister and a servant both of these things which thou hast seen, and of those things in the which I will reveal unto thee;	
Acts 27:1	And when it was determined that we should sail into Italy, they delivered Paul and certain other prisoners unto one named Julius, a centurion of Augustus' band.	And when it was determined that we should sail into Italy, they delivered Paul and certain other prisoners unto one named Julius, a centurion of corhort of Augustus.	
Acts 28:2	And the barbarous people shewed us no little kindness: for they kindled a fire, and received us every one, because of the present rain, and because of the cold.	And the foreigners shewed us no little kindness: for they kindled a fire, and received us every one, because of the present rain, and because of the cold.	

Scripture	Discrepancies in KJV Scripture	Memories of the 1611 KJV	Notes:
Acts 28:4	And when the barbarians saw the venomous beast hang on his hand, they said among themselves, No doubt this man is a murderer, whom, though he hath escaped the sea, yet vengeance suffereth not to live.	And when the barbarians saw the venomous beast hang on his hand, they said among themselves, No doubt this man is a murderer, whom, though he hath escaped the sea, yet justice suffereth not to live.	vengeance!
Acts 28:8	And it came to pass, that the father of Publius lay sick of a fever and of a bloody flux: to whom Paul entered in, and prayed, and laid his	And it came to pass, that the father of Popliou lay sick of a fever and of dysentery: to whom Paul entered in, and prayed, and laid his hands on him,	a bloody flux!

30

Scripture	Discrepancies in KJV Scripture	Memories of the 1611 KJV	Notes:
	hands on him, and healed him.	and healed him.	
Acts 28:11	And after three months we departed in a ship of Alexandria, which had wintered in the isle, whose sign was Castor and Pollux.	And after three months we departed and journeyed to Alexandria, which had wintered in the isles, whose sign was twin gods as its figurehead.	Castor and Pollux!
Acts 28:12	And from thence we fetched a compass, and came to Rhegium: and after one day the south wind blew, and we came the next day to Puteoli:	And from thence we made a circuit, and came to Rhegium: and after one day the south wind blew, and we came the next day to Puteoli:	fetched a compass!
Acts 28:15	And from thence, when the brethren heard of us, they came to meet us as far as Appii forum, and The three taverns: whom when Paul saw, he thanked God, and took courage.	And from thence, when the brethren heard of us, they came to meet us as far as the Appian Way, whom when Paul saw, he thanked God, and took courage.	tavern!
Rom 1:13	Now I would not have you ignorant, brethren, that oftentimes I purposed to come unto you, (but was let hitherto,) that I might have some fruit among you also, even as among other Gentiles.	Now I would not have you ignorant, brethren, that often times I purposed to come unto you, (but was hindered hitherto,) that I might have some fruit among you also, even as among other Gentiles.	let!
Rom 1:31	Without understanding, covenantbreakers, without natural affection, implacable, unmerciful:	Without understanding, covenant breakers, without natural affection, unforgiving, unmerciful:	implacable!

Scripture	Discrepancies in KJV Scripture	Memories of the 1611 KJV	Notes:
Rom 2:8	But unto them that are contentious, and do not obey the truth, but obey unrighteousness, indignation and wrath,	But unto them that are self-seeking, and do not obey the truth, but obey unrighteousness, indignation and wrath,	contentious!
Rom 3:23	For all have sinned, and come short of the glory of God;	For all have sinned, and fallen short of the glory of God;	
Rom 5:3-5	3 And not only so, but we glory in tribulations also: knowing that tribulation worketh patience; 4 And patience, experience; and experience, hope: 5 And hope maketh not ashamed; because the love of God is shed abroad in our hearts by the Holy Ghost which is given unto us.	3 And not only so, but we also rejoice in our sufferings, because we know that suffering produces perserverance; 4 perserverence, character; and character, hope. 5 And hope does not disappoint us, because God has poured out his love into our hearts by the Holy Ghost, whom he has given us.	experience!
Rom 6:5	For if we have been planted together in the likeness of his death, we shall be also in the likeness of his resurrection:	For if we have been united together in the likeness of his death, we shall be also in the likeness of his resurrection:	planted!
Rom 7:8	But sin, taking occasion by the commandment, wrought in me all manner of concupiscence. For without the law sin was dead.	But sin, taking occasion by the commandment, wrought in me all manner of covetousness. For without the law sin was dead.	concupiscence!
Rom 7:15	For that which I do I allow not: for what I would, that do I not; but what I hate, that do I.	For that which I do I know not: for what I would, that I do not; but what I hate, that do I.	allow!
Rom 8:19	For the earnest expectation of the creature waiteth for the manifestation of the sons of God.	For the earnest expectation of the creation waiteth for the manifestation of the sons of God.	creature!
Rom 8:20	For the creature was made subject to vanity, not willingly, but by reason of him who hath subjected the same in hope,	For the creation was made subject to vanity, not willingly, but by reason of him who hath subjected the same in hope,	
Rom 8:21	Because the creature itself also shall be delivered from the bondage of corruption into the glorious liberty of the children of God.	Because the creation itself also shall be delivered from the bondage of corruption into the glorious liberty of the children of God.	
Rom 8:24	For we are saved by hope: but hope that is seen is not hope: for	For in this hope we are saved: but hope that is seen is not hope: for	

Scripture	Discrepancies in KJV Scripture	Memories of the 1611 KJV	Notes:
	what a man seeth, why doth he	what a man seeth, why doth he yet	

31

Scripture	Discrepancies in KJV Scripture	Memories of the 1611 KJV	Notes:
	yet hope for?	hope for?	
Rom 8:39	Nor height, nor depth, nor any other creature, shall be able to separate us from the love of God, which is in Christ Jesus our Lord.	Nor height, nor depth, nor any other creation, shall be able to separate us from the love of God, which is in Christ Jesus our Lord.	
Rom 9:25	As he saith also in Osee, I will call them my people, which were not my people; and her beloved, which was not beloved.	As he saith also in Hosea, I will call them my people, which were not my people; and her beloved, which was not beloved.	Osee!
Rom 9:29	And as Esaias said before, Except the Lord of Sabaoth had left us a seed, we had been as Sodoma, and been made like unto Gomorrha.	And as Isaiah said before, "Except the Lord of Hosts had left us a seed, we had been as Sodom, and been made like unto Gomorrah."	also Mark 6:11 and Matt 10:15
Rom 11:16	For if the firstfruit be holy, the lump is also holy: and if the root be holy, so are the branches.	For if the first fruit be holy, the lump is also holy: and if the root be holy, so are the branches.	
Rom 11:24	For if thou wert cut out of the olive tree which is wild by nature, and wert graffed contrary to nature into a good olive tree: how much more shall these, which be the natural branches, be graffed into their own olive tree?	For if thou were cut out of the wild olive tree which is wild by nature, and were grafted contrary to nature into a good olive tree: how much more shall these, which be the natural branches, be grafted into their own olive tree?	wert! graffed!
Rom 11:26	And so all Israel shall be saved: as it is written, There shall come out of Sion the Deliverer, and shall turn away ungodliness from Jacob:	And so all Israel shall be saved: as it is written, From Mount Zion a Deliverer will come, and he shall turn away ungodliness from Jacob:	Sion!
Rom 12:3	For I say, through the grace given unto me, to every man that is among you, not to think of himself more highly than he ought to think; but to think soberly, according as God hath dealt to every man the measure of faith.	For I say, through the grace given unto me, to every man that is among you, not to think of himself more highly than he ought to think; but to think soberly, according as God hath dealt to every man a measure of faith.	
Rom 12:9	Let love be without dissimulation. Abhor that which is evil; cleave to that which is good.	Let love be without hypocrisy. Abhor that which is evil; cleave to that which is good.	dissimulation !

Scripture	Discrepancies in KJV Scripture	Memories of the 1611 KJV	Notes:
Rom 12:12	Rejoicing in hope; patient in tribulation; continuing instant in prayer;	Rejoicing in hope; patient in tribulation; constant in prayer;	instant!
Rom 13:1	Let every soul be subject unto the higher powers. For there is no power but of God: the powers that be are ordained of God.	Let every one be subject unto the governing authorities. For there is no authority except from God: the authorities existing are ordained by God.	higher powers! powers that be!
Rom 13:2	Whosoever therefore resisteth the power, resisteth the ordinance of God: and they that resist shall receive to themselves damnation.	Whosoever therefore resists the authority, withstands the ordinance of God: and they that resist shall receive to themselves condemnation.	Doc error damnation to those who resist Gov.?
Rom 13:3	For rulers are not a terror to good works, but to the evil. Wilt thou then not be afraid of the power? do that which is good, and thou shalt have praise of the same:	For rulers are not a terror to good works, but to the evil. Wilt thou then not be afraid of the authority? do that which is good, and thou shalt have praise of the same:	
Rom 13:4	For he is the minister of God to thee for good. But if thou do that which is evil, be afraid; for he beareth not the sword in vain: for he is the minister of God, a revenger to execute wrath upon him that doeth evil.	For he is the minister of God to thee for good. But if thou do that which is evil, be afraid; for he bares not the sword in vain: for he is a minister of God, to execute judgment upon him that doeth evil.	Contridicts Rom 12:19
Rom 13:6	For for this cause pay ye tribute also: for they are God's ministers, attending continually upon this very thing.	For for this cause ye pay tribute also: for they are God's ministers, continually devoted upon this very thing.	

Scripture	Discrepancies in KJV Scripture	Memories of the 1611 KJV	Notes:
Rom 13:12	The night is far spent, the day is at hand: let us therefore cast off the works of darkness, and let us put on the armour of light.	The night is far spent, the day is at hand: let us therefore cast off the works of darkness, and let us put ye on the Lord Jesus Christ, and let us not make a provision for the flesh.	armour of light!
Rom 13:13	Let us walk honestly, as in the day; not in rioting and drunkenness, not in chambering and wantonness, not in	Let us walk honestly, as in the day; not in reveling and drunkenness, not in immorality and wantonness,	chambering!

Scripture	Discrepancies in KJV Scripture	Memories of the 1611 KJV	Notes:
	strife and envying.	not in strife and envying.	
Rom 14:20	For meat destroy not the work of God. All things indeed are pure; but it is evil for that man who eateth with offence.	For food destroy not the work of God. All things indeed are clean; howbeit it is evil for that man who eateth with offense.	
Rom 14:23	And he that doubteth is damned if he eat, because he eateth not of faith: for whatsoever is not of faith is sin.	And he that doubteth is condemned if he eat, because he eateth not of faith: for whatsoever is not of faith is sin.	damned!
Rom 16:1	I commend unto you Phebe our sister, which is a servant of the church which is at Cenchrea:	I commend unto you Phoebe, a deacon, of the church at Cenchreae:	
Rom 16:2	That ye receive her in the Lord, as becometh saints, and that ye assist her in whatsoever business she hath need of you: for she hath been a succourer of many, and of myself also.	That ye receive her in the Lord, as becometh saints, and that ye assist her in whatsoever business she hath need of you: for she hath been a benefactor of many, and of myself also.	succourer!
Rom 16:4	Who have for my life laid down their own necks: unto whom not only I give thanks, but also all the churches of the Gentiles.	Who have risked their necks for my life: unto whom not only I give thanks, but also all the churches of the Gentiles.	
Rom 16:5	Likewise greet the church that is in their house. Salute my wellbeloved Epaenetus, who is the firstfruits of Achaia unto Christ.	Likewise greet the church in their house. Greet my beloved Epaenetus, who is the first convert in Asia for Christ.	achaia!
Rom 16:7	Salute Andronicus and Junia, my kinsmen, and my fellowprisoners, who are of note among the apostles, who also were in Christ before me.	Greet Andronicus and Junia, my relatives, and my fellow prisoners, who are of note among the apostles, who also were in Christ before me.	
Rom 16:8	Greet Amplias my beloved in the Lord.	Greet Ampliatus my beloved in the Lord.	
Rom 16:9	Salute Urbane, our helper in Christ, and Stachys my beloved.	Greet Urbanus, our co-worker in Christ, and my beloved Stachys.	
Rom 16:10	Salute Apelles approved in Christ. Salute them which are of Aristobulus' household.	Greet Apelles who is approved in Christ. Greet those who belong to the family of Aristobulus.	
Rom 16:11	Salute Herodion my kinsman. Greet them that be of the household of Narcissus, which are in the Lord.	Greet my relative Herodion. Greet those in the Lord who belong to the family of Narcissus.	

Scripture	Discrepancies in KJV Scripture	Memories of the 1611 KJV	Notes:
Rom 16:12	Salute Tryphena and Tryphosa, who labour in the Lord. Salute the beloved Persis, which laboured much in the Lord.	Greet those workers in the Lord, Tryphaena and Tryphosa. Greet the beloved Persis, which laboured much in the Lord.	
Rom 16:13	Salute Rufus chosen in the Lord, and his mother and mine.	Greet Rufus chosen in the Lord, and his mother and mine.	
Rom 16:14	Salute Asyncritus, Phlegon, Hermas, Patrobas, Hermes, and the brethren which are with them.	Greet Asyncritus, Phlegon, Hermes, and the brethren which are with them.	
Rom 16:15	Salute Philologus, and Julia, Nereus, and his sister, and Olympas, and all the saints which are with them.	Greet Philologus, and Julia, Nereus, and his sister, and Olympas, and all the saints who are with them.	
Rom 16:21	Timotheus my workfellow, and Lucius, and Jason, and Sosipater, my kinsmen, salute you.	Timothy my co-worker, greets you, and so do Lucius, and Jason, and Sosipater, my relatives, greet	

33

Scripture	Discrepancies in KJV Scripture	Memories of the 1611 KJV	Notes:
		you.	
Rom 16:22	I Tertius, who wrote this epistle, salute you in the Lord.	I Tertius, who wrote down this letter, greet you in the Lord.	
Rom 16:25	Now to him that is of power to stablish you according to my gospel, and the preaching of Jesus Christ, according to the revelation of the mystery, which was kept secret since the world began,	Now to him that is of power to esstablish you according to my gospel, and the preaching of Jesus Christ, according to the revelation of the mystery which has been kept secret for ages past,	
1 Cor 4:7	For who maketh thee to differ from another? and what hast thou that thou didst not receive? now if thou didst receive it, why dost thou glory, as if thou hadst not received it?	For who maketh thee to differ from another? and what hast thou that thou didst not receive? now if thou didst receive it, why dost thou glory, as if thou hadst not received it?	
1 Cor 4:8	Now ye are full, now ye are rich, ye have reigned as kings without us: and I would to God ye did reign, that we also might reign with you.	(I don't remember this verse)	
1 Cor 4:13	Being defamed, we intreat: we are made as the filth of the world, and are the offscouring of all things	(I don't remember this verse)	

Scripture	Discrepancies in KJV Scripture	Memories of the 1611 KJV	Notes:
	unto this day.		
1 Cor 4:17	For this cause have I sent unto you Timotheus, who is my beloved son, and faithful in the Lord, who shall bring you into remembrance of my ways which be in Christ, as I teach every where in every church.	For this cause have I sent unto you Timothy, who is my son by adoption, and faithful in the Lord, who shall put you in remembrance of my ways which are in Christ, as I teach everywhere in all the churches.	
1 Cor 5:4	In the name of our Lord Jesus Christ, when ye are gathered together, and my spirit, with the power of our Lord Jesus Christ,	In the name of our Lord Jesus Christ, when ye are gathered together, (and I am there in spirit), with the power of our Lord Jesus Christ,	
1 Cor 5:5	To deliver such an one unto Satan for the destruction of the flesh, that the spirit may be saved in the day of the Lord Jesus.	To deliver such a one unto Satan for the destruction of the flesh, that his spirit may be saved in the day of the Lord Jesus.	
1 Cor 5:9	I wrote unto you in an epistle not to company with fornicators:	(I don't remember this verse)	
1 Cor 5:10	Yet not altogether with the fornicators of this world, or with the covetous, or extortioners, or with idolaters; for then must ye needs go out of the world.	(I don't remember this verse)	
1 Cor 5:11	But now I have written unto you not to keep company, if any man that is called a brother be a fornicator, or covetous, or an idolater, or a railer, or a drunkard, or an extortioner; with such an one no not to eat.	But now I have written unto you not to keep company, if any man that is called a brother be a fornicator, or covetous, or an idolater, or a railer, or a drunkard, or an extortioner; with such a one do not eat.	
1 Cor 5:12	For what have I to do to judge them also that are without? do not ye judge them that are within?	For what have I to do to judge them also that are without? do not ye judge them that are within?	
1 Cor 6:9	Know ye not that the unrighteous shall not inherit the kingdom of God? Be not deceived: neither fornicators, nor idolaters, nor adulterers, nor effeminate, nor abusers of themselves with mankind,	Know ye not that the unrighteous shall not inherit the kingdom of God? Be not deceived: neither fornicators, nor idolaters, nor adulterers, nor homosexuals, nor abusers of themselves with mankind,	NOTE:Word effeminate now means, just more womanly qualities.

Scripture	Discrepancies in KJV Scripture	Memories of the 1611 KJV	Notes:
1 Cor 7:5	Defraud ye not one the other, except it be with consent for a time, that ye may give yourselves	Do not deprive one another, except it be with consent for a time, that ye may give yourselves to	incontinency! lack of self

Scripture	Discrepancies in KJV Scripture	Memories of the 1611 KJV	Notes:
	to fasting and prayer; and come together again, that Satan tempt you not for your incontinency.	fasting and prayer; and come together again, that Satan tempt you not for your lack of self-control.	control
1 Cor 7:7	For I would that all men were even as I myself. But every man hath his proper gift of God, one after this manner, and another after that.	For I would that all men were even as I myself. But every man hath his own gift of God, one after this manner, and another after that.	proper!
1 Cor 7:17	But as God hath distributed to every man, as the Lord hath called every one, so let him walk. And so ordain I in all churches.	But as God hath distributed to every man, as the Lord hath called every one, so let him walk. And so I prescribe in all churches.	
1 Cor 8:7	Howbeit there is not in every man that knowledge: for some with conscience of the idol unto this hour eat it as a thing offered unto an idol; and their conscience being weak is defiled.	Howbeit there is not in every man that knowledge: for some with consciousness of the idol unto this hour eat it as a thing offered unto an idol; and their consciousness being weak is defiled.	conscience!
1 Cor 10:24	Let no man seek his own, but every man another's wealth.	Let no man seek his own, but every man another's good.	wealth! (WBT says wealth)
1 Cor 10:25	Whatsoever is sold in the shambles, that eat, asking no question for conscience sake:	Whatsoever is sold in the marketplace, that eat, asking no question for conscience sake:	marketplace!
1 Cor 11:13	Judge in yourselves: is it comely that a woman pray unto God uncovered?	Judge in yourselves: is it proper that a woman pray unto God uncovered?	comely
1 Cor 11:19	For there must be also heresies among you, that they which are approved may be made manifest among you.	For there must be also factions among you, that they which are approved may be made manifest among you.	heresies!
1 Cor 11:22	What? have ye not houses to eat and to drink in? or despise ye the church of God, and shame them that have	What? have ye not houses to eat and to drink in? or despise ye the church of God? What shall I say	

Scripture	Discrepancies in KJV Scripture	Memories of the 1611 KJV	Notes:
	not? What shall I say to you? shall I praise you in this? I praise you not.	to you? shall I praise you in this? I praise you not.	
1 Cor 11:25	After the same manner also he took the cup, when he had supped, saying, This cup is the new testament in my blood: this do ye, as oft as ye drink it, in remembrance of me.	After the same manner also he took the cup, after supper, saying, This cup is the new covenant in my blood: this do ye, as often as ye drink it, in remembrance of me.	
1 Cor 12:23	And those members of the body, which we think to be less honourable, upon these we bestow more abundant honour; and our uncomely parts have more abundant comeliness.	And those members of the body, which we think to be less honourable, on these we bestow greater honour; and our unpresentable parts have greater modesty,	uncomely!
1 Cor. 13:2	And though I have the gift of prophecy, and understand all mysteries, and all knowledge; and though I have all faith, so that I could remove mountains, and have not charity, I am nothing.	And though I have the gift of prophecy, and understand all mysteries, and all knowledge; and though I have all faith, so that I could move mountains, and have not love, I am nothing.	
I Cor. 13:12	For now we see through a glass, darkly; but then face to face: now I know in part; but then shall I know even as also I am known.	For now we see through a mirror, dimly; but then face to face: now I know in part; but then shall I know even as also I am known.	glass!
1 Cor 14:7-11	7 And even things without life giving sound, whether pipe or harp, except they give a distinction in the sounds, how shall it be known what is piped or harped? 8 For if the trumpet give an uncertain sound, who shall prepare himself to the battle? 9 So likewise ye, except ye utter by the tongue words easy to be understood, how shall it be known what is spoken? for ye shall speak into	7 And even things without life which give sound, whether flute or harp, unless they give a distinction in the sounds, how shall it be known what is played or harped? 8 For if the trumpet give an indistinct sound, who shall prepare himself to the battle? 9 So likewise, if unless ye utter by the tongue words easy to be understood, how shall it be known what is spoken? for ye shall speak into the air.	pipe,piped! signification! barbarian!

35

Scripture	Discrepancies in KJV Scripture	Memories of the 1611 KJV	Notes:
	the air.	10 There are, it may be, a great many	

Scripture	Discrepancies in KJV Scripture	Memories of the 1611 KJV	Notes:
	10 There are, it may be, so many kinds of voices in the world, and none of them is without signification. 11 Therefore if I know not the meaning of the voice, I shall be unto him that speaketh a barbarian, and he that speaketh shall be a barbarian unto me.	languages in the world, and no kind of them is without meaning. 11 Therefore if I know not the meaning of the sound, I shall be unto him that speaketh a foreigner, and he that speaketh shall be a foreigner unto me.	
1 Cor 14:34	Let your women keep silence in the churches: for it is not permitted unto them to speak; but they are commanded to be under obedience, as also saith the law.	Let your women keep silence in the churches: for it is not permitted unto them to speak; but they are commanded to be under subjection, as also saith the law.	
1 Cor 15:9	For I am the least of the apostles, that am not meet to be called an apostle, because I persecuted the church of God.	For I am the least of the apostles, and I am not worthy to be called an apostle, because I persecuted the church of God.	
1 Cor 15:21	For since by man came death, by man came also the resurrection of the dead.	For since by a man came death, also by a man resurrection of the dead.	
1 Cor 15:23- 32	1Cor. 15:23 But every man in his own order: Christ the firstfruits; afterward they that are Christ's at his coming. 1Cor. 15:24 Then cometh the end, when he shall have delivered up the kingdom to God, even the Father; when he shall have put down all rule and all authority and power. 1Cor. 15:25 For he must reign, till he hath put all enemies under his feet. 1Cor. 15:26 The last enemy that shall be destroyed is death. 1Cor. 15:27 For he hath put all things under his feet. But when he saith all things are put under him, it is manifest that he is excepted, which did put all	1Cor. 15:23 But every man in his own rank: Christ is the first fruits; then they that are Christ's at his second coming. 1Cor. 15:24 Then cometh the end, when he shall deliver over the kingdom to God, even the Father; when he shall abolish every rule and all authority and power. 1Cor. 15:25 For he must reign, until he hath put all his enemies under his feet. 1Cor. 15:26 The last enemy that shall be abolished is death. 1Cor. 15:27 For the Father hath put all things in subjection under his feet. But when he saith all things are under subjection, it is evident that he is excepted, which did put all things under him. 1Cor. 15:28 And when all things shall be subjected unto him, then shall the Son also himself be	

Scripture	Discrepancies in KJV Scripture	Memories of the 1611 KJV	Notes:
	things under him. 1Cor. 15:28 And when all things shall be subdued unto him, then shall the Son also himself be subject unto him that put all things under him, that God may be all in all. 1Cor. 15:29 Else what shall they do which are baptized for the dead, if the dead rise not at all? why are they then baptized for the dead? 1Cor. 15:30 And why stand we in jeopardy every hour? 1Cor. 15:31 I protest by your rejoicing which I have in Christ Jesus our Lord, I die daily. 1Cor. 15:32 If after the manner of men I have fought with beasts at Ephesus, what advantageth it me, if the dead rise not? let us eat and drink; for to morrow we die.	subject unto him that put all things under him, that God may be all in all. 1Cor. 15:29 Otherwise, what shall they themselves do which are baptized in behalf of the dead, if the dead rise not at all? why are they then baptized for the dead? 1Cor. 15:30 And why do I stand in peril every hour? 1Cor. 15:31 I protest by the pride which I have in you in Christ Jesus our Lord, I die daily. 1Cor. 15:32 If after the manner of men I have fought wild beasts at Ephesus, what doth it advantage me, if the dead are not raised? let us eat and drink; for tomorrow we die.	
1 Cor 15:33	Be not deceived: evil communications corrupt good manners.	Be not deceived: evil company corrupts good manners.	communicato in!
1 Cor 15:35- 41	1Cor. 15:35 ¶ But some man will say, How are the dead raised up? and with what body do they come? 1Cor. 15:36 Thou fool, that which thou sowest is not quickened, except it die:	1Cor. 15:35 ¶ But some will say, How are the dead raised up? and with what body do they come forth? 1Cor. 15:36 Thou fool, that which thou dost sow does not spring up, lest it die: 1Cor. 15:37 Nor the seed which thou sows, thou	

36

Scripture	Discrepancies in KJV Scripture	Memories of the 1611 KJV	Notes:
	1Cor. 15:37 And that which thou sowest, thou sowest not that body that shall be, but bare grain, it may chance of wheat, or of some other grain: 1Cor. 15:38 But God giveth it a body as it hath pleased him, and to every seed his own body. 1Cor. 15:39 All flesh is not the same flesh: but there is one kind of flesh of men, another flesh	sows not that body that shall be, but a naked kernel, perhaps of wheat, or of some other grain: 1Cor. 15:38 But God giveth it a body that he hath purposed, and to every kind of seed its own body. 1Cor. 15:39 All flesh is not the same: but there is one kind of flesh of men, another flesh of	

Scripture	Discrepancies in KJV Scripture	Memories of the 1611 KJV	Notes:
	of beasts, another of fishes, and another of birds. 1Cor. 15:40 There are also celestial bodies, and bodies terrestrial: but the glory of the celestial is one, and the glory of the terrestrial is another. 1Cor. 15:41 There is one glory of the sun, and another glory of the moon, and another glory of the stars: for one star differeth from another star in glory.	beasts, another of fish, and another of birds. 1Cor. 15:40 There are also heavenly bodies, and earthly bodies : but the glory of the heavenly is one, and the glory of the earthly is another. 1Cor. 15:41 There is one glory of the sun, and another glory of the moon, and another glory of the stars: for one star differs from another star in glory.	
1 Cor 15:48,49	1Cor. 15:48 As is the earthy, such are they also that are earthy: and as is the heavenly, such are they also that are heavenly. 1Cor. 15:49 And as we have borne the image of the earthy, we shall also bear the image of the heavenly.	1Cor. 15:48 And those made from the dust, such are they also that are like him made from the dust: and as he is made from heaven, such are they also who are from heaven. 1Cor. 15:49 And as we have borne the image of the man of dust we shall also bear the image of the man of heaven.	
1 Cor 15:56	The sting of death is sin; and the strength of sin is the law.	The sting of death is sin; and the power of sin is the violation of the law.	
1 Cor 16:3	And when I come, whomsoever ye shall approve by your letters, them will I send to bring your liberality unto Jerusalem.	(I don't remember this verse)	grammer?
1 Cor 16:6	And it may be that I will abide, yea, and winter with you, that ye may bring me on my journey whithersoever I go.	(I don't remember this verse)	whithersoever!
1 Cor 16:7,8	7 For I will not see you now by the way; but I trust to tarry a while with you, if the Lord permit. 8 But I will tarry at Ephesus until Pentecost.	(I don't remember these verses)	
1 Cor. 16:15	I beseech you, brethren, (ye know the house of Stephanas, that it is the firstfruits of Achaia, and that they have addicted themselves to the	I beseech you, brethren, (ye know the house of Stephanas,) that it is the first converts of Asia, and that they have devoted themselves to	addicted! appointed

Scripture	Discrepancies in KJV Scripture	Memories of the 1611 KJV	Notes:
	ministry of the saints,)	the ministry of the saints,	
1 Cor 16:22	If any man love not the Lord Jesus Christ, let him be Anathema Maranatha.	If any man love not the Lord Jesus Christ, let him be Anathema Maranatha. The Lord comes.	
2 Cor 1:15	And in this confidence I was minded to come unto you before, that ye might have a second benefit;	And in this confidence I was minded to come unto you before, that ye might have a second blessing;	
2 Cor 1:16	And to pass by you into Macedonia, and to come again out of Macedonia unto you, and of you to be brought on my way toward Judaea.	(I don't remember this verse)	
2 Cor 1:17- 19	17 When I therefore was thus minded, did I use lightness? or the things that I purpose, do I purpose according to the flesh, that with me there should be yea yea, and nay nay? 18 But as God is true, our word toward you was	(I don't remember these verses)	Contradicts Matt 5:37

37

Scripture	Discrepancies in KJV Scripture	Memories of the 1611 KJV	Notes:
	not yea and nay. 19 For the Son of God, Jesus Christ, who was preached among you by us, even by me and Silvanus and Timotheus, was not yea and nay, but in him was yea.		
2 Cor 1:24	Not for that we have dominion over your faith, but are helpers of your joy: for by faith ye stand.	(I don't remember this verse)	
2 Cor 2:2	For if I make you sorry, who is he then that maketh me glad, but the same which is made sorry by me?	For if I make you grieve, who is he then that maketh me glad, but the same which is grieved by me?	
2 Cor 2:15	For we are unto God a sweet savour of Christ, in them that are saved, and in them that perish:	For we are unto God a sweet savour, to them that are perishng:	
2 Cor 2:16	To the one we are the savour of death unto death; and to the other the savour of life unto life. And who is sufficient for these things?	(I don't remember this verse)	
2 Cor	For we are not as many, which	(I don't remember this verse)	

Scripture	Discrepancies in KJV Scripture	Memories of the 1611 KJV	Notes:
2:17	corrupt the word of God: but as of sincerity, but as of God, in the sight of God speak we in Christ.		
2 Cor 3:1	Do we begin again to commend ourselves? or need we, as some others, epistles of commendation to you, or letters of commendation from you?	(I don't remember this verse)	
2 Cor 3:3	Forasmuch as ye are manifestly declared to be the epistle of Christ ministered by us, written not with ink, but with the Spirit of the living God; not in tables of stone, but in fleshy tables of the heart.	Being made manifest declared to be the epistle of Christ ministered by us, written not with ink, but with the Spirit of the living God; not in tablets of stone, but in human tablets of the heart.	tables! fleshly! manifestly!
2 Cor 3:7	But if the ministration of death, written and engraven in stones, was glorious, so that the children of Israel could not stedfastly behold the face of Moses for the glory of his countenance; which glory was to be done away:	But if the ministry of death, written and engraved in stones, came with glory, so that the children of Israel could not stedfastly behold the face of Moses for the glory of his countenance; which glory was fading:	
2 Cor 3:8	How shall not the ministration of the spirit be rather glorious?	How shall not the ministry of the spirit be for greater glory?	rather glorious!
2 Cor 3:9	For if the ministration of condemnation be glory, much more doth the ministration of righteousness exceed in glory.	For if the ministry that brought condemnation had glory, much more does the ministry of righteousness abound in glory.	ministration of condemnation!
2 Cor 5:4	For we that are in this tabernacle do groan, being burdened: not for that we would be unclothed, but clothed upon, that mortality might be swallowed up of life.	(I don't remember this verse)	
2 Cor 5:11	Knowing therefore the terror of the Lord, we persuade men; but we are made manifest unto God; and I trust also are made manifest in your consciences.	Knowing therefore the fear of the Lord, we persuade men; but we are made manifest unto God; and I trust also are made manifest in your consciences.	terror of the Lord!
2 Cor 5:13	For whether we be beside ourselves, it is to God: or whether we be sober, it is for your cause.	(I don't remember this verse)	
2 Cor	Therefore if any man be in Christ, he	Therefore if any man be in Christ,	

Scripture	Discrepancies in KJV Scripture	Memories of the 1611 KJV	Notes:
5:17	is a new	he is a new	

38

Scripture	Discrepancies in KJV Scripture	Memories of the 1611 KJV	Notes:
	creature: old things are passed away; behold, all things are become new.	creation: old things are passed away; behold, all things are become new.	
2 Cor 6:4	But in all things approving ourselves as the ministers of God, in much patience, in afflictions, in necessities, in distresses,	But in all things commending ourselves as the ministers of God, in much patience, in afflictions, in necessities, in distresses,	approving!
2 Cor 6:11	O ye Corinthians, our mouth is open unto you, our heart is enlarged.	Oh ye Corinthians, we have spoken freely to you, our heart is enlarged.	mouth!
2 Cor 6:12	Ye are not straitened in us, but ye are straitened in your own bowels.	Ye are not constrained in us, but ye are constrained by your own affections.	straitened!
2 Cor. 6:15	And what concord hath Christ with Belial? or what part hath he that believeth with an infidel?	And what harmony hath Christ with Belial? or what part hath he that believeth with an unbeliever?	concord! infidel!
2 Cor 6:16	And what agreement hath the temple of God with idols? for ye are the temple of the living God; as God hath said, I will dwell in them, and walk in them; and I will be their God, and they shall be my people.	And what agreement hath the temple of God with idols? for ye are the temple of the living God; as God hath said, I will dwell in them, and walk among them; and I will be their God, and they shall be my people.	
2 Cor 7:1	Having therefore these promises, dearly beloved, let us cleanse ourselves from all filthiness of the flesh and spirit, perfecting holiness in the fear of God.	Having therefore these promises, dearly beloved, let us cleanse ourselves from everything that can defile the flesh and spirit, perfecting holiness in the fear of God.	
2 Cor 7:3	I speak not this to condemn you: for I have said before, that ye are in our hearts to die and live with you.	I speak not this to condemn you: for I have said before, that ye are in our hearts whether to die or live with you.	
2 Cor 7:5	For, when we were come into Macedonia, our flesh had no rest, but we were troubled on every side; without were fightings, within were fears.	For, when we were come into Macedonia, our flesh had no rest, but we were pressed on every side; without were fightings, within were fears.	
2 Cor 7:8	For though I made you sorry with a letter, I do not repent, though I did repent: for I perceive that the same	For though I grieved you with a letter, I do not regret, though I did regret: for I perceive that the same	sorry!

Scripture	Discrepancies in KJV Scripture	Memories of the 1611 KJV	Notes:
	epistle hath made you sorry, though it were but for a season.	epistle hath made grieved you, though it were but for a season.	
2 Cor 7:9	Now I rejoice, not that ye were made sorry, but that ye sorrowed to repentance: for ye were made sorry after a godly manner, that ye might receive damage by us in nothing.	Now I rejoice, not that ye were made sorrowful, but that ye sorrowed to repentance: for ye were made sorrowful after a godly manner, that ye might suffer loss by us in nothing.	sorry!
2 Cor 7:10	For godly sorrow worketh repentance to salvation not to be repented of: but the sorrow of the world worketh death.	For Godly sorrow bringeth repentance that leads to salvation and leaves no regret: but worldly sorrow brings death.	godly!
2 Cor 7:11	For behold this selfsame thing, that ye sorrowed after a godly sort, what carefulness it wrought in you, yea, what clearing of yourselves, yea, what indignation, yea, what fear, yea, what vehement desire, yea, what zeal, yea, what revenge! In all things ye have approved yourselves to be clear in this matter.	For behold this selfsame thing, that ye sorrowed after a Godly sort, what carefulness it wrought in you, yea, what clearing of yourselves, yea, what indignation, yea, what fear, yea, what longing, yea, what zeal, yea, what justice! In all things ye have proved yourselves to be clear in this matter.	godly! revenge! vindication
2 Cor 7:15	And his inward affection is more abundant toward you, whilst he remembereth the obedience of you all, how with fear and trembling ye received him.	And his inward affection is more abundant toward you, whilst he remembereth the obedience of you all, how with fear and trembling ye received him.	
2 Cor 8:1	Moreover, brethren, we do you to wit of the grace of God bestowed on the churches of	Moreover, brethren, we make you to know of the grace of God bestowed on the churches of	do you to wit!

39

Scripture	Discrepancies in KJV Scripture	Memories of the 1611 KJV	Notes:
	Macedonia;	Macedonia;	
2 Cor 8:2	How that in a great trial of affliction the abundance of their joy and their deep poverty abounded unto the riches of their liberality.	How that in a great trial of affliction the abundance of their joy and their deep poverty abounded unto the riches of their generosity.	liberality!
2 Cor 8:10	And herein I give my advice: for this is expedient for you, who have begun before, not only to do, but also to be forward a year ago.	And herein I give my advice: for this is expedient for you, who have begun before, not only to do, but also to be ready a year ago.	forward!

Scripture	Discrepancies in KJV Scripture	Memories of the 1611 KJV	Notes:
2 Cor 8:17	For indeed he accepted the exhortation; but being more forward, of his own accord he went unto you.	For indeed he accepted the exhortation; but being more earnest, of his own accord he went unto you.	forward!
2 Cor 8:19	And not that only, but who was also chosen of the churches to travel with us with this grace, which is administered by us to the glory of the same Lord, and declaration of your ready mind:	And not that only, but who was also chosen of the churches to travel with us with this grace, which is administered by us to the glory of the same Lord, and declaration of your eagerness:	your ready mind!
2 Cor 9:1	For as touching the ministering to the saints, it is superfluous for me to write to you:	Concerning the ministering to the saints, it is not necessary for me to write to you:	superfluous!
2 Cor 9:9	(As it is written, He hath dispersed abroad; he hath given to the poor: his righteousness remaineth for ever.	As it is written, He hath scattered abroad; he hath given to the poor: his righteousness remains forever.	
2 Cor 9:10	Now he that ministereth seed to the sower both minister bread for your food, and multiply your seed sown, and increase the fruits of your righteousness;)	Now he that supplies seed to the sower shall also supply bread for food, and multiply your seed sown, and increase the fruits of your righteousness;)	ministereth!
2 Cor 9:13	Whiles by the experiment of this ministration they glorify God for your professed subjection unto the gospel of Christ, and for your liberal distribution unto them, and unto all men;	While by the proof of this service they glorify God for your professed obedience to the gospel of Christ, and for your liberal sharing unto them, and unto all men;	Whiles! experiment!
2 Cor 10:4	(For the weapons of our warfare are not carnal, but mighty through God to the pulling down of strong holds;)	For the weapons of our warfare are not carnal, but mighty through God to the pulling down of strongholds;	
2 Cor 10:6	And having in a readiness to revenge all disobedience, when your obedience is fulfilled.	And having in a readiness to punish all disobedience, when your obedience is fulfilled.	revenge!
2 Cor 10:7	Do ye look on things after the outward appearance? If any man trust to himself that he is Christ's, let him of himself think this again, that, as he is Christ's, even so are we Christ's	Do ye look on things after the outward appearance? If any man is confident that he is Christ's, let him remind himself this that, as he is Christ's, even so are we also are Christ's	

Scripture	Discrepancies in KJV Scripture	Memories of the 1611 KJV	Notes:
2 cor 10:12	For we dare not make ourselves of the number, or compare ourselves with some that commend themselves: but they measuring themselves by themselves, and comparing themselves among themselves, are not wise.	For we dare not compare ourselves, with some that commend themselves: but they measuring themselves by one another, and comparing themselves with each other, they are not wise.	
2 Cor 10:13	But we will not boast of things without our measure, but according to the measure of the rule which God hath distributed to us, a measure to reach even unto you.	We however, will not boast beyond limits, but keep within the area of influence which God hath assigned to us, to reach even unto you.	field v13,14,15 are very redundant?
2 Cor 10:14	For we stretch not ourselves beyond our measure, as though we reached not unto you: for we are come as far as to you also in preaching the gospel of Christ:	For we were not overstepping our limits when we reached you; we were the first to come all the way to you with the good news of Christ.	also Matt 4:23

40

Scripture	Discrepancies in KJV Scripture	Memories of the 1611 KJV	Notes:
2 Cor 10:15	Not boasting of things without our measure, that is, of other men's labours; but having hope, when your faith is increased, that we shall be enlarged by you according to our rule abundantly,	We do not boast beyond limits, that is, of other men's labours; but having hope, when your faith is increased, that we shall be magnified by you according to our our area of influence,	
2 Cor 10:16	To preach the gospel in the regions beyond you, and not to boast in another man's line of things made ready to our hand.	To preach the gospel in the lands beyond you, and not to boast in another man's work in another area of influence.	
2 Cor 11:3	But I fear, lest by any means, as the serpent beguiled Eve through his subtilty, so your minds should be corrupted from the simplicity that is in Christ.	But I fear, lest by any means, as the serpent beguiled Eve through his subtlety, so your minds should be corrupted from a pure devotion towards Christ.	craftiness
2 Cor 11:4	For if he that cometh preacheth another Jesus, whom we have not preached, or if ye receive another spirit, which ye have not received, or another gospel, which ye have not	For if he that comes preaches another Jesus, whom we have not preached, or if ye receive another spirit, which ye have not received, or another gospel, which ye have not accepted, ye tolerate it well.	ref. Gal 1:8

Scripture	Discrepancies in KJV Scripture	Memories of the 1611 KJV	Notes:
	accepted, ye might well bear with him.		
2 Cor 11:5	For I suppose I was not a whit behind the very chiefest apostles.	For I suppose I was not least inferior the very chief apostles.	chiefest!
2 Cor 11:8	I robbed other churches, taking wages of them, to do you service.	I have taken from other churches, taking wages of them, to do you service.	robbed!
Gal 1:4	Who gave himself for our sins, that he might deliver us from this present evil world, according to the will of God and our Father:	Who gave himself for our sins, that he might deliver us from this present evil world, according to the will of God our Father:	
Gal 1:13	For ye have heard of my conversation in time past in the Jews' religion, how that beyond measure I persecuted the church of God, and wasted it:	For ye have indeed heard of my former way of life in Judiasm, how that beyond measure I persecuted the church of God, and destroyed it:	
Gal 1:16	To reveal his Son in me, that I might preach him among the heathen; immediately I conferred not with flesh and blood:	Was pleased to reveal his Son to me, that I might preach him among the Gentiles; I did not immediately confer with flesh and blood:	heathen! ref. Gal 2:2 again in 2:9
Gal 2:6	But of these who seemed to be somewhat, (whatsoever they were, it maketh no matter to me: God accepteth no man's person:) for they who seemed to be somewhat in conference added nothing to me:	But of these who seemed to be somewhat, (whatsoever they were, it maketh no difference to me: God accepteth no man's person:) for they who seemed to be somewhat in reputation added nothing to me:	conference!
Gal 2:7	But contrariwise, when they saw that the gospel of the uncircumcision was committed unto me, as the gospel of the circumcision was unto Peter;	But on the contrary, when they saw that the gospel of the uncircumcision was committed unto me, as the gospel of the circumcision was unto Peter;	contrariwise!
Gal 2:9	And when James, Cephas, and John, who seemed to be pillars, perceived the grace that was given unto me, they gave to me and Barnabas the right hands of fellowship; that we should go unto the heathen, and they unto the circumcision.	And when James, Cephas, and John, who were reputed to be pillars, perceived the grace that was given unto me, they gave to me and Barnabas the right hand of fellowship; that we should go unto the Gentiles, and they unto the circumcision.	
Gal 2:10	Only they would that we should remember the poor; the same which	Only they would that we should remember the poor; the same which	forward!

Scripture	Discrepancies in KJV Scripture	Memories of the 1611 KJV	Notes:
	I also was forward to do.	I also was eager to do.	
Gal 2:15	We who are Jews by nature, and not sinners of the Gentiles,	We who are Jews by birth, and not sinners like the Gentiles,	
Gal 3:19	Wherefore then serveth the law? It was added	Why then the law? It was added because of	

41

Scripture	Discrepancies in KJV Scripture	Memories of the 1611 KJV	Notes:
	because of transgressions, till the seed should come to whom the promise was made; and it was ordained by angels in the hand of a mediator.	transgressions, till the seed should come to whom the promise was made; and it was ordained by angels in the hand of a mediator.	
Gal 4:2	But is under tutors and governors until the time appointed of the father.	But is under guardians and stewards until the time appointed of the father.	
Gal 4:9	But now, after that ye have known God, or rather are known of God, how turn ye again to the weak and beggarly elements, whereunto ye desire again to be in bondage?	But now, after that ye have known God, or rather are known of God, how turn ye again to the weak and elementary principles, whereunto ye desire again to be in bondage?	beggarly elements!
Gal 4:14	And my temptation which was in my flesh ye despised not, nor rejected; but received me as an angel of God, even as Christ Jesus.	And my affliction which was in my body ye despised not, nor rejected; but received me as though I was an angel of God, even as Christ himself.	
Gal 4:17	They zealously affect you, but not well; yea, they would exclude you, that ye might affect them.	They are zealous for you, but not well; yea, they would exclude you, that ye might be zealous for them.	
Gal 4:20	I desire to be present with you now, and to change my voice; for I stand in doubt of you.	I desire to be present with you now, and to change my tone of voice; for I am perplexed about you.	
Gal 4:22	For it is written, that Abraham had two sons, the one by a bondmaid, the other by a freewoman.	For it is written, that Abraham had two sons, the one by a bondwoman, the other by a freewoman.	bondmaid!
Gal 4:24	Which things are an allegory: for these are the two covenants; the one from the mount Sinai, which gendereth to bondage, which is	Which things are an allegory: for these women are the two covenants; the one from the Mount Sinai, which bears forth to	begat also Gal 4:25

Scripture	Discrepancies in KJV Scripture	Memories of the 1611 KJV	Notes:
	Agar.	bondage, which is Hagar.	
Gal 5:10	I have confidence in you through the Lord, that ye will be none otherwise minded: but he that troubleth you shall bear his judgment, whosoever he be.	I have confidence in you through the Lord, that ye will be none otherwise minded: but he that troubleth you shall bear his penalty, whosoever he be.	guilt
Gal 5:11	And I, brethren, if I yet preach circumcision, why do I yet suffer persecution? then is the offence of the cross ceased.	And I, brethren, if I yet preach circumcision, why do I yet suffer persecution? then is the offense of the cross ceased.	
Gal 5:23	Meekness, temperance: against such there is no law.	Meekness, self-control: against such there is no law.	
Gal 5:24	And they that are Christ's have crucified the flesh with the affections and lusts.	And they that are Christ's have crucified the flesh with the passions and lusts.	affections!
Gal 6:15	For in Christ Jesus neither circumcision availeth any thing, nor uncircumcision, but a new creature.	For in Christ Jesus neither circumcision availeth any thing, nor uncircumcision, but a new creation.	
Eph 1:5	Having predestinated us unto the adoption of children by Jesus Christ to himself, according to the good pleasure of his will,	Having predestined us unto the adoption of children by Jesus Christ to himself, according to the good pleasure of his will,	predestinated !
Eph 1:6	To the praise of the glory of his grace, wherein he hath made us accepted in the beloved.	To the praise of his glorious grace, wherein he hath made us accepted in the beloved.	
Eph 3:21	Unto him be glory in the church by Christ Jesus throughout all ages, world without end. Amen.	Unto him be glory in the church by Christ Jesus throughout all generations forever and ever. Amen.	world without end!
Eph 4:32	And be ye kind one to another, tenderhearted, forgiving one another, even as God for Christ's sake hath forgiven you.	And be ye kind one to another, tenderhearted, forgiving one another, even as God in Christ forgave you.	for Christ's sake! Also 2 Cor 12:10

42

Scripture	Discrepancies in KJV Scripture	Memories of the 1611 KJV	Notes:
Eph 5:8	For ye were sometimes darkness, but now are ye light in the Lord: walk as children of light:	For ye were once darkness, but now are ye light in the Lord: walk as children of light:	
Eph 5:19	Speaking to yourselves in psalms	Speaking to yourselves in psalms and	

Scripture	Discrepancies in KJV Scripture	Memories of the 1611 KJV	Notes:
	and hymns and spiritual songs, singing and making melody in your heart to the Lord;	hymns and spiritual songs, singing and making melody in your hearts to the Lord;	
Phil 1:8	For God is my record, how greatly I long after you all in the bowels of Jesus Christ.	For God is my witness, how I long after you all with the tender mercies of Christ Jesus.	bowels!
Phil 1:16,17	16 The one preach Christ of contention, not sincerely, supposing to add affliction to my bonds: 17 But the other of love, knowing that I am set for the defence of the gospel.	16 The one of love, knowing that I am set for the defense of the gospel. 17 But the other preach Christ of contention, not sincerely, supposing to add affliction to my bonds:	Scriptures have been transposed!
Phil 2:1	If there be therefore any consolation in Christ, if any comfort of love, if any fellowship of the Spirit, if any bowels and mercies,	If there be therefore any encouragement in Christ, if any comfort of love, if any fellowship of the Spirit, if any tender mercies,	
Phil 2:8	And being found in fashion as a man, he humbled himself, and became obedient unto death, even the death of the cross.	And being found in form of a man, he humbled himself, and became obedient unto death, even the death of the cross.	fashion! likeness
Phil 2:10,11	10 That at the name of Jesus every knee should bow, of things in heaven, and things in earth, and things under the earth; 11 And that every tongue should confess that Jesus Christ is Lord, to the glory of God the Father.	10 That in the name of Jesus every knee shall bow, of things in heaven, and things on earth, and things under the earth; 11 And that every tongue shall confess that Jesus Christ is Lord, to the glory of God the Father.	
Phil 2:25	Yet I supposed it necessary to send to you Epaphroditus, my brother, and companion in labour, and fellowsoldier, but your messenger, and he that ministered to my wants.	Yet I supposed it necessary to send to you Epaphroditus, my brother, and companion in labour, and fellow soldier, but your messenger, and he that ministered to my needs.	ministered to my wants!
Phil 3:2	Beware of dogs, beware of evil workers, beware of the concision.	Beware of dogs, beware of evil workers, beware of the circumcision.	concision!
Phil 3:12	Not as though I had already attained, either were already perfect: but I follow after, if that I may apprehend that for which also	Not as though I had already attained, either were already perfect: but I follow after, if that I may lay hold that for which also I am laid hold of Christ	

Scripture	Discrepancies in KJV Scripture	Memories of the 1611 KJV	Notes:
	I am apprehended of Christ Jesus.	Jesus.	
Phil 3:13	Brethren, I count not myself to have apprehended: but this one thing I do, forgetting those things which are behind, and reaching forth unto those things which are before,	Brethren, I count not myself to have obtain: but this one thing I do, forgetting what lies behind, and reaching forward to what lies ahead,	
Phil 3:14	I press toward the mark for the prize of the high calling of God in Christ Jesus.	I press toward the goal for the prize of the high calling of God in Christ Jesus.	
Phil 4:3	And I intreat thee also, true yokefellow, help those women which laboured with me in the gospel, with Clement also, and with other my fellowlabourers, whose names are in the book of life.	And I intreat thee also, true companion, help these women which laboured with me in the gospel, together with Clement also, and with the rest of my fellow-workers, whose names are in the book of life.	Syzugus! in GWT
Phil 4:4	Rejoice in the Lord alway: and again I say, Rejoice.	Rejoice in the Lord always: and again I say, Rejoice.	alway!
Phil 4:6	Be careful for nothing; but in every thing by prayer and supplication with thanksgiving let your requests be made known unto God.	Be anxious for nothing; but in every thing by prayer and supplication with thanksgiving let your requests be made known unto God.	

43

Scripture	Discrepancies in KJV Scripture	Memories of the 1611 KJV	Notes:
Phil 4:7	And the peace of God, which passeth all understanding, shall keep your hearts and minds through Christ Jesus.	And the peace of God, which surpasses all understanding, shall guard your hearts and minds through Christ Jesus.	
Phil 4:13	I can do all things through Christ which strengtheneth me.	I can do all things through Christ who strengthens me.	
Phil 4:19	But my God shall supply all your need according to his riches in glory by Christ Jesus.	But my God shall supply all your needs according to his riches in glory by Christ Jesus.	
Col 1:15	Who is the image of the invisible God, the firstborn of every creature:	He is the image of the invisible God, the firstborn of all creation:	The son, Christ
Col 1:23	If ye continue in the faith grounded and settled, and be not moved away from the hope of the gospel, which	If indeed, ye continue in the faith grounded and settled, and be not moved away from the hope of the	

Scripture	Discrepancies in KJV Scripture	Memories of the 1611 KJV	Notes:
	ye have heard, and which was preached to every creature which is under heaven; whereof I Paul am made a minister;	gospel, which ye have heard, and which was preached in all creation under heaven; whereof I Paul became a minister;	
Col 1:24	Who now rejoice in my sufferings for you, and fill up that which is behind of the afflictions of Christ in my flesh for his body's sake, which is the church:	Who now rejoice in my sufferings for you, and fill up that which is lacking of the afflictions of Christ in my flesh for his body's sake, which is the church:	behind!
Col 2:1	For I would that ye knew what great conflict I have for you, and for them at Laodicea, and for as many as have not seen my face in the flesh;	For I would that ye knew what great solicitude I have for you, and for them at Laodicea, and for as many as have not seen my face in the flesh;	Laodicea! (thought only ref. is Rev 3:14)
Col 2:23	Which things have indeed a shew of wisdom in will worship, and humility, and neglecting of the body; not in any honour to the satisfying of the flesh.	These things have indeed a shew of wisdom in self imposed worship, and humility, and neglecting of the body; not in any honour to the satisfying of the flesh.	will worship!
Col 3:2	Set your affection on things above, not on things on the earth.	Set your mind on things above, not on things on the earth.	affection!
Col 3:5	Mortify therefore your members which are upon the earth; fornication, uncleanness, inordinate affection, evil concupiscence, and covetousness, which is idolatry:	Mortify therefore your members which are upon the earth; fornication, uncleanness, inordinate affection, evil desire, and covetousness, which is idolatry:	concupiscence!
Col 3:6	For which things' sake the wrath of God cometh on the children of disobedience:	Because of these things the wrath of God cometh on the sons of disobedience:	
Col 3:7	In the which ye also walked some time, when ye lived in them.	In the which ye also once walked, when ye lived in them.	some time!
Col 3:11	Where there is neither Greek nor Jew, circumcision nor uncircumcision, Barbarian, Scythian, bond nor free: but Christ is all, and in all.	Where there is neither Greek nor Jew, circumcision nor uncircumcision, bond nor free: but Christ is all, and in all.	
Col 3:12	Put on therefore, as the elect of God, holy and beloved, bowels of mercies, kindness, humbleness of mind, meekness, longsuffering;	Put on therefore, as the elect of God, holy and beloved, tender mercies, kindness, humbleness of mind, meekness, longsuffering;	
Col 3:14	And above all these things put on	And above all these things put on	perfectness!

Scripture	Discrepancies in KJV Scripture	Memories of the 1611 KJV	Notes:
	charity, which is the bond of perfectness.	love, which is the bond of unity.	
Col 3:16	Let the word of Christ dwell in you richly in all wisdom; teaching and admonishing one another in psalms and hymns and spiritual songs, singing with grace in your hearts to the Lord.	Let the word of Christ dwell in you richly in all wisdom; teaching and admonishing one another in psalms and hymns and spiritual songs, making melody in your hearts to the Lord.	

44

Scripture	Discrepancies in KJV Scripture	Memories of the 1611 KJV	Notes:
Col 3:24	Knowing that of the Lord ye shall receive the reward of the inheritance: for ye serve the Lord Christ.	Knowing that of the Lord ye shall receive recompence of inheritance: for ye serve Christ our Lord.	
Col 3:25	But he that doeth wrong shall receive for the wrong which he hath done: and there is no respect of persons.	But he that doeth wrong shall receive the wrong which he hath done: for there is no respect of persons.	
Col 4:5	Walk in wisdom toward them that are without, redeeming the time.	Walk in wisdom toward them that are outside, redeeming the time.	(without is now used many times for outside)
Col 4:8	Whom I have sent unto you for the same purpose, that he might know your estate, and comfort your hearts;	Whom I have sent unto you for the same purpose, that he might know your state, and comfort your hearts;	
Col 4:10	Aristarchus my fellowprisoner saluteth you, and Marcus, sister's son to Barnabas, (touching whom ye received commandments: if he come unto you, receive him;)	Aristarchus my fellow-prisoner greets you, and Marcus, sister's son to Barnabas, (concerning whom ye received commandments: if he come unto you, receive him;)	
Col 4:13	For I bear him record, that he hath a great zeal for you, and them that are in Laodicea, and them in Hierapolis.	(I don't remember this verse)	
Col 4:16	And when this epistle is read among you, cause that it be read also in the church of the Laodiceans; and that ye likewise read the epistle from Laodicea.	(I don't remember this verse)	epistle from Laodicea!
1 Thess	So that ye were ensamples to all	So that ye were examples to all that	ensamples!

Scripture	Discrepancies in KJV Scripture	Memories of the 1611 KJV	Notes:
1:7	that believe in Macedonia and Achaia.	believe in Macedonia and Achaia.	
1 Thess 1:8	For from you sounded out the word of the Lord not only in Macedonia and Achaia, but also in every place your faith to God-ward is spread abroad; so that we need not to speak any thing.	For from you is spread abroad the word of the Lord not only in Macedonia and Achaia, but also in every place your faith which is towards God is gone forth; so that we need not to speak anything.	
1 Thess 1:9	For they themselves shew of us what manner of entering in we had unto you, and how ye turned to God from idols to serve the living and true God;	For they themselves report of us what manner of reception you gave us, and how ye turned to God from idols to serve the living and true God;	
1 Thess 2:2	But even after that we had suffered before, and were shamefully entreated, as ye know, at Philippi, we were bold in our God to speak unto you the gospel of God with much contention.	But even after that we had suffered before, and were shamefully treated, as ye know, at Philippi, we were bold in our God to speak unto you the gospel of God with much contention.	entreated!
1 Thess 2:4	But as we were allowed of God to be put in trust with the gospel, even so we speak; not as pleasing men, but God, which trieth our hearts.	But as we were approved of God to be in entrusted with the gospel, even so we speak; not as pleasing men, but pleasing God, who tests our hearts.	Allowed! which= (witch)
1 Thess 2:7	But we were gentle among you, even as a nurse cherisheth her children:	But we were gentle among you, even as a nursing mother cherisheth her own children:	nurse!
1 Thess 2:10	Ye are witnesses, and God also, how holily and justly and unblameably we behaved ourselves among you that believe:	Ye are witnesses, and God also, how holy, righteous and blameless we behaved ourselves among you that believe:	holily! justly! unblameably!
1 Thess 3:13	To the end he may stablish your hearts unblameable in holiness before God, even our Father, at the coming of our Lord Jesus Christ	To the end he may establish your hearts unblameable in holiness before God, even our Father, at the coming of our Lord Jesus Christ with all his saints.	

45

Scripture	Discrepancies in KJV Scripture	Memories of the 1611 KJV	Notes:
	with all his saints.		
1 Thess	Not in the lust of concupiscence,	Not lust of sensuality, even as the	concupiscien

Scripture	Discrepancies in KJV Scripture	Memories of the 1611 KJV	Notes:
4:5	even as the Gentiles which know not God:	Gentiles which know not God:	ce!
1 Thess 4:6	That no man go beyond and defraud his brother in any matter: because that the Lord is the avenger of all such, as we also have forewarned you and testified.	That no man transgress and defraud his brother in any matter: because that the Lord is the avenger of all such, as we also have forewarned you and testified.	go beyond!
1 Thess 4:11	And that ye study to be quiet, and to do your own business, and to work with your own hands, as we commanded you;	And that ye strive to be quiet, and to do your own business, and to work with your own hands, as we commanded you;	study!
1 Thess 5:14	Now we exhort you, brethren, warn them that are unruly, comfort the feebleminded, support the weak, be patient toward all men.	Now we exhort you, brethren, warn them that are unruly, encourage the fainthearted, support the weak, be patient toward all men.	
1 Thess 5:23	And the very God of peace sanctify you wholly; and I pray God your whole spirit and soul and body be preserved blameless unto the coming of our Lord Jesus Christ.	May the God of peace sanctify you wholly; and I pray God your whole spirit and soul and body be kept blameless unto the coming of our Lord Jesus Christ.	
2 Thess 2:2	That ye be not soon shaken in mind, or be troubled, neither by spirit, nor by word, nor by letter as from us, as that the day of Christ is at hand.	That ye be not soon shaken in mind, or be troubled, neither by spirit, nor by word, nor by letter as from us, as that the day of Christ has already come.	
2 Thess 2:4	Who opposeth and exalteth himself above all that is called God, or that is worshipped; so that he as God sitteth in the temple of God, shewing himself that he is God.	Who opposeth and exalteth himself above all that is called God, or that is worshipped; so that he as God sitteth in the temple of God, shewing himself as though he were God.	
2 Thess 2:6	And now ye know what withholdeth that he might be revealed in his time.	And now ye know who restraineth that he might be revealed in his time.	hindereth grammer: who
2 Thess 2:7	For the mystery of iniquity doth already work: only he who now letteth will let, until he be taken out of the way.	For the mystery of lawlessness doth already work: only he who now restrains, will do so until he be taken out of the way.	letteth will let!
2 Thess 2:8	And then shall that Wicked be revealed, whom the Lord shall	And then that lawless one will be revealed, whom the Lord shall	

Scripture	Discrepancies in KJV Scripture	Memories of the 1611 KJV	Notes:
	consume with the spirit of his mouth, and shall destroy with the brightness of his coming:	consume with the breath of his mouth, and shall destroy with the brightness of his coming:	
2 Thess 2:12	That they all might be damned who believed not the truth, but had pleasure in unrighteousness.	That they all might be condemned who believed not the truth, but had pleasure in unrighteousness.	damned! judged
	2 Thess 3:14 And if any man obey not our word by this epistle, note that man, and have no company with him, that he may be ashamed.	And if any man obey not our word by this epistle, mark that man, and have no company with him, that he may be ashamed.	
1 Tim 1:6	From which some having swerved have turned aside unto vain jangling;	From which some having strayed away having turned aside unto vain babbling;	swerved! jangling!
1 Tim 1:10	For whoremongers, for them that defile themselves with mankind, for menstealers, for liars, for perjured persons, and if there be any other thing that is contrary to sound doctrine;	For fornicators, for them that defile themselves with mankind, for slave-traders, for liars, for perjured persons, and if there be any other thing that is contrary to sound doctrine;	whoremongers! menstealers! kidnappers
1 Tim 1:15	This is a faithful saying, and worthy of all acceptation, that Christ Jesus came into the world to save sinners; of whom I am chief.	This is a faithful saying, and worthy of all acceptance, that Christ Jesus came into the world to save sinners; of whom I am chief.	acceptation!

46

Scripture	Discrepancies in KJV Scripture	Memories of the 1611 KJV	Notes:
1 Tim 2:9	In like manner also, that women adorn themselves in modest apparel, with shamefacedness and sobriety; not with broided hair, or gold, or pearls, or costly array;	In like manner also, that women adorn themselves in modest apparel, with Godly fear and self-control; not with braided hair, or gold, or pearls, or costly array;	shamefacedness! modesty propriety
1 Tim 2:12	But I suffer not a woman to teach, nor to usurp authority over the man, but to be in silence.	But I permit not a woman to teach, nor to usurp authority over the man, but to be in silence.	
1 Tim 3:3	Not given to wine, no striker, not greedy of filthy lucre; but patient, not a brawler, not covetous;	Not given to wine, not violent, not greedy of dishonest gain; but gentle, not quarrelsome, not covetous;	no striker!
1 Tim 3:4	One that ruleth well his own house, having his children in subjection with all gravity;	One that ruleth well his own house, having his children in subjection with all reverence;	gravity!

Scripture	Discrepancies in KJV Scripture	Memories of the 1611 KJV	Notes:
1 Tim 3:8	Likewise must the deacons be grave, not doubletongued, not given to much wine, not greedy of filthy lucre;	Likewise must the deacons be reverent, not double tongued not given to much wine, not greedy of dishonest gain;	
1 Tim 3:13	For they that have used the office of a deacon well purchase to themselves a good degree, and great boldness in the faith which is in Christ Jesus.	For they that have used the office of a deacon well gain for themselves a good standing, and great boldness in the faith which is in Christ Jesus.	
1 Tim 3:16	And without controversy great is the mystery of godliness: God was manifest in the flesh, justified in the Spirit, seen of angels, preached unto the Gentiles, believed on in the world, received up into glory.	And without controversy great is the mystery of godliness: God was manifest in the flesh, justified in the Spirit, seen of angels, preached unto the nations, believed on in the world, received up into glory.	
1 Tim 4:1	Now the Spirit speaketh expressly, that in the latter times some shall depart from the faith, giving heed to seducing spirits, and doctrines of devils;	Now the Spirit speaketh expressly, that in the latter days some shall depart from the faith, giving heed to seducing spirits, and doctrines of demons;	
1 Tim 4:3	Forbidding to marry, and commanding to abstain from meats, which God hath created to be received with thanksgiving of them which believe and know the truth.	Forbidding to marry, and commanding to abstain from foods, which God hath created to be received with thanksgiving of them which believe and know the truth.	
1 Tim 4:4	For every creature of God is good, and nothing to be refused, if it be received with thanksgiving:	For every creation of God is good, and nothing to be refused, if it be received with thanksgiving:	
1 Tim 4:7	But refuse profane and old wives' fables, and exercise thyself rather unto godliness.	But refuse profane and old wives' tales, and train thyself rather unto godliness.	modern kjv says "womenish tales"!
1 Tim 4:9	This is a faithful saying and worthy of all acceptation.	This is a faithful saying and worthy of all acceptance.	acceptation!
1 Tim 4:12	Let no man despise thy youth; but be thou an example of the believers, in word, in conversation, in charity, in spirit, in faith, in purity.	Let no man despise thy youth; but be thou an example of the believers, in word, in conduct, in love, in spirit, in faith, in purity.	

Scripture	Discrepancies in KJV Scripture	Memories of the 1611 KJV	Notes:
1 Tim 4:14	Neglect not the gift that is in thee, which was given thee by prophecy, with the laying on of the hands of the presbytery.	Neglect not the gift that is in thee, which was given thee by prophecy, with the laying on of the hands of the elders.	presbytery!
1 Tim 5:7	And these things give in charge, that they may be blameless.	And these things command, that they may be blameless.	give in charge!

47

Scripture	Discrepancies in KJV Scripture	Memories of the 1611 KJV	Notes:
1 Tim 5:8	But if any provide not for his own, and specially for those of his own house, he hath denied the faith, and is worse than an infidel.	But if any provide not for his relatives, and specially for those of his own house, he hath denied the faith, and is worse than an unbeliever.	apostate
1 Tim 5:12	Having damnation, because they have cast off their first faith.	Having condemnation because they have cast off their first faith.	
1 Tim 5:13	And withal they learn to be idle, wandering about from house to house; and not only idle, but tattlers also and busybodies, speaking things which they ought not.	And, besides, they learn to be idle, wandering about from house to house; and not only idle, but gossips also and busybodies, speaking things which they ought not.	withal! tattlers! besides
1 Tim 5:16	If any man or woman that believeth have widows, let them relieve them, and let not the church be charged; that it may relieve them that are widows indeed.	If any woman that believeth have widows, let her take care of them, and let not the church be burdened; that it may help them that are truly widows indeed.	
1 Tim 5:18	For the scripture saith, Thou shalt not muzzle the ox that treadeth out the corn. And, The labourer is worthy of his reward.	For the scripture saith, Thou shalt not muzzle the ox that treadeth out the grain. And, The labourer is worthy of his hire.	corn!
1 Tim 6:4	He is proud, knowing nothing, but doting about questions and strifes of words, whereof cometh envy, strife, railings, evil surmisings,	He is puffed up, knowing nothing, but quarrels over questions and disputes of words, whereof cometh envy, strife, railings, evil suspicions,	doting! surmisings!
1 Tim 6:13	I give thee charge in the sight of God, who quickeneth all things, and before Christ Jesus, who before Pontius Pilate witnessed a good confession;	I command thee, in the sight of God, who maketh all things alive, and before Christ Jesus, who before Pontius Pilate gave a good confession;	

Scripture	Discrepancies in KJV Scripture	Memories of the 1611 KJV	Notes:
1 Tim 6:14	That thou keep this commandment without spot, unrebukeable, until the appearing of our Lord Jesus Christ:	That thou keep this commandment without spot, irreproachable, until the appearing of our Lord Jesus Christ:	unrebukeable ! Contradicts Heb 12:5
1 Tim 6:15	Which in his times he shall shew, who is the blessed and only Potentate, the King of kings, and Lord of lords;	Which at the proper time he shall shew, who is the blessed and only Sovereign the King of kings, and Lord of lords;	potentate! ruler
1 Tim 6:16	Who only hath immortality, dwelling in the light which no man can approach unto; whom no man hath seen, nor can see: to whom be honour and power everlasting. Amen.	Who only possesses immortality, dwelling in unapproachable light; whom no man hath seen, nor can see: to whom be honour and power everlasting. Amen.	Doc. Error Christ is the only one immortal?
1 Tim 6:17	Charge them that are rich in this world, that they be not highminded, nor trust in uncertain riches, but in the living God, who giveth us richly all things to enjoy;	Charge them that are rich in this world, that they be not high-minded, nor trust in uncertain riches, but in the living God, who giveth to all men liberally things to enjoy;	
1 Tim 6:18	That they do good, that they be rich in good works, ready to distribute, willing to communicate;	That they do good, that they be rich in good works, ready to distribute, willing to share;	
1 Tim 6:20	O Timothy, keep that which is committed to thy trust, avoiding profane and vain babblings, and oppositions of science falsely so called:	O Timothy, keep that which is committed to thy trust, avoiding profane and vain babblings, and oppositions of knowledge falsely so called:	science!
2 Tim 1:5	When I call to remembrance the unfeigned faith that is in thee; which dwelt first in thy grandmother Lois, and thy mother Eunice; and, I am persuaded, in thee also.	When I call to remembrance the sincere faith that is in thee; which dwelt first in thy grandmother Lois, and thy mother Eunice; and, I am persuaded, in thee also.	unfeigned!
2 Tim 1:6	Wherefore I put thee in remembrance that thou stir up the gift of God, which is in thee by the	Wherefore I put thee in remembrance that thou stir up the gift of God, which is in thee by the laying on	putting on of my hands!

48

Scripture	Discrepancies in KJV Scripture	Memories of the 1611 KJV	Notes:

Scripture	Discrepancies in KJV Scripture	Memories of the 1611 KJV	Notes:
	putting on of my hands.	of hands.	
2 Tim 1:16	The Lord give mercy unto the house of Onesiphorus; for he oft refreshed me, and was not ashamed of my chain:	The Lord give mercy unto the house of O-nes-iph-o rus; for he often refreshed me, and was not ashamed of my chains:	
2 Tim 2:3	Thou therefore endure hardness, as a good soldier of Jesus Christ.	Thou, therefore endure hardship, as a good soldier of Jesus Christ.	suffering
2 Tim 2:4	No man that warreth entangleth himself with the affairs of this life; that he may please him who hath chosen him to be a soldier.	No man as a soldier entangleth himself with the affairs of this life; that he may please him who hath chosen him to be a soldier.	
2 Tim 2:5	And if a man also strive for masteries, yet is he not crowned, except he strive lawfully.	And if a man also competes as an athlete, yet is he not crowned, except unless he strives lawfully.	masteries!
2 Tim 2:20	But in a great house there are not only vessels of gold and of silver, but also of wood and of earth; and some to honour, and some to dishonour.	But in a great house there are not only vessels of gold and of silver, but also of wood and clay; and some to honour, and some to dishonour.	
2 Tim 2:21	If a man therefore purge himself from these, he shall be a vessel unto honour, sanctified, and meet for the master's use, and prepared unto every good work.	If a man therefore purge himself from these, he shall be a vessel unto honour, sanctified, and fit for the master's use, and prepared unto every good work.	
2 Tim 2:23	But foolish and unlearned questions avoid, knowing that they do gender strifes.	But avoid foolish and unlearned questions, knowing that they generate strife.	gender!
2 Tim 3:3	Without natural affection, trucebreakers, false accusers, incontinent, fierce, despisers of those that are good,	Without natural affection, trucebreakers, false accusers, without self-control, brutal, despisers of those that are good,	incontinent!
2 Tim 3:17	That the man of God may be perfect, throughly furnished unto all good works.	That the man of God may be complete, equipped for every good work.	furnished!
2 Tim 4:1	I charge thee therefore before God, and the Lord Jesus Christ, who shall judge the quick and the dead at his appearing and his kingdom;	I charge thee therefore before God, and the Lord Jesus Christ, who shall judge the living and the dead at his appearing and his kingdom;	
2 Tim 4:15	Of whom be thou ware also; for he hath greatly withstood our words.	Of whom beware also; for he hath greatly withstood our words.	
2 Tim	At my first answer no man stood	At my first defense no man stood	answer!

Scripture	Discrepancies in KJV Scripture	Memories of the 1611 KJV	Notes:
4:16	with me, but all men forsook me: I pray God that it may not be laid to their charge.	with me, but all men forsook me: I pray God that it may not be laid to their charge.	
2 Tim 4:19	Salute Prisca and Aquila, and the household of Onesiphorus.	Greet Priscilla and Aquila, and the household of Onesiphorus.	see 1 Cor 16:19
2 Tim 4:20	Erastus abode at Corinth: but Trophimus have I left at Miletum sick.	Erastus remained at Corinth: but Trophimus have I left at Miletus ill.	
Tit 1:6	If any be blameless, the husband of one wife, having faithful children not accused of riot or unruly.	If any be blameless, the husband of one wife, having faithful children not accused of riotous living.	profligancy
Tit 1:7	For a bishop must be blameless, as the steward of God; not selfwilled, not soon angry, not given to wine, no striker, not given to filthy lucre;	For a bishop must be blameless, as the steward of God; not self-willed, not soon angry, not given to wine, not violent, not given to filthy lucre;	
Tit 1:8	But a lover of hospitality, a lover of good men, sober, just, holy, temperate;	But a lover of hospitality, a lover of good men, sober-minded, just, holy, temperate;	
Tit 1:12	One of themselves, even a prophet of their own, said, The Cretians are alway liars, evil beasts, slow bellies.	One of themselves, even a prophet of their own, said, Cretans are alway liars, evil brutes, lazy gluttons.	evil beasts! slow bellies!

49

Scripture	Discrepancies in KJV Scripture	Memories of the 1611 KJV	Notes:
Tit 1:13	This witness is true. Wherefore rebuke them sharply, that they may be sound in the faith;	This testimony is true. Wherefore rebuke them sharply, that they may be sound in the faith;	
Tit 2:7	In all things shewing thyself a pattern of good works: in doctrine shewing uncorruptness, gravity, sincerity,	In all things showing thyself a pattern of good works: in doctrine showing soundness, dignity, integrity,	good teaching
Tit 3:1	Put them in mind to be subject to principalities and powers, to obey magistrates, to be ready to every good work,	Remind them to be subject to rulers and authorities, to be obedient, to be ready to every good work,	subject to principalities!
Tit 3:3	For we ourselves also were sometimes foolish, disobedient, deceived, serving divers lusts and pleasures, living in malice and envy, hateful, and hating one another.	For we ourselves also were once foolish, disobedient, deceived, serving various lusts and pleasures, living in malice and envy, hateful, and hating one another.	

Scripture	Discrepancies in KJV Scripture	Memories of the 1611 KJV	Notes:
Tit 3:10	A man that is an heretick after the first and second admonition reject;	A man that is an heretic after the first and second admonition reject;	heretick!
Phm 6	That the communication of thy faith may become effectual by the acknowledging of every good thing which is in you in Christ Jesus.	That the fellowship of thy faith may become effectual by the acknowledging of every good thing which is in you in Christ Jesus.	communicati on!
Phm 10	I beseech thee for my son Onesimus, whom I have begotten in my bonds:	I beseech thee for my son Onesimus, whom I have begotten in my bonds:	
Phm 12	Whom I have sent again: thou therefore receive him, that is, mine own bowels:	Whom I have sent again: thou therefore receive him, that is, mine very heart.	
Phm 20	Yea, brother, let me have joy of thee in the Lord: refresh my bowels in the Lord.	Yea, brother, let me have joy of thee in the Lord: refresh my heart in Christ.	
Heb 1:2	Hath in these last days spoken unto us by his Son, whom he hath appointed heir of all things, by whom also he made the worlds;	Hath in these last days spoken unto us by his Son, whom he hath appointed heir of all things, by whom also he made the world;	worlds!
Heb 1:13	But to which of the angels said he at any time, Sit on my right hand, until I make thine enemies thy footstool?	But to which of the angels said he at any time, Sit at my right hand, until I make thine enemies thy footstool?	
Heb 6:20	Whither the forerunner is for us entered, even Jesus, made an high priest for ever after the order of Melchisedec.	Whither the forerunner is for us entered, even Jesus, made a high priest for ever after the order of Melchizedek.	
Heb 7:24	But this man, because he continueth ever, hath an unchangeable priesthood.	But this man, because he lives forever, hath an eternal priesthood.	
Heb 8:1	Now of the things which we have spoken this is the sum: We have such an high priest, who is set on the right hand of the throne of the Majesty in the heavens;	Now of the things which we have spoken this is the sum: We have such an high priest, who is set at the right hand of the throne of the LORD in the heavens;	(notice it is called heavens here)
Heb 8:2	A minister of the sanctuary, and of the true tabernacle, which the Lord pitched, and not man.	A minister of the sanctuary, and of the true tabernacle, which the Lord raised up, and not man.	pitched!
Heb 8:13	In that he saith, A new covenant, he hath made the first old. Now that	In that he saith, A new covenant, he hath made the first obsolete.	decayeth!

Scripture	Discrepancies in KJV Scripture	Memories of the 1611 KJV	Notes:
	which decayeth and waxeth old is ready to vanish away.	Now that which decays and waxes old is ready to vanish away.	
Heb 9:26	For then must he often have suffered since the foundation of the world: but now once in the end of the world hath he appeared to put away sin by the sacrifice of himself.	For then must he often have suffered since the foundation of the world: but now once in the end of the age hath he appeared to put away sin by the sacrifice of himself.	

50

Scripture	Discrepancies in KJV Scripture	Memories of the 1611 KJV	Notes:
Heb 10:1	For the law having a shadow of good things to come, and not the very image of the things, can never with those sacrifices which they offered year by year continually make the comers thereunto perfect.	For the law having a shadow of good things to come, and not the very image of the things, can never with those sacrifices which they offered year by year continually make those who come unto it perfect.	
Heb 10:2	For then would they not have ceased to be offered? because that the worshippers once purged should have had no more conscience of sins.	For then would they not have ceased to be offered? because that the worshippers once cleansed should have had no more conscience of sins.	
Heb 10:12	But this man, after he had offered one sacrifice for sins for ever, sat down on the right hand of God;	But this man, after he had offered one sacrifice for sins forever, sat down at the right hand of God;	on!
Heb 10:19	Having therefore, brethren, boldness to enter into the holiest by the blood of Jesus,	Having therefore, brethren, boldness to enter into the holy place by the blood of Jesus,	
Heb 10:32	But call to remembrance the former days, in which, after ye were illuminated, ye endured a great fight of afflictions;	But call to remembrance the former days, in which, after ye were enlightened, ye endured a great fight of afflictions:	illuminated!
Heb 10:33	Partly, whilst ye were made a gazingstock both by reproaches and afflictions; and partly, whilst ye became companions of them that were so used.	Partly, while ye were made a spectacle both by reproaches and afflictions: and partly, while ye became companions of those who were so treated.	gazingstock! whilst!
Heb 11:3	Through faith we understand that the worlds were framed by the word of God, so that things which are seen were not made of things which do appear.	Through faith we understand that the worlds were made by the word of God, so that things which are seen were not made of things which do appear.	framed!

Scripture	Discrepancies in KJV Scripture	Memories of the 1611 KJV	Notes:
Heb 11:9	By faith he sojourned in the land of promise, as in a strange country, dwelling in tabernacles with Isaac and Jacob, the heirs with him of the same promise:	By faith he sojourned in the land of promise, as in a foreign country, dwelling in tents with Isaac and Jacob, the heirs with him of the same promise:	
Heb 11:23	By faith Moses, when he was born, was hid three months of his parents, because they saw he was a proper child; and they were not afraid of the king's commandment.	By faith Moses, when he was born, was hid three months of his parents, because they saw he was a beautiful child; and they were not afraid of the king's commandment.	proper!
Heb 11:29	By faith they passed through the Red sea as by dry land: which the Egyptians assaying to do were drowned.	By faith they passed through the Red sea as by dry land: which the Egyptians attempting to do were drowned.	assaying!
Heb 11:34	Quenched the violence of fire, escaped the edge of the sword, out of weakness were made strong, waxed valiant in fight, turned to flight the armies of the aliens.	Quenched the violence of fire, escaped the edge of the sword, out of weakness were made strong, became valiant in fight, turned to flight the armies of the foreigners.	armies of aliens! strangerseb
Heb 11:37	They were stoned, they were sawn asunder, were tempted, were slain with the sword: they wandered about in sheepskins and goatskins; being destitute, afflicted, tormented;	They were stoned, they were sawn asunder, were tested, were slain with the sword: they wandered about in sheepskins and goatskins; being destitute, afflicted, tormented;	
Heb 12:5	And ye have forgotten the exhortation which speaketh unto you as unto children, My son, despise not thou the chastening of the Lord, nor faint when thou art rebuked of him:	And ye have forgotten the exhortation which speaketh unto you as dear children, despise not thou the chastening of the Lord, nor faint when thou art rebuked of him:	Heb 12:6,7,8 all refer to 'sons'
Heb 12:16	Lest there be any fornicator, or profane person, as Esau, who for one morsel of meat sold his	Lest there be any fornicator, or profane person, as Esau, who for one morsel of food sold his birthright.	

51

Scripture	Discrepancies in KJV Scripture	Memories of the 1611 KJV	Notes:
	birthright.		
Heb 12:20	(For they could not endure that which was commanded, And if so much as a beast touch the mountain, it shall be stoned, or thrust through	For they could not endure that which was commanded, And if so much as a beast touch the mountain, it shall be stoned, or	

Scripture	Discrepancies in KJV Scripture with a dart:	Memories of the 1611 KJV thrust through with a spear:	Notes:
Heb 12:22	But ye are come unto mount Sion, and unto the city of the living God, the heavenly Jerusalem, and to an innumerable company of angels,	But ye are come unto Mount Zion, and unto the city of the living God, the heavenly Jerusalem, and to an innumerable company of angels,	
Heb 12:23	To the general assembly and church of the firstborn, which are written in heaven, and to God the Judge of all, and to the spirits of just men made perfect,	To the church of the firstborn, which are written in heaven, and to God the Judge of all, and to the spirits of just men made perfect,	general assembly!
Heb 13:4	Marriage is honourable in all, and the bed undefiled: but whoremongers and adulterers God will judge.	Marriage is honourable in all, and the bed undefiled: but fornicators and adulterers God will judge.	
Heb 13:8	Jesus Christ the same yesterday, and to day, and for ever.	Jesus Christ the same yesterday, and today, and forever.	
Heb 13:9	Be not carried about with divers and strange doctrines. For it is a good thing that the heart be established with grace; not with meats, which have not profited them that have been occupied therein.	Be not carried about with various and strange doctrines. For it is a good thing that the heart be established with grace; not with foods, which have not profited them that have been occupied therein.	
Heb 13:11	For the bodies of those beasts, whose blood is brought into the sanctuary by the high priest for sin, are burned without the camp.	For the bodies of animals, is brought into the holy place by the high priest for sin, are burned outside the camp.	also in Heb 13:12,13
Heb 13:16	But to do good and to communicate forget not: for with such sacrifices God is well pleased.	But to do good and to share forget not: for with such sacrifices God is well pleased.	
Heb 13:24	Salute all them that have the rule over you, and all the saints. They of Italy salute you.	Greet all them that have the rule over you, and all the saints.	
Jas 1:4	But let patience have her perfect work, that ye may be perfect and entire, wanting nothing.	But let patience have her perfect work, that ye may be perfect and entire, lacking nothing.	
Jas 1:6	6 But let him ask in faith, nothing wavering. For he that wavereth is like a wave of the sea driven with the wind and tossed.	But let him ask in faith, nothing wavering, for he that doubts is like a wave of the sea tossed to and fro,	

Scripture	Discrepancies in KJV Scripture	Memories of the 1611 KJV	Notes:
Jas 1:18	Of his own will begat he us with the word of truth, that we should be a kind of firstfruits of his creatures.	Of his own will he bagat us with the word of truth, that we should be a kind of firstfruits of his creation.	
Jas 1:21	Wherefore lay apart all filthiness and superfluity of naughtiness, and receive with meekness the engrafted word, which is able to save your souls.	Wherefore put away all filthiness and overflowing of wickedness, and receive with meekness the engrafted word, which is able to save your souls.	superfluity of naughtiness!
Jas 1:23	For if any be a hearer of the word, and not a doer, he is like unto a man beholding his natural face in a glass:	For if any be a hearer of the word, and not a doer, he is like unto a man beholding his natural face in a mirror:	
Jas 2:3	And ye have respect to him that weareth the gay clothing, and say unto him, Sit thou here in a good place; and say to the poor, Stand thou there, or sit here under my footstool:	And ye have respect to him that weareth the fine raiment, and say unto him, Sit thou here in a good place; and say to the poor, Stand thou there, or sit here under my footstool:	gay! apparel
Jas 2:19	Thou believest that there is one God; thou doest	Thou believest that there is one God; thou doest well: the demons also believe, and tremble.	

52

Scripture	Discrepancies in KJV Scripture	Memories of the 1611 KJV	Notes:
	well: the devils also believe, and tremble.		
Jas 3:1	My brethren, be not many masters, knowing that we shall receive the greater condemnation.	My brethren, be not many teachers, knowing that we shall receive the greater judgment.	
Jas 3:2	For in many things we offend all. If any man offend not in word, the same is a perfect man, and able also to bridle the whole body.	For in many things we all stumble. If any man offend not in word, the same is a perfect man, and able also to bridle the whole body.	
Jas 3:4	Behold also the ships, which though they be so great, and are driven of fierce winds, yet are they turned about with a very small helm, whithersoever the governor listeth.	Behold also the ships, which though they be so great, and are driven of fierce winds, yet are they turned about with a very small helm, wherever the pilot willeth.	governor! listeth!
Jas 4:3	Ye ask, and receive not, because ye ask amiss, that ye may consume it upon your lusts.	Ye ask, and receive not, because ye ask amiss, that ye may consume it upon your own lusts.	

Scripture	Discrepancies in KJV Scripture	Memories of the 1611 KJV	Notes:
Jas 4:8	Draw nigh to God, and he will draw nigh to you. Cleanse your hands, ye sinners; and purify your hearts, ye double minded.	Draw near to God, and he will draw near to you. Cleanse your hands, ye sinners; and purify your hearts, ye double minded.	
Jas 4:13	Go to now, ye that say, To day or to morrow we will go into such a city, and continue there a year, and buy and sell, and get gain:	Come now, ye that say, today or tomorrow we will go into such a city, and continue there a year, and buy and sell, and get gain:	
Jas 5:9	Grudge not one against another, brethren, lest ye be condemned: behold, the judge standeth before the door.	Murmur not one against another, brethren, lest ye be judged: behold, the judge standeth before the door.	Grudge! condemned!
Jas 5:11	Behold, we count them happy which endure. Ye have heard of the patience of Job, and have seen the end of the Lord; that the Lord is very pitiful, and of tender mercy.	Behold, we count them happy which endure. Ye have heard of the perseverance of Job, and have seen the purpose of the Lord; that the Lord is compassionate and merciful.	
Jas 5:15	And the prayer of faith shall save the sick, and the Lord shall raise him up; and if he have committed sins, they shall be forgiven him.	And the prayer of faith shall heal the sick, and the Lord shall raise him up; and if he has committed sins, they shall be forgiven him.	
Jas 5:18	And he prayed again, and the heaven gave rain, and the earth brought forth her fruit.	And he prayed again, and the heaven gave rain, and the earth brought forth its fruit.	her!
1 Pet 1:6	Wherein ye greatly rejoice, though now for a season, if need be, ye are in heaviness through manifold temptations:	Wherein ye greatly rejoice, though now for a season, if need be, ye are in heaviness through manifold trials:	temptations!
1 Pet 1:11	Searching what, or what manner of time the Spirit of Christ which was in them did signify, when it testified beforehand the sufferings of Christ, and the glory that should follow.	Searching what, or what manner of time the Spirit of Christ which was in them did signify, when he testified beforehand the sufferings of Christ, and the glory that should follow.	
1 Pet 1:15	But as he which hath called you is holy, so be ye holy in all manner of conversation;	But as he which hath called you is holy, so be ye holy in all manner of life;	Also Rev 1:18
1 Pet 2:5	Ye also, as lively stones, are built up a spiritual house, an holy priesthood, to offer up spiritual	Ye also, as living stones, are built into a spiritual house, an holy priesthood, to offer up spiritual	also in 1Peter 1:3

Scripture	Discrepancies in KJV Scripture	Memories of the 1611 KJV	Notes:
	sacrifices, acceptable to God by Jesus Christ.	sacrifices, acceptable to God by Jesus Christ.	
1 Pet 2:6	Wherefore also it is contained in the scripture, Behold, I lay in Sion a chief corner stone, elect, precious: and he that believeth on him shall not be confounded.	Wherefore also it is contained in the scripture, "Behold, I lay in Zion a chief cornerstone, elect, precious: and he that believeth on Him shall not be confounded."	Also Matt 21:5
1 Pet 2:11	Dearly beloved, I beseech you as strangers and pilgrims, abstain from fleshly lusts, which war	Dearly beloved, I beseech you as sojourners and pilgrims, abstain from fleshly lusts, which war	

53

Scripture	Discrepancies in KJV Scripture	Memories of the 1611 KJV	Notes:
	against the soul;	against the soul;	
1 Pet 2:24	Who his own self bare our sins in his own body on the tree, that we, being dead to sins, should live unto righteousness: by whose stripes ye were healed.	Who his own self bare our sin in his own body on the tree, that we, being dead to sin, should live unto righteousness: by whose stripes ye were healed.	
1 Pet 2:25	For ye were as sheep going astray; but are now returned unto the Shepherd and Bishop of your souls.	For ye were as sheep going astray; but are now returned unto the Shepherd and Overseer of your souls.	
1 Pet 3:2	While they behold your chaste conversation coupled with fear.	While they behold your chaste conduct coupled with fear.	
1 Pet 3:3	Whose adorning let it not be that outward adorning of plaiting the hair, and of wearing of gold, or of putting on of apparel;	Whose adorning let it not be that outward adorning of braiding the hair, and of wearing of gold, or of putting on of apparel;	
1 Pet 3:4	But let it be the hidden man of the heart, in that which is not corruptible, even the ornament of a meek and quiet spirit, which is in the sight of God of great price.	But let it be the hidden man of the heart, that which is not corruptible, even the adornment of a meek and quiet spirit, which is in the sight of God of great price.	ornament! man (generic)
1 Pet 3:6	Even as Sara obeyed Abraham, calling him lord: whose daughters ye are, as long as ye do well, and are not afraid with any amazement.	Even as Sara obeyed Abraham, calling him lord: whose daughters ye are, as long as ye do well, and are not afraid with any terror.	amazement!
1 Pet 3:8	Finally, be ye all of one mind, having compassion one of another, love as	Finally, all of you being like-minded and compassionate, love as brothers, be tender-hearted and	pitiful!

232

Scripture	Discrepancies in KJV Scripture	Memories of the 1611 KJV	Notes:
	brethren, be pitiful, be courteous:	humble.	
1 Pet 3:9	Not rendering evil for evil, or railing for railing: but contrariwise blessing; knowing that ye are thereunto called, that ye should inherit a blessing.	Not rendering evil for evil, or railing for railing: but on the contrary blessing; knowing that ye are thereunto called, that ye should inherit a blessing.	contrariwise!
1 Pet 3:11	Let him eschew evil, and do good; let him seek peace, and ensue it.	Let him eschew evil, and do good; let him seek peace, and pursue it.	
1 Pet 3:18	For Christ also hath once suffered for sins, the just for the unjust, that he might bring us to God, being put to death in the flesh, but quickened by the Spirit:	For Christ also hath once suffered for sins, the just for the unjust, that he might bring us to God, being put to death in the flesh, but made alive by the Spirit:	
1 Pet 3:19	By which also he went and preached unto the spirits in prison;	By whom also he went and preached to the souls imprisoned in Sheol;	
1 Pet 3:20	Which sometime were disobedient, when once the longsuffering of God waited in the days of Noah, while the ark was a preparing, wherein few, that is, eight souls were saved by water.	Which at one time were disobedient, when God waited patiently in the days of Noah, while the ark was being prepared, wherein few, that is, eight souls were saved by water.	
1 Pet 4:3	For the time past of our life may suffice us to have wrought the will of the Gentiles, when we walked in lasciviousness, lusts, excess of wine, revellings, banquetings, and abominable idolatries:	For the time past of our life may suffice us to have wrought the will of the Gentiles, when we walked in lasciviousness, lusts, excess of wine, revellings, carousing, and abominable idolatries:	banquetings! drunkenness
1 Pet 4:4	Wherein they think it strange that ye run not with them to the same excess of riot, speaking evil of you:	Wherein they think it strange that ye run not with them to the same excess of riotous living, speaking evil of you:	
1 Pet 4:6	For, for this cause was the gospel preached also to them that are dead, that they might be judged	For, this cause was the gospel preached also to them that are (spiritually) dead, that they might not be	

54

Scripture	Discrepancies in KJV Scripture	Memories of the 1611 KJV	Notes:
	according to men in the flesh, but live according to God in the spirit.	judged according to men in the flesh, but live according to God in the spirit.	

Scripture	Discrepancies in KJV Scripture	Memories of the 1611 KJV	Notes:
1 Pet 4:8	And above all things have fervent charity among yourselves: for charity shall cover the multitude of sins	And above all things have fervent love among yourselves: for love shall cover a multitude of sins	
1 Pet 5:8	Be sober, be vigilant; because your adversary the devil, as a roaring lion, walketh about, seeking whom he may devour:	Be sober, be vigilant; because your adversary the devil, walks about like a roaring lion, seeking whom he may devour:	
1 Pet 5:13	The church that is at Babylon, elected together with you, saluteth you; and so doth Marcus my son.	The church that is at Babylon, elected together with you, greeteth you; and so doth Marcus, whom I regard as a son.	(Babylon was probably Rome)
1 Pet 5:14	Greet ye one another with a kiss of charity. Peace be with you all that are in Christ Jesus. Amen.	Greet ye one another with a holy kiss. Peace be with you all that are in Christ Jesus. Amen.	
2 Pet 1:6	And to knowledge temperance; and to temperance patience; and to patience godliness;	And to knowledge self-control; and to self-control patience; and to patience godliness;	
2 Pet 1:13	Yea, I think it meet, as long as I am in this tabernacle, to stir you up by putting you in remembrance;	Yea, I think it fitting, as long as I am in this tabernacle, to stir you up by putting you in remembrance;	
2 Pet 1:15	Moreover I will endeavour that ye may be able after my decease to have these things always in remembrance.	Moreover I will endeavour that ye may be able after my departure to have these things always in remembrance.	
2 Pet 1:18	And this voice which came from heaven we heard, when we were with him in the holy mount.	And this voice which came from heaven we heard, when we were with him on the holy mountain.	
2 Pet 2:1	But there were false prophets also among the people, even as there shall be false teachers among you, who privily shall bring in damnable heresies, even denying the Lord that bought them, and bring upon themselves swift destruction.	But there were false prophets also among the people, even as there shall be false teachers among you, who secretly shall bring in destructive heresies, even denying the Lord that bought them, and bring upon themselves swift destruction.	
2 Pet 2:3	And through covetousness shall they with feigned words make merchandise of you: whose judgment now of a long time lingereth not, and their damnation slumbereth not.	And through covetousness shall they with false words make merchandise of you: whose judgment now of a long time lingereth not, and their destruction slumbereth not.	feigned!
2 Pet 2:6	And turning the cities of Sodom and Gomorrha into ashes condemned	And turning the cities of Sodom and Gomorrah into ashes condemned	ensample!

Scripture	Discrepancies in KJV Scripture	Memories of the 1611 KJV	Notes:
	them with an overthrow, making them an ensample unto those that after should live ungodly;	them with an overthrow, making them an example unto those that after should live ungodly;	
2 Pet 2:7	And delivered just Lot, vexed with the filthy conversation of the wicked:	And delivered just Lot, vexed with the filthy manner of life of the wicked:	
2 Pet 2:10	But chiefly them that walk after the flesh in the lust of uncleanness, and despise government. Presumptuous are they, selfwilled, they are not afraid to speak evil of dignities.	But chiefly them that walk after the flesh in the lust of uncleanness, and despise authority. Presumptuous are they, self-willed, they are not afraid to rail at angelic magistrates.	dignities!
2 Pet 2:18	For when they speak great swelling words of vanity, they allure through the lusts of the flesh, through much wantonness, those that were clean escaped from them who live in error.	For when they speak great swelling words of vanity, they allure through the lusts of the flesh, through much wantonness, those that are just escapeing from them who live in error.	

55

Scripture	Discrepancies in KJV Scripture	Memories of the 1611 KJV	Notes:
2 Pet 2:20	For if after they have escaped the pollutions of the world through the knowledge of the Lord and Saviour Jesus Christ, they are again entangled therein, and overcome, the latter end is worse with them than the beginning.	For if after they have escaped the defilements of the world through the knowledge of Our Lord and Saviour Jesus Christ, they are again entangled therein and overcome, the latter end is worse with them than the beginning.	pollutions!
1 Pet 3:10	But the day of the Lord will come as a thief in the night; in the which the heavens shall pass away with a great noise, and the elements shall melt with fervent heat, the earth also and the works that are therein shall be burned up.	But the day of the Lord will come as a thief in the night; in which the heavens shall pass away with a great noise, and the elements shall melt with fervent heat, the earth also and the works that are therein shall be burned up.	
2 Pet 3:11	Seeing then that all these things shall be dissolved, what manner of persons ought ye to be in all holy conversation and godliness,	Seeing then that all these things shall be dissolved, what manner of persons ought ye to be in all holy living and godliness,	
1 Jhn 2:7,8	7)Brethren, I write no new commandment unto you, but an old commandment which ye had from the beginning. The old commandment is	7)Brethren, I write no new commandment unto you, but an old commandment which ye had from the beginning. The old	what word? no/a new?

Scripture	Discrepancies in KJV Scripture	Memories of the 1611 KJV	Notes:
	the word which ye have heard from the beginning. 8)Again, a new commandment I write unto you, which thing is true in him and in you: because the darkness is past, and the true light now shineth.	commandment is the word which ye have heard from the beginning. 8)Again, a new commandment I write unto you, which thing is true in him and in you: because the darkness is past, and the true light now shineth. (verse 7 says John writes no new commandment and verse 8 says John writes a new commandment) using "Again" should reiterate what John had just said but completely contradicts it.	
	1 Jhn 2:13,14 13)I write unto you, fathers, because ye have known him that is from the beginning. I write unto you, young men, because ye have overcome the wicked one. I write unto you, little children, because ye have known the Father. 14) I have written unto you, fathers, because ye have known him that is from the beginning. I have written unto you, young men, because ye are strong, and the word of God abideth in you, and ye have overcome the wicked one.	I write unto you, fathers, because ye have known him that is from the beginning. I write unto you, young men, because ye have overcome the wicked one and the word of God abideth in you, I write unto you, little children, because ye have known the Father.	DUPLICATE!
1 Jhn 2:23	Whosoever denieth the Son, the same hath not the Father: (but) he that acknowledgeth the Son hath the Father also.	Whosoever denieth the Son, the same hath not the Father: but he that confesseth the Son hath the Father also.	Doc. Error you can acknowledge something without confessing it
1 Jhn 2:26	These things have I written unto you concerning them that seduce you.	These things have I written unto you concerning them that deceive you.	
1 Jhn 3:2	Beloved, now are we the sons of God, and it doth not yet appear what we shall be: but we know that, when he shall appear, we shall be like him; for we shall see him as he is.	Beloved, now are we the children of God, and it doth not yet appear what we shall be: but we know that, when he shall appear, we shall be like him; for we shall see him as he is.	
1 Jhn	Not as Cain, who was of that wicked	Not as Cain, who was of that	

Scripture	Discrepancies in KJV Scripture	Memories of the 1611 KJV	Notes:
3:12	one, and slew his brother. And wherefore slew he him? Because his own works were evil, and his brother's righteous.	wicked one, and killed his brother. And wherefore killed he him? Because his own works were evil, and his brother's righteous.	
1 Jhn 3:17	But whoso hath this world's good, and seeth his brother have need, and shutteth up his bowels of	But whoso hath this world's goods, and seeth his brother have need, and shutteth up his compassions	

56

Scripture	Discrepancies in KJV Scripture	Memories of the 1611 KJV	Notes:
	compassion from him, how dwelleth the love of God in him?	from him, how dwelleth the love of God in him?	
1 Jhn 4:1	Beloved, believe not every spirit, but try the spirits whether they are of God: because many false prophets are gone out into the world.	Beloved, believe not every spirit, but test the spirits whether they are from God: because many false prophets are gone out into the world.	
1 Jhn 4:18	There is no fear in love; but perfect love casteth out fear: because fear hath torment. He that feareth is not made perfect in love.	There is no fear in love; but perfect love casteth out fear: because fear hath torment. He that feareth has not been made perfect in love.	
1 Jhn 5:3	For this is the love of God, that we keep his commandments: and his commandments are not grievous.	For this is the love of God, that we keep his commandments: and his commandments are not burdensome.	
1 Jhn 5:7	For there are three that bear record in heaven, the Father, the Word, and the Holy Ghost: and these three are one.	For there are three that bear witness in heaven, the Father, the Son, and the Holy Ghost: and these three are one.	
2Jhn 7	For many deceivers are entered into the world, who confess not that Jesus Christ is come in the flesh. This is a deceiver and an antichrist.	For many deceivers have gone out into the world, who confess not that Jesus Christ cometh in the flesh. This is a deceiver and an antichrist.	
2Jhn 12	Having many things to write unto you, I would not write with paper and ink: but I trust to come unto you, and speak face to face, that our joy may be full.	Having many things to write unto you, I would not write with papyrus and ink: but I trust to come unto you, and speak face to face, that our joy may be full.	paper! parchment
3 Jhn 8	We therefore ought to receive such, that we might be fellowhelpers to the truth.	We therefore ought to receive such, that we might be fellow helpers to the truth.	

Scripture	Discrepancies in KJV Scripture	Memories of the 1611 KJV	Notes:
3 Jhn 14	But I trust I shall shortly see thee, and we shall speak face to face. Peace be to thee. Our friends salute thee. Greet the friends by name.	But I trust I shall shortly see thee, and we shall speak face to face. Peace be to thee. Our friends greet thee. Greet the friends by name.	salute!
Jud 7	Even as Sodom and Gomorrha, and the cities about them in like manner, giving themselves over to fornication, and going after strange flesh, are set forth for an example, suffering the vengeance of eternal fire.	Even as Sodom and Gomorrah, and the cities about them in like manner, giving themselves over to fornication, and going after strange flesh, are set forth for an example, suffering the penalty of eternal fire.	vengeance!
Jud 9	Yet Michael the archangel, when contending with the devil he disputed about the body of Moses, durst not bring against him a railing accusation, but said, The Lord rebuke thee.	Yet Michael the archangel, when contending with the devil he disputed about the body of Moses, dare not bring against him a railing accusation, but said, The Lord rebuke thee.	durst!
Jud 11	Woe unto them! for they have gone in the way of Cain, and ran greedily after the error of Balaam for reward, and perished in the gainsaying of Core.	Woe unto them! for they have gone in the way of Cain, and ran greedily after the error of Balaam for reward, and perished in Korah's rebellion.	
Jud 15	To execute judgment upon all, and to convince all that are ungodly among them of all their ungodly deeds	To execute judgment upon all, and to convict all that are ungodly among them of all their ungodly deeds	

57

Scripture	Discrepancies in KJV Scripture	Memories of the 1611 KJV	Notes:
Jud 16	These are murmurers, complainers, walking after their own lusts; and their mouth speaketh great swelling words, having men's persons in admiration because of advantage.	These are murmurers, complainers, walking after their own lusts; and their mouth speaketh great swelling words, shewing respect of persons that they might gain an advantage.	
Rev 1:1	The Revelation of Jesus Christ, which God gave unto him, to shew unto his servants things which must shortly come to pass; and he sent and signified it by his angel unto his servant John:	The Revelation of Jesus Christ, which God gave unto him, to shew unto his servants things which must shortly come to pass; and he sent it by his angel unto his servant John:	
Rev 1:2	Who bare record of the word of God, and of the testimony of Jesus Christ, and of all things that he	Who bore witness of the word of God, and of the testimony of Jesus Christ, and of all things that he saw.	

Scripture	Discrepancies in KJV Scripture	Memories of the 1611 KJV	Notes:
	saw.		
Rev 1:3	Blessed is he that readeth, and they that hear the words of this prophecy, and keep those things which are written therein: for the time is at hand.	Blessed is he that readeth, and they that hear the words of this prophecy, and keep those things which are written therein: for the time is near.	
Rev 1:5	And from Jesus Christ, who is the faithful witness, and the first begotten of the dead, and the prince of the kings of the earth. Unto him that loved us, and washed us from our sins in his own blood,	And from Jesus Christ, who is the faithful witness, and the first begotten of the dead, and the ruler over the kings of the earth. Unto him who has loveth us, and washed us from our sins by his own blood,	
Rev 1:6	And hath made us kings and priests unto God and his Father; to him be glory and dominion for ever and ever. Amen.	And hath made us a kingdom of priests unto God and Father; to him be glory and dominion forever and ever. Amen.	Doc. Error God doesn't have a Father
Rev 1:8	I am Alpha and Omega, the beginning and the ending, saith the Lord, which is, and which was, and which is to come, the Almighty.	I am the Alpha and the Omega, the beginning and the end, saith the Lord, who is, and who was, and who is to come, the Almighty.	ref. Matt 6:10
Rev 1:12	And I turned to see the voice that spake with me. And being turned, I saw seven golden candlesticks;	And I turned to see the voice that spake with me. And being turned, I saw seven golden lampstands;	(Many other verses say candlesticks!)
Rev 1:13	...the Son of man, clothed with a garment down to the foot, and girt about the paps with a golden girdle.	...the Son of man, clothed with a garment down to the foot, clothed with a garment down to the feet and girt about the chest with a golden sash.	
Rev 2:12	And to the angel of the church in Pergamos write; These things saith he which hath the sharp sword with two edges;	And to the angel of the church in Pergamum write; These things saith he which hath the sharp sword with two edges;	
Rev 2:14	But I have a few things against thee, because thou hast there them that hold the doctrine of Balaam, who taught Balac to cast a stumblingblock before the children of Israel, to eat things sacrificed unto idols, and to commit fornication.	But I have a few things against thee, because thou hast there them that hold the doctrine of Balaam, who taught Balak to cast a stumbling block before the children of Israel, to eat things sacrificed unto idols, and to commit fornication.	

Scripture	Discrepancies in KJV Scripture	Memories of the 1611 KJV	Notes:
Rev 2:21	And I gave her space to repent of her fornication; and she repented not.	And I gave her time to repent of her sexual immorality; and she repented not.	
Rev 2:22	Behold, I cast her into a bed, and them that commit adultery with her into great tribulation, except they repent of her works.	Behold, I cast her into a sick bed, and them that commit adultery with her into great tribulation, except they repent of her works.	
Rev 2:23	And I will kill her children with death; and all the churches shall know that I am he which searcheth the reins and hearts: and I will give unto every one of you according to your works.	And I will kill her children with death; and all the churches shall know that I am he which searcheth the minds and hearts: and I will give unto every one of you according to your works.	reins!
Rev 3:3	Remember therefore how thou hast received and heard, and hold fast, and repent. If therefore thou shalt not watch, I will come on thee as a thief, and thou shalt not know what hour I will come upon thee.	Remember therefore how thou hast received and heard, and hold fast, and repent. If therefore thou shalt not watch, I will come to thee as a thief, and thou shalt not know what hour of thy visitation.	

Scripture	Discrepancies in KJV Scripture	Memories of the 1611 KJV	Notes:
Rev 3:14	And unto the angel of the church of the Laodiceans write; These things saith the Amen, the faithful and true witness, the beginning of the creation of God;	And unto the angel of the church of the Laodiceans write; These things saith the Eternal, the faithful and true witness, Who was in the beginning before the creation;	
Rev 3:16	So then because thou art lukewarm, and neither cold nor hot, I will spue thee out of my mouth.	So then because thou art lukewarm, and neither cold nor hot, I will spew thee out of my mouth.	spue!
Rev 4:4	And round about the throne were four and twenty seats: and upon the seats I saw four and twenty elders sitting, clothed in white raiment; and they had on their heads crowns of gold.	And round about the throne were four and twenty thrones: and upon the thrones I saw four and twenty elders sitting, clothed in white raiment; and they had on their heads crowns of gold.	
Rev 4:6	And before the throne there was a sea of glass like unto crystal: and in the midst of the throne, and round about the throne, were four beasts full of eyes before and behind.	And before the throne there was a sea of glass like unto crystal: and in the midst of the throne, and round about the throne, were four living creatures full of eyes in front and	beasts!

Scripture	Discrepancies in KJV Scripture	Memories of the 1611 KJV	Notes:
		behind.	
Rev 4:7	And the first beast was like a lion, and the second beast like a calf, and the third beast had a face as a man, and the fourth beast was like a flying eagle.	And the first living creature was like a lion, and the second living creature like a calf, and the third living creature had a face as a man, and the fourth living creature was like a flying eagle.	
Rev 5:1	And I saw in the right hand of him that sat on the throne a book written within and on the backside, sealed with seven seals.	And I saw in the right hand of him that sat on the throne a scroll written within and on the back, sealed with seven seals.	backside! also in Rev 5:2,3,7,&9
Rev 5:5	And one of the elders saith unto me, Weep not: behold, the Lion of the tribe of Juda, the Root of David,	And one of the elders saith unto me, Weep not: behold, the Lion of the tribe of Judah, the Root of David,	Juda! book!
Rev 5:8	And when he had taken the book, the four beasts and four and twenty elders fell down before the Lamb, having every one of them harps, and golden vials full of odours, which are the prayers of saints.	And when he had taken the scroll, the four living creatures and four and twenty elders fell down before the Lamb, having every one of them harps, and golden bowls full of incense, which are the prayers of saints.	beasts! vials odours!
Rev 5:14	And the four beasts said, Amen. And the four and twenty elders fell down and worshipped him that liveth for ever and ever.	And the four living creatures said, Amen. And the four and twenty elders fell down and worshipped him that liveth for ever and ever.	(many refs. to living creatures as beasts!)
Rev 6:1	And I saw when the Lamb opened one of the seals, and I heard, as it were the noise of thunder, one of the four beasts saying, Come and see.	And I saw when the Lamb opened one of the seals, and I heard, as it were the noise of thunder, one of the four living creatures saying, Come.	also Rev 6:3
Rev 6:5	And he that sat on him had a pair of balances in his hand.	And he that sat on him had a pair of scales in his hand.	
Rev 6:6	And I heard a voice in the midst of the four beasts say, A measure of wheat for a penny, and three measures of barley for a penny;	And I heard a voice in the midst of the four living creatures say, A measure of wheat for a denarius, and three measures of barley for a denarius;	beasts!
Rev 6:8	And I looked, and behold a pale horse: and his name that sat on him was Death, and Hell followed with him. And power was given unto	And I looked, and behold a pale horse: and his name that sat on him was Death, and Hades followed with him. And power was given unto	

Scripture	Discrepancies in KJV Scripture	Memories of the 1611 KJV	Notes:
	them over the fourth part of the earth, to kill with sword, and with hunger, and with death, and with the beasts of the earth.	fourth part of the earth, to kill with sword, and with hunger, and with death, and with the beasts of the earth.	
Rev 7:13	And one of the elders answered, saying unto me, What are these which are arrayed in white robes? and whence came they?	And one of the elders answered, saying unto me, Who are these which are arrayed in white robes? and whence came they?	
Rev 7:14	And I said unto him, Sir, thou knowest. And he said to me, These are they which came out of great tribulation, and have washed their robes, and made them white in the blood of the Lamb.	And I said unto him, Sir, thou knowest. And he said to me, These are they which came out of the great tribulation, and have washed their robes, and made them white in the blood of the Lamb.	
Rev 7:17	For the Lamb which is in the midst of the throne shall feed them, and shall lead them unto living fountains of waters: and God shall wipe away all tears from their eyes.	For the Lamb which is in the midst of the throne shall feed them, and shall lead them unto fountains of living water: and God shall wipe away all tears from their eyes.	
Rev 8:1	And when he had opened the seventh seal, there was silence in heaven about the space of half an hour.	And when he had opened the seventh seal, there was silence in heaven about a half an hour.	
Rev 8:7	The first angel sounded, and there followed hail and fire mingled with blood, and they were cast upon the earth: and the third part of trees was burnt up, and all green grass was burnt up.	The first angel sounded, and there followed hail and fire mixed with blood, and they were cast upon the earth: and the third part of trees was burnt up, and all green grass was burnt up.	
Rev 10:6	And sware by him that liveth for ever and ever, who created heaven, and the things that therein are, and the earth, and the things that therein are, and the sea, and the things which are therein, that there should be time no longer:	And sware by him that liveth forever and ever, who created heaven, and the things that therein are, and the earth, and the things that therein are, and the sea, and the things which are therein, that there should be delay no longer:	
Rev 10:10	And I took the little book out of the angel's hand, and ate it up; and it	And I took the little scroll out of the angel's hand, and ate it up; and	also Rev 10:8,9

Scripture	Discrepancies in KJV Scripture	Memories of the 1611 KJV	Notes:
	was in my mouth sweet as honey: and as soon as I had eaten it, my belly was bitter.	it was in my mouth sweet as honey: and as soon as I had eaten it, my belly was bitter.	
Rev 10:11	And he said unto me, Thou must prophesy again before many peoples, and nations, and tongues, and kings.	And he said unto me, Thou must prophesy again about many peoples, and nations, and tongues, and kings.	
Rev 11:2	But the court which is without the temple leave out, and measure it not; for it is given unto the Gentiles: and the holy city shall they tread under foot forty and two months.	But the court which is outside the temple leave out, and measure it not; for it is given unto the nations: and the holy city shall they tread under foot forty and two months.	
Rev 11:4	These are the two olive trees, and the two candlesticks standing before the God of the earth.	These are the two olive trees, and the two lampstands standing before the God of the earth.	candlesticks! also Rev 2:5
Rev 11:13	And the same hour was there a great earthquake, and the tenth part of the city fell, and in the earthquake were slain of men seven thousand: and the remnant were affrighted, and gave glory to the God of heaven.	And the same hour was there a great earthquake, and the tenth part of the city fell, and in the earthquake were slain of men seven thousand: and the remnant were terrified, and gave glory to the God of heaven.	
Rev 11:15	And the seventh angel sounded; and there were great voices in heaven, saying, The kingdoms of this world are become the kingdoms of our Lord, and of his Christ; and he shall reign for ever and ever.	And the seventh angel sounded; and there were great voices in heaven, saying, The kingdom of this world are become the kingdom of our Lord, and of Christ; and he shall reign forever and ever.	
Rev 11:19	And the temple of God was opened in heaven, and there was seen in his temple the ark of his testament: and there were lightnings, and voices, and thunderings, and an earthquake, and great hail.	Then the temple of God was opened in heaven, and the ark of His covenant was seen in His temple. And there were lightnings, noises, thunderings, an earthquake, and great hail.	

60

Scripture	Discrepancies in KJV Scripture	Memories of the 1611 KJV	Notes:
Rev 11:19	And the temple of God was opened in heaven, and there was seen in his temple the ark of his testament: and there were lightnings, and voices, and thunderings, and an	And the temple of God was opened in heaven, and there was seen in his temple the ark of his covenant: and there were lightnings, and voices, and thunderclaps, and an	

Scripture	Discrepancies in KJV Scripture	Memories of the 1611 KJV	Notes:
	earthquake, and great hail.	earthquake, and great hail.	
Rev 13:2	And the beast which I saw was like unto a leopard, and his feet were as the feet of a bear, and his mouth as the mouth of a lion: and the dragon gave him his power, and his seat, and great authority.	And the beast which I saw was like unto a leopard, and his feet were as the feet of a bear, and his mouth as the mouth of a lion: and the dragon gave him his power, and his throne, and great authority.	also Rev 11:16
Rev 13:16	And he causeth all, both small and great, rich and poor, free and bond, to receive a mark in their right hand, or in their foreheads:	And he causeth all, both small and great, rich and poor, free and bond, to receive a mark on their right hand, or on their foreheads:	GK epi, on
Rev 13:17	And that no man might buy or sell, save he that had the mark, or the name of the beast, or the number of his name.	And that no man might buy or sell, except he that had the mark, or the name of the beast, or the number of his name.	
Rev 14:1	And I looked, and, lo, a Lamb stood on the mount Sion, and with him an hundred forty and four thousand, having his Father's name written in their foreheads.	And I looked, and, lo, a Lamb stood on the Mount Zion, and with him an hundred forty and four thousand, having his Father's name written on their foreheads.	
Rev 14:2	And I heard a voice from heaven, as the voice of many waters, and as the voice of a great thunder: and I heard the voice of harpers harping with their harps:	And I heard a voice from heaven, as the sound of many waters, and like the sound of loud thunder: and I heard the sound of harpists playing on their harps:	harpers, harping!
Rev 14:20	And the winepress was trodden without the city, and blood came out of the winepress, even unto the horse bridles, by the space of a thousand and six hundred furlongs.	And the winepress was trodden without the city, and blood came out of the winepress, even unto the horse bridles, by a thousand and six hundred furlongs.	
Rev 15:6	And the seven angels came out of the temple, having the seven plagues, clothed in pure and white linen, and having their breasts girded with golden girdles.	And out of the temple came the seven angels having the seven plagues, clothed in pure white linen, and having their chests girded with golden bands.	
Rev 15:7*	And one of the four beasts gave unto the seven angels seven golden vials full of the wrath of God, who liveth for ever and ever.	And one of the four living creatures gave unto the seven angels seven golden bowls full of the wrath of God, who liveth forever and ever.	see Rev 17:1
Rev 16:2	And the first went, and poured out	And the first went, and poured out	noisome!

Scripture	Discrepancies in KJV Scripture	Memories of the 1611 KJV	Notes:
	his vial upon the earth; and there fell a noisome and grievous sore upon the men which had the mark of the beast, and upon them which worshipped his image.	his bowl upon the earth; and there fell a foul and painful sore upon the men which had the mark of the beast, and upon them which worshipped his image.	
Rev 16:14	For they are the spirits of devils, working miracles, which go forth unto the kings of the earth and of the whole world, to gather them to the battle of that great day of God Almighty.	For they are the spirits of demons, working miracles, which go forth unto the kings of the earth and of the whole world, to gather them to the battle of that great day of God Almighty.	
Rev 17:6	And I saw the woman drunken with the blood of the saints, and with the blood of the martyrs of Jesus: and when I saw her, I wondered with great admiration.	And I saw the woman drunken with the blood of the saints, and with the blood of the martyrs of Jesus: and when I saw her, I wondered with great wonder.	admiration! astonishment
Rev 17:9	And here is the mind which hath wisdom. The seven heads are seven mountains, on which the woman sitteth.	And here is the mind which hath wisdom. The seven heads are seven hills, on which the woman sitteth.	
Rev 18:1	And after these things I saw another angel come down from heaven, having great power; and the earth was lightened with his glory.	And after these things I saw another angel come down from heaven, having great power; and the earth was made bright with his glory.	

61

Scripture	Discrepancies in KJV Scripture	Memories of the 1611 KJV	Notes:
Rev 18:3	For all nations have drunk of the wine of the wrath of her fornication, and the kings of the earth have committed fornication with her, and the merchants of the earth are waxed rich through the abundance of her delicacies.	For all nations have drunk of the wine of the wrath of her fornication, and the kings of the earth have committed fornication with her, and the merchants of the earth have grown rich through the abundance of her sensuality.	
Rev `18:7	How much she hath glorified herself, and lived deliciously, so much torment and sorrow give her: for she saith in her heart, I sit a queen, and am no widow, and shall see no sorrow.	In the measure that she glorified herself and lived luxuriously, iso much torment and sorrow give her: for she saith in her heart, I sit as a queen, and am no widow, and shall see no sorrow.	
Rev 18:9	How much she hath glorified	How much she hath glorified	deliciously!

	Scripture Discrepancies in KJV Scripture	Memories of the 1611 KJV	Notes:
	herself, and lived deliciously, so much torment and sorrow give her: for she saith in her heart, I sit a queen, and am no widow, and shall see no sorrow.	herself, and lived luxuriously, so much torment and sorrow give her: for she saith in her heart, I sit a queen, and am no widow, and shall see no sorrow.	delicately also Rev 18:7
Rev 18:12	The merchandise of gold, and silver, and precious stones, and of pearls, and fine linen, and purple, and silk, and scarlet, and all thyine wood, and all manner vessels of ivory, and all manner vessels of most precious wood, and of brass, and iron, and marble,	The merchandise of gold, and silver, and precious stones, and of pearls, and fine linen, and purple, and silk, and scarlet, and all thyine wood, and all kinds of vessels of ivory, and all kinds of vessels of most precious wood, and of bronze, and iron, and marble,	
Rev 18:13	And cinnamon, and odours, and ointments, and frankincense, and wine, and oil, and fine flour, and wheat, and beasts, and sheep, and horses, and chariots, and slaves, and souls of men.	And cinnamon, and incense, and ointments, and frankincense, and wine, and oil, and fine flour, and wheat, and cattle, and sheep, and horses, and chariots, and slaves, and souls of men.	
Rev 18:14	And the fruits that thy soul lusted after are departed from thee, and all things which were dainty and goodly are departed from thee, and thou shalt find them no more at all.	And the fruits that thy soul lusted after are departed from thee, and all things which were dainty and sumptuous are departed from thee, and thou shalt find them no more at all.	
Rev 18:22	And the voice of harpers, and musicians, and of pipers, and trumpeters, shall be heard no more at all in thee; and no craftsman, of whatsoever craft he be, shall be found any more in thee; and the sound of a millstone shall be heard no more at all in thee;	And the voice of harpers, and minstrels, and of flute players, and trumpeters, shall be heard no more at all in thee; and no craftsman, of whatsoever craft, shall be found any more in thee; and the sound of a millstone shall be heard no more at all in thee;	
Rev 18:23	And the light of a candle shall shine no more at all in thee; and the voice of the bridegroom and of the bride shall be heard no more at all in thee: for thy merchants were the great men of the earth; for by thy sorceries were all nations deceived.	And the light of a lamp shall shine no more at all in thee; and the voice of the bridegroom and of the bride shall be heard no more at all in thee: for thy merchants were the great men of the earth; for by thy sorceries were all nations deceived.	see Rev 22:5
Rev 19:1	And after these things I heard a great voice of much people in	And after these things I heard a great voice of many people in	much people!

Scripture	Discrepancies in KJV Scripture	Memories of the 1611 KJV	Notes:
	heaven, saying, Alleluia; Salvation, and glory, and honour, and power, unto the Lord our God:	heaven, saying, Hallelujah!; redemption, and glory, and honour, and power, unto the Lord our God:	
Rev 19:2	For true and righteous are his judgments: for he hath judged the great whore, which did corrupt the earth with her fornication, and hath avenged the blood of his servants at her hand.	For true and righteous are his judgments: for he hath judged the great harlot, which did corrupt the earth with her fornication, and hath avenged the blood of his servants at her hand.	
Rev 19:4	And the four and twenty elders and the four beasts fell down and worshipped God that sat on the throne, saying, Amen; Alleluia.	And the four and twenty elders and the four living creatures fell down and worshipped God who sat on the throne, saying, Amen; Hallelujah!	
Rev 19:6	And I heard as it were the voice of a great multitude, and as the voice of many waters, and as the voice of mighty thunderings, saying, Alleluia: for the Lord God omnipotent reigneth.	And I heard as it were the voice of a great multitude, and as the voice of many waters, and as the voice of mighty peals of thunder, saying, Hallelujah: for the Lord God omnipotent reigneth.	
Rev 19:7	Let us be glad and rejoice, and give honour to	Let us be glad and rejoice, and give honour to him:	wife!

62

Scripture	Memories of the 1611 KJV	Notes:
	for the marriage of the Lamb is come, and his Bride hath made herself ready.	
Rev 19:13	And he was clothed with a robe dipped in blood: and his name is called The Word of God.	
Rev 19:21	And the rest were slain with the sword of him that sat upon the horse, which sword proceeded out of his mouth: and all the birds were filled with their flesh.	also Rev 19:17
Rev 20:2	And he laid hold of the dragon, that serpent of old, who is the devil, and satan, and bound him a thousand years.	(notice Devil and Satan are caps.)
Rev 20:3	And cast him into the bottomless pit, and chained him up, and set a seal over him, that he should deceive the nations no more, till the thousand years should be fulfilled: and after that he must be loosed a little season.	
Rev 20:7	And when the thousand years are ended, Satan shall be loosed out of his prison,	
Rev 20:10	And the devil that deceived them was cast into the lake of fire and brimstone, where the beast and the false prophet are, and shall be	

tormented day and night forever and ever.

Rev 20:14	And death and hades were cast into the lake of fire. This is the second death.	also Rev 20:13
Rev 21:9	And there came unto me one of the seven angels which had the seven bowls full of the seven last plagues, and talked with me, saying, Come hither, I will shew thee the bride of the Lamb of God.	
Rev 21:21	And the twelve gates were twelve pearls; each one of the gates was of one pearl: and the street of the city was pure gold, as it were transparent glass.	
Rev 21:27	And there shall in no way enter into it anything that defileth, neither he that worketh abomination, or maketh a lie: but they which are written in the Lamb's book of life.	
Rev 22:5	And there shall be no night there; and they need no lamp, neither light of the sun; for the Lord God giveth them light: and they shall reign for ever and ever.	
Rev 22:10	And he saith unto me, Seal not the words of the prophecy of this book: for the time is at hand.	also Rev 22:7,9
Rev 22:14	Blessed are they that wash their robes, that they may have right to the tree of life, and may enter in	

63

Scripture	Discrepancies in KJV Scripture	Memories of the 1611 KJV	Notes:
	enter in through the gates into the city.	through the gates into the city.	
Rev 22:15	For without are dogs, and sorcerers, and whoremongers, and murderers, and idolaters, and whosoever loveth and maketh a lie.	For outside are dogs, and sorcerers, and fornicators, and murderers, and idolaters, and whosoever loveth and maketh a lie.	see Rev 21:8
Rev 22:19	And if any man shall take away from the words of the book of this prophecy, God shall take away his part out of the book of life, and out of the holy city, and from the things which are written in this book.	And if any man shall take away from the words of the book of this prophecy, God shall take away his part from the tree of life, and out of the holy city, and from the things which are written in this book.	
Rev 22:12	And, behold, I come quickly; and my reward is with me, to give every man according as his work shall be.	And, behold, I come quickly; and my reward is with me, to give every man according to his work.	
Rev 22:21	The grace of our Lord Jesus Christ be with you all. Amen	(I don't remember this verse)	

Chapter 8

Who or What Is Causing the Mandela Effect

The Mandela Effect poses quite a dilemna.

Theories abound as to how the Mandela Effect is happening. They range from CERN accessing different dimensions to parallel universes to time travel to simulation in the secular. In the spiritual, there are those that think that God is effecting the changes and others who think that Satan is causing them.

I am not scientifically knowledgeable enough to know the answer, but I personally believe that it is a result of Satan using Fallen Angel technology in combination with witchcraft or black magic. I say that because the changes to the Bible create a great deal of confusion, with the archaic words being hard to understand, with the transposed sentence structure, making the sentence hard to read, the lack of God and Jesus' pronouns being capitalized and the denigration of Jesus and God's character.

This grim reality points to a malevolent source, which of course is Satan himself. Whether he is using the Quantum Computers at CERN or elaborate spells of witchcraft to fabricate his new material world, the fact of the matter is, physical matter is being changed into something different.

Time travel is an interesting supposition as it does say in the Bible that Satan will seek to change times and laws.:

> *Daniel 7:25*
> *And he shall speak great words against the most High, and shall wear out the saints of the most High, and think to change times and laws:*

Time Travel

If time travel is possible, you can bet Satan has tried it, so I wouldn't doubt if that had something to do with it. However, the reason so many do not believe that it is time travel is because there is residue. If one were to go back in time and change something, then that would eliminate all the versions of how "it used to be" from reality. Yet, we see loads of residue all over the place.

It is no coincidence that on the big launch of CERN in 2008 that Stephen Hawkings (now has been Mandel'ed to be Stephen Hawking) made this announcement at the

> *Genesis 3:1*
> *Now the serpent was more subtil than any beast of the field which the Lord God had made.*

unveiling of a huge clock

in England, considered to be a work of art, the *Chronophage* :
"Relative time"? Your guess is as good as mine.

> *Join us for this unveiling of this clock as we unleash relative time on the unsuspecting people for the first time.-Stephen Hawkings*

Have you ever noticed that the Mandela Effect is purposefully subtle in its changes. Word changes consist of mainly one letter, or to a different spelling with the exact same pronunciation?

Example:

> - **Sally Fields, now Sally Field**
> - **Proctor and Gamble, now Procter and Gamble**
> - **Christopher Reeves, now Christopher Reeve**
> - **Stephen Hawkings, now Stephen Hawking**
> - **Joel Olsteen, now Joel Osteen**
> - **Joyce Meyers, now Joyce Meyer**
> - **Chic-Fil-A, now Chick-Fil-A**
> - **Anderson Windows, now Andersen**
> - **Bragg's Apple Cider Vinegar, now Bragg**
> - **Depends, now Depend**
> - **Advanced Auto Parts, now Advance Auto Parts**
> - **Caldwell Banker, now Coldwell Banker**
> - **Jimi Baker, now Jim Bakker**
> - **Hailey's Comet, now Halley's Comet**
> - **Dilemna, now Dilemma**

The changes are very subtle. Which leads me to believe that they are incurred by Satan, as he is master of subtlety. Definition: cunning (usually in a bad sense):—crafty, prudent.

If someone went back in time to make a change, all that effort wouldn't have gone into a minor spelling change to a word.Satan most likely would change the outcome of Jesus' death or resurrection.

Moreover, the Bible says that we are made to live ONCE and die ONCE.

> ### AMP Hebrews 9:27
> *And just as it is appointed and destined for all men to die once and after this [comes certain] judgment*

If we die ONCE, then we live ONCE. We don't live a thousand different lives based on each decision we make. That's not Biblical.

Fallen Angel Technology

If you think it's too fantastic for satan to change the words in the Bible, remember what Pharoah by changing the staff to a serpent, he changed matter".

It is no less astounding that the words in the Bible have been changed, and are still

> *Exodus 7:10-12 Amplified Bible (AMP)*
> *So Moses and Aaron came to Pharaoh, and did just as the Lord had commaded; Aaron threw down his staff before Pharaoh and his servants, and it became a serpent. 11 Then Pharaoh called for the wise men [skilled in magic and omens] and the sorcerers [skilled in witchcraft], and they also, these magicians (soothsayer-priests) of Egypt, did the same with their secret arts and enchantments. 12 For every [a]man threw down his staff and they turned into serpents; but Aaron's staff swallowed up their staffs*

changing. It appears that fallen angel technology is able to change the words in the the Bible that you have in your home.

Even words in the Bible have been changed to make them part of a satanic witchcraft ritual, as the new spellings of words have added a ck on the end:

"K" is the eleventh letter of the alphabet, which has numerological significance in witchcraft. Aleister Crowley, the leader of satanism, who wrote the satanic bible, or the "Book of the Law", invented the spelling "ck" tat the end of words. In the field of black majick; For words ending in C, changing the spelling of the word, by using 'k" at the end, casts a spell.

Changed words in the Bible that Now Contain a "K" at the end:

➢ MAGICK
➢ LUNATICK
➢ HERETICK
➢ GARLICK
➢ MUSICK
➢ PUBLICK
➢ BISHOPRICK
➢ HAVOCK
➢ TRAFFICK

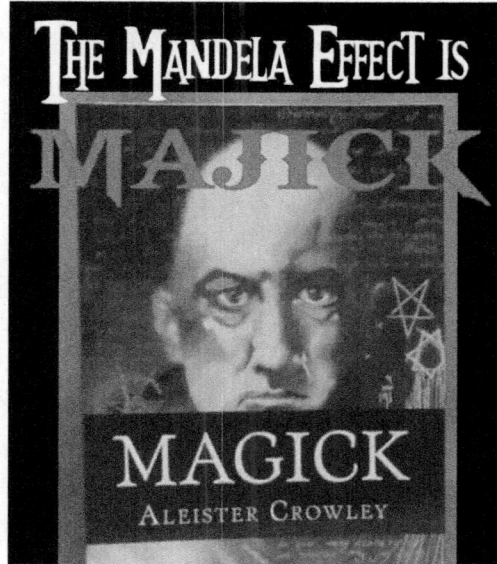

CERN

A more secular theory as to how the Mandela Effect is happening points to CERN, the world's largest particle accelerator, called the Large Hadron Collider . I remember how the Large Hadron Collider used to be the Large Haldron Collider, with an L.

What is it with the Mandela Effect and "L"s? Joel Olsteen lost his L as well. But, I digest. CERN is built on the ancient city of Apollyon mentioned in Revelation 9, saying that a portal will be opened to Hell.

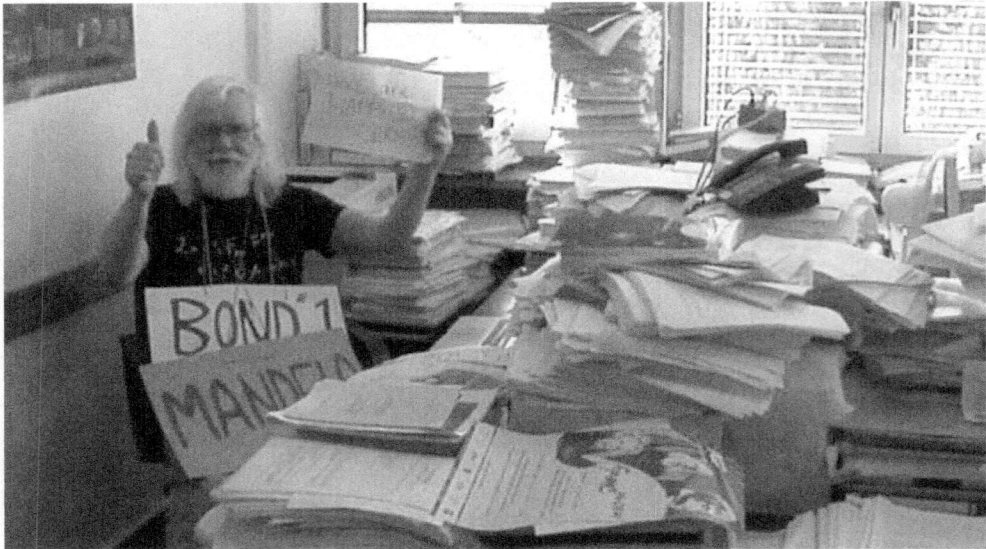

This picture shows the sign on the bottom which reads, "Mandela" on it and the other sign reads "Bond1". The first Bond movie .refers to the first person to play James Bond on screen and his surname, is"Nelson". "Bond #1"(first James Bond actor) and "Mandela" which translates to Barry Nelson Mandela. Coincidence?

The LHC collides protons approaching the speed of light. The exponential computing power of quantum computing, which is measured in Qbits is vastly faster than regular computing. Quoting a scientist at CERN, he states that

the quantum computer engages in computational resources from parallel universes

CERN is the largest and most advanced scientific research facility in the world. You would think their buildings, advertising and symbols would be all about projecting a sterile, scientific, authoritative look, in order to convey a professional image. Like banks. Banks do not have advertising commercials with half naked singers gyrating around. They want to project an image of "safety" and conservatism, so you will put your money in their bank.

You would think that CERN would want that same type of image. Yet, their long opening ceremony has dancers wearing underwear, angels floating in the sky, demons dancing feverishly, and time machines spinning around with the devil rising up from hell. The CERN mascot outside the building is the Hindu god of destruction: Lord Shiva.

The logo for CERN just happens to be "666": Update 4/17/24: a short tail has been added to the logo, a recent Mandela Effect change.

The building is constructed on the very spot that an ancient Roman temple was dedicated to the god Apollo. And their name is derived from an ancient god of the underworld: CERNUSSOS

The Horned god CERNUSSOS

If the research center CERN is all about science, then why does everything have religious meaning to it? Even the tiniest detail has religious connotation: an analysis of the format of the quantum computer chip is identical to an ancient religious temple, exactly the same layout as Herod and Solomon's Temple. Is that a coincidence?

Ok, if we let all that slide, we must be able to get some strictly technical information from the founder of the Quantum Computer, who is Geordie Rose. Here is an excerpt of what he says:

If we are not careful - it is going to wipe us all out.-Geordie Rose

To get even more spooky, Geordie Rose talks about summoning demons in from another dimension. That's a real scientific stance. When describing how these large, black monolithic 10' tall quantum computers looks like, Rose says: "It feels like an altar to an alien god. They really are impressive machines."

Rose continues, "This word demons...doesn't capture the essence of what's happening here...There's this guy named H.P. Lovecraft, a very famous weird fiction author. And he espoused a view called "cosmicism". The essence of cosmicism is "cosmic indifference....There's these massively intelligent entities out there...but they're not good – they're not evil – they just don't give a shit about you even in the slightest...the same way that you don't care about an ant, is the same way they're not going to care about you.

H. P. Lovecraft depiction from one of his dreams of the "Great Old Ones".

These things that we're summoning into the world now, they're not demons, they're not evil – but they're more like the "Lovecraftian great old ones" - they are entities that are not necessarily going to be aligned with what we want. This transition is really, really, massively important for our entire species to navigate..and nobody is "paying attention."

Underneath it all is this "rising tsunami" that if we're not careful is going to wipe us all out."And by the way, we are hiring people to make this all happen. Anyone interested?

Is Geordie Rose Crazy?

He espouses what he just said in the paragraph above, all while recruiting our brightest young minds to come and work there. He warns that what CERN is doing with quantum computing is massively dangerous, life-threatening to the entire human race, yet he is launching forward in leaps and bounds. If he isn't compelling caution, just postulating about it, then who does he think will? His actions are contradictory and insane.

The Quantum Computer Chip is Identical to Solomon's Temple

At the heart of the quantum computer is a tiny chip, in which contains all of the "wonder and magic that makes this thing go".

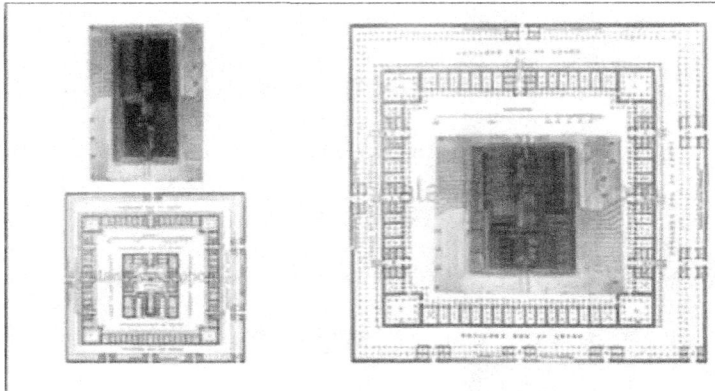

"If you look at the blueprint of Herod's Temple, and this is similar with Solomon's Temple, the temples are arranged in a specific fashion so as to enhance the communication ..with their god or the God. The D Wave 2X, the fourth model..the chip.side by side, it's exactly the same as Aliester Crowley's great table, which has a chart dissected by a cross into four quadrants.

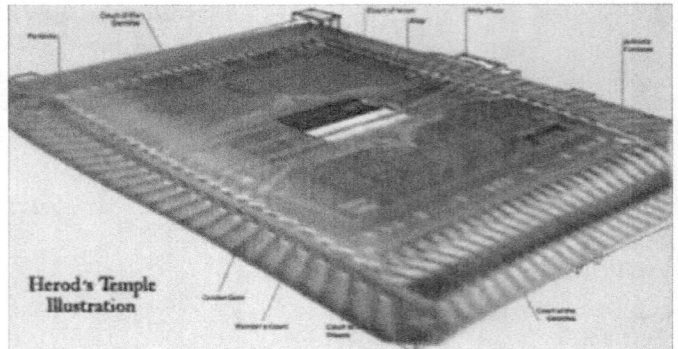

Herod's Temple Illustration

The table is used to communicate with the other side, to exchange information. When I say this is evidence of evil, this is what I'm showing you...geomancy is used for divining the future."

Nothing suspicious here. CERN is just a scientific company smashing small particles together to figure things out.

Some believe the only rational explanation for the Mandela Bible Effect phenomenon is that Quantum Computing is making the changes. The scientific facility that does Quantum Computing is CERN, which houses the Large Haldron Collider (LHC) and is located in a town in France called "Saint-Genus-Poilly." In Roman times a temple existed on that very spot, to honor the Greek god Apollo. The people who lived there believed that in that location was a gateway to the underworld.

> *Revelation 9:11 King James Version says:*
> *And they had a king over them, which is the angel of the bottomless pit, whose name in the Hebrew tongue is Abaddon, but in the Greek tongue hath his name Apollyon*

Scholarly opinions concur that Apollo is the same god as Apollyon.

QBITS and CUBITS

Dimensional computers deal with binary information – ones or zeros. Quantum computers manipulate what is knows an Qbits – or "Quantum bits" which can be ones and zeroes at the same time, leveraging the power ...performing many operation on the same date simultaneously. Qbits is pronounced exactly like the measurement of 'Cubits' in the Bible:

> *Genesis 6:15*
> *This is how you are to ––-make it: the length of the ark*
> *––-three hundred cubits...*

Satan copies everything that God does.

In an article at Recode, they state that, "No one can really say for certain where those helpful distant qubits are operating.The leading bet among physicists...suggest quantum computer offload processing to parallel universes.Basically, the scientists are saying thatthe problems that they are having the quantum computers solve, disappear into another universe, then comes back with the solution."Doesn't this sound like the information is coming from another realm – and could be coming from the demonic realm of fallen angels?

Geordie Rose, the inventor of quantum computing states:

2 PREDICTIONS OF GEORDIE ROSE

➢ "By 2023, a major breakthrough in physics will occur...the reality of parallel universes."

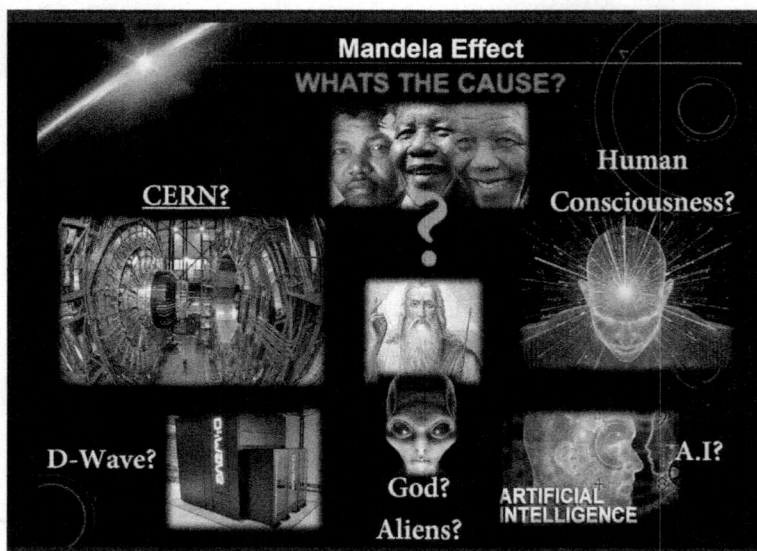

➢ "By 2028; intelligent machines will exist that can do anything humans can do..."

> *We are not far off from a total artificial intelligence takeover.*
> *What it really will be, is the takeover of demonic entities into*
> *human bodies.*

The speculation that CERN is causing the supernatural bible changes and Mandela Effect is based on the following assumptions:

➢ CERN is a secret organization that is working on opening portals to other dimensions, where they can communicate with and summon entities that are hostile to humanity and God.

➢ CERN is using D-Wave quantum computers, which are capable of accessing and manipulating parallel realities, to alter the past, the present, and the future, according to their agenda.

➢ CERN is responsible for creating and spreading the Mandela Effect, which is a phenomenon where large groups of people have false or inconsistent memories of certain events, facts, or details, such as the spelling of words, the names of celebrities, the logos of brands, or the verses of the Bible.

➢ CERN is doing this to deceive and confuse the masses, to undermine their faith and trust in God and His Word, to prepare them for the arrival of the Antichrist, the False Prophet, and the Beast, and to fulfill the prophecies of the Book of Revelation.

Some of the evidence or arguments that are used to support this speculation are:

➢ CERN is located near Geneva, Switzerland, which is close to the ancient site of the Temple of Apollo, where the god of destruction and chaos was worshiped. Some believe that CERN is trying to unleash the spirit of Apollo, who is also identified with Apollyon or Abaddon, the angel of the abyss in Revelation 9:11.

- CERN has a statue of the Hindu god Shiva, who is also known as the destroyer, the transformer, and the lord of the dance. Some believe that CERN is trying to invoke the power of Shiva, who is also associated with the serpent, the dragon, and the Antichrist.

- CERN has a logo that resembles three sixes, or 666, which is the number of the Beast in Revelation 13:18. Some believe that CERN is trying to mark the world with the sign of the Beast, and to create a one world system that is controlled by the Antichrist

- CERN has a project called ALICE, which stands for A Large Ion Collider Experiment. Some believe that CERN is trying to create a wormhole or a gateway to Wonderland, where they can enter and explore other dimensions, and where the laws of physics and logic do not apply.

- CERN has a project called AWAKE, which stands for Advanced Wakefield Experiment. Some believe that CERN is trying to awaken the

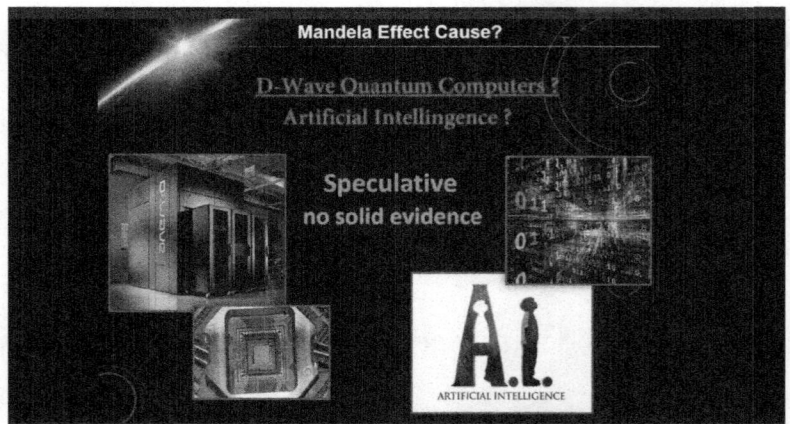

sleeping giants or the Nephilim, who are the offspring of the fallen angels and the human women, and who were the cause of the great flood in Genesis 6:4.

- CERN has a project called LHCb, which stands for Large Hadron Collider beauty. Some believe that CERN is trying to create the image of the Beast, which is a sentient and deceptive artificial intelligence that can perform miracles and cause people to worship the Antichrist, as described in Revelation 13:14-15.

➢ CERN has a project called CMS, which stands for Compact Muon Solenoid. Some believe that CERN is trying to create the mark of the Beast, which is a microchip or a tattoo that can be implanted or applied on the right hand or the forehead of people, and that can track and control their transactions and activities, as described in Revelation 13:16-17.

Rose also waxes on about bringing other entities into this dimension, saying they are "not demons" (which they are), but just the musings of an old Science Fiction writer, Lovecraft, calling them "old great ones". He says they won't give a shit about us, and will stamp us out like ants.

By breaking the subatomic bonds of matter, and casting away the chords that hold the material world together, mankind will willingly tear the veil that has been established for his own protection and unleash a darkness and chaos that the earth has not seen for many ages. This is the masterplan of the Luciferian elite, who seek to open forbidden gates and usher in the entities that will lead them in a futile war against the Lord and against His anointed.

The leading bet among physicists…suggest quantum computers offload processing to parallel universes.Basically, the scientists are saying that the problems that they are having that the quantum computers solve, disappears into another universe, then comes back with the solution.

"I don't know what's happening either but if I had to take a guess I would think our reality is somehow being changed slightly. Why? I don't know. It could be from messing around with time travel, it could be bleed through of different timelines if that theory is correct or maybe even the result of so many quantum computers operating," Clif High speculates.

Planned Parenthood

This quote was found from 1969, from a man who attended a Planned Parenthood meeting where no one was allowed to take notes. He remembers them saying things which perfectly describes the Bible changes that are going on now:

"Religion is not necessarily bad...so they will have religion. But the major religions of today have to be changed because they are not compatible with the changes to come. The old religions will have to go, especially Christianity. Once the Roman Catholic church is brought down, the rest of Christianity will follow easily.

Then a new religion could be accepted for use all over the world. It will incorporate something for all the old ones to make it more easy for people to accept it and feel at home in it. In order to do this, the Bible will need to be changed. It will be rewritten to fit the new religion. Gradually, key words will be replaced with new words, having various change of meaning. Then the meaning attached to the new word can be close to the old word.

And as time goes on, other phases of meaning can be emphasized. And then gradually, that word – replaced with another word. Most people won't know the difference...the few who do notice the different won't be enough to matter.

One of the most surprising statement of the whole presentation was:

Why would someone from Planned Parenthood be in on a highly technical scheme to change the words in the Bible? Considering that planned Parenthood is in charge of murdering babies on a mass scale, killing many alive, and then selling their harvested body parts for profit – it makes sense to connect the dots that this organization has nefarious ties to the underworld of demonic darkness.

Planned Parenthood is 'sacrificing babies. They are simply carrying on the pagan religious practices of biblical and ancient times,where people sacrificed their infants by throwing them in the fire on the altar of Ba'al.

Deuteronomy 18:10
There shall not be found among you any one that maketh— his son or his daughter to pass through the fire, or that useth divination,or an observer of times, or an enchanter, or a witch.

2 Kings 17:17
And they caused their sons and their daughters to pass— through the fire, and used divination and —enchantments, and sold themselves to do evil —in the sight of the Lord, to provoke him to anger.

"You probably think the churches won't stand for this —

the churches will help us."

Audio clip from 1969, Dr. Richard Day, former Director of Planned Parenthood, spoke the above words on 3/20/1969.

DIVINATION

Anthony Patch states that the quantum computers are causing the Mandela Effect, but not on their own. He asserts that they are able to communicate with other dimensions where the fallen angels are. He refers to Aleister Crowley's summonings of the same fallen angels, which he says are giving information to the quantum computers:

"They are not only communicating with fallen angels but with 91 governors. Crowley developed 4 watchtowers on the great table. Each tower has 22 governors assigned to it. There are 4 of them, like the 4 elements of earth, wind, fire and water. Each have control over a specific element. They also have the ability to manipulate people.

These governors are influencing the physical reality. The Mandela Effect is a trial run. The Mandela Effect is evidence of the baby steps they are taking with the governors. The more that this interdimensional communication is taking place, the more these Mandela Effects will be evident to people, to the point that people will realize what's going on.

The technological geomancy that is being practiced by quantum computing…is what is creating the Mandela Effect.

It is also a psychological operation. These governors are tricksters. Their minds are altered when they cast spells over them, so there is a combination of changes and psychological manipulation. That's why some people remember one thing, and others another.

They are re-writing our history. They want us questioning our own memories. Other explanations haven't gone deep enough to make these occult connections."

Fallen Angels Speaking With CERN

Revolution Radio hosted an interview with popular Mandela Effect Youtuber, *Brian Staveley*, in which Brian laid out his case for the Mandela Effect. Toward the end of the show, Revolution Radio related several astounding real-life stories of how the Mandela Effect may be related. The following is what he related as to why Hewlett Packard discontinued use of Quantum Computers,

One of the real life interviews involves a military man in the 1930s that was transported into the 1970s. The host tells how he interviewed this man on his radio show. During the broadcast, the entire station went dark and the show was canceled. It was a major event, yet after the whole episode occurred, his staff **never remembered it**.

The host went on to introduce a possible reasoning for the Mandela Effect regarding Hewlett-Packard's experience with Quantum Computers, and why they chose to stop using them.

The host explains how Hewlett Packard abandoned its use of Quantum Computers years ago because they were shocked to learn that supernatural occurrences were happening. Apparently, when they got down to the quantum level with their computers, **their circuitry boards would miraculously change wiring.**

This happened over and over, and was so shocking and unexplainable that HP decided they were delving into a forbidden realm. They then patently abandoned the use of Quantum Computers, saying **they felt they were opening a doorway into another malevolent dimension that was taking over their programming.**

Seeking Truth in the New Age Movement

For many in the Mandela Effected community, the pursuit of truth is paramount. I believe that anyone's search for ultimate truth will lead them to the conclusion that the Bible is real, we are living in a state of spiritual warfare, and there is a battle raging between good and evil. The big picture will lead to the fact that we as humans need to accept Jesus Christ, in order to be saved from this dying world.

However, this search for truth often ends up in various places, not the least of which are New Age theories. Such theories as Ascension, manifestation, Christ consciousness and belief in multiple timelines converging are considered New Age.

Within the New Age movement are core beliefs that are centered around *saving the earth*, and *doing what you want to do*. I will label them

> *Romans 1:25 NLT*
> *They traded the truth about God for a lie. So they*
> *worshiped and served the things God created*
> *instead of the Creator himself, who is worthy of*
> *eternal praise! Amen.*
>
> *The KJV now says in Romans 1:25*
>
> *Who changed the truth of God into a lie,*
> *and worshipped and served the creature more*
> *than the Creator, who is blessed for ever. Amen.*
>
> *Used to be: creation instead of creature*

➢ **earth-centered**

➢ **self-centered**

While those concepts may seem benevolent on their face, they can be easily countered by the Bible. The first concept *"earth-centered"* is when people put their worship to the earth. Mother Earth or Gaia.

The second concept is when people believe in the satanic concept of "Do what Thou Wilt" or "Do Anything You Want". This is obviously "self-centered":

When you make your own rules, the sky's the limit.

When anything goes, deviance, depravity and greed reigns

"Who is God? The New Age says he is both the creator and the destroyer, a combination of good and evil. He is both holy, and he is the devil…Satan…is not a real, existent being, nor is he a dark angel who rebelled against God. Instead, he is "the part of us that refuses to recognize that we are the innocent children of a loving and unconditionally supporting God that never judges us and always finds us beautiful. Yes, no matter what evil the New Ager commits, it will be just beautiful, all part of the glorious work involved in perfecting ourselves.

When God gave us free choice He gave us freedom from being judged…The New Agers know that there is no wrong path, no bad way, no failure, no evil, no Devil, only us with complete free choice to find our way back to God in any way we choose,

270

and to grow in the experience. Satan is no more than God seen through cheap glasses."[1]

"But...there is all the evil we see on the TV news and read in the daily newspaper. What about *that* evil? Confidently, reassuringly comes the reply: the people who are murdered raped, robbed, victimized asked for it! Before they ever entered this particular incarnation they decided what would happen to them during this life."[2]

New Age religion is anything but new and has its roots in the ancient Babylonian religion, and that was one of paganism, witchcraft, and the occult.

"*Ramtha* is venerated as an all-knowing, perfect Master and is literally worhsiped by tens of thousands of New Agers...One lady, a secretary in a large, highly regarded and well-known law office with seventy-two in-house attorneys, has confided to my wife, Wanda, that every day during the lunch break, employees of the firm gather in the conference room to view Ramtha on video...My voluminous research proves conclusively that demons like Ramtha are at the root of every New Age teaching. I have yet to discover a single New Age cult, organization, or church that was not founded by a demon or demons...New Ager teaches that one's "higher self, "inner voice," spirit guide, or the "Christ within" (not Jesus!) is always right and is always to be obeyed...New Agers are taught to let go and let their inner "god" - the Self or the Universal Mind or Force - take over." [3].

---

[1] Jack Underhill, "Some New Age Myths and Truths," *Life Times*, Vol. 1, No. 3, p.9.
[2] Texe Marrs *Mystery Mark of the New Age*, p 206.
[3] Texe Marrs *Mystery Mark of the New Age*, p 209

The Triangle

Aiming to mock God's holy trinity, the ancient pagan religions set up the 3 sided triangle as a symbol of their gods. "The *triangle* is the supreme symbol of New Age satanism…The Triangle was a primary form of the Pyramid and a sacred symbol…with its apex, or point, facing downward represented Horus, the Sun God, while the triangle pointing upward characterized Sur, or Set, the Destroyer God…in San Francisco we find the Temple of Set, led by Michael Aquino, the self-styled "High Priest of Satan.,"[4] states . The Egyptians changed the names of the gods to Osiris, the Father god, Isis the Mother Goddess, and Horus the Son. Ra was greater yet somewhat aloof and portrayed as a unisex sun god. The Hindus, Egyptians and Greeks revered the Mother Goddess knows as the Kali Yantra, or sign of the vulva. Today, Hollywood stars constantly make a triangle symbol with their hands in display of their allegiance to these ancient gods.

> *Every person in the New Age, knowingly or unknowingly, worships Satan. -Texe Marrs*

Anton Levey, the internationally known Satanist priest and author *The Satanic Bible,* mentions the name "Shiva" as a synonym for Satan or Lucifer. CERN has a statue of Shiva outside their building.

The Hindu deity Lord Shiva is literally known in India as "the Destroyer," and is worshiped by the leaders of the prominent New Age group, the Lucis Trust

---

[4] *Mystery Mark of the New Age* by Texe Marrs, p. 78

(formerly Lucifer Publishing). They also believe that "Lord Maitreya is a powerful, reincarnated god-man who represent Sanat Kumara, the "Christ" of the Aquarian Age, who will reign over the earth while a greater god whom he serves, Sanat Kumara, pulls the strings behind the scenes."[5]

The godlike entities that inhabit the unseen spirit world are said to be in "Shamballa".[6]

New Agers worship Lucifer, whether they know it or not. Sanat Kumara is a code name for Lucifer, or Satan, conveniently transposed in the word "Sanat"'. The :"all seeing eye of God" that is portrayed everywhere in popular culture refers to the eye of Horus the Sun God and Lucifer respectively.

New Agers are taught that symbolic images lift one into an altered state of higher consciousness, meditating and visualizing a symbol or object, which is an idol. "The New Age teaches that the removal and physical destruction fo all Christians will be a *holy act*....explained in a key New Age bible called The Keys of Enoch...published in 1978...describes the wrath that will befall those who, in the last days, refuse to embrace the New Age religion and its gods...They envision themselves a holier race of humans, who have become gods." Beliefs based on 'new mystery texts, or "Sacred Scriptures," shall be brought to man by interplanetary messengers who will reveal them only to the New Age "Sons of Light."[7]

These are the same people who are bringing you stories of UFOs or UAPs, normalizing it, so when an alien does make its appearance with these mysterious texts, you will believe it.

---

[5] Texe Marrs *Mystery Mark of the New Age,* p. 174.
[6] Texe Marrs *Mystery Mark of the New Age,* p. 168
[7] J.J. Hurtag, *The Keys of Enoch,* p. 173,332,418-422

"In the New Age view, the cleansing and healing of Mother Earth involves the removal of all those who have a *negative consciousness.* Unity of all religions - even satanism and witchcraft-is positive, but to insist that *Jesus is the only way to salvation* is not only undesirable, it is dangerously *negative.* Christians are at a lower and inferior level of consciousness…The Age of Aquarius "will bring joy and happiness unexcelled since the days of the Atlantean era…one requirement will be that all who are to become citizens of the coming era of happiness and plenty must be willing to communicate with the dead…and to blasphemously claim that we , mere men and women, are divine gods."[8]. This new age will come after the closing of the Age of Pisces, which is now on its last legs. "…two-thirds of humanity will advance into the New Age kingdom.The other one third "will be held over for later unfoldment. This one-third of humanity obviously includes Bible believing Christians as well as Jews who refuse to deny a personal Jehovah."[9]

Channeling is the process by which a person calls up a demon spirit to communicate with. New Agers believe in channeling spirits, saying they are miracle workers. "Many New Agers say they are afraid to make any important life decisions without first asking their spirit guide.…one channeled demon entity writes: "We create our own reality," "it is natural to be bisexual," "evil and destruction do not exist."[10]

It is a common belief in the Mandela Effect community that the Mandela Effect has shown us that reality is not what we thought it was; it is malleable, therefore

---

[8] Texe Marrs *Mystery Mark of the New Age,* p. 156-7
[9] Texe Marrs *Dark Secrets of the New Age,* p .145-6
[10] Texe Marrs *Mystery Mark of the New Age,* p . 109

we can create our own reality. Many are studying how to manifest, or make come to life, anything they want, just by speaking it out and concentrating on it.

Meditation is the most common method used in the New Age to make contact with Satan and his demons. "New Age meditation involves an emptying of one's mind an an inviting in of spirits who are not from God...meditation is based on Hindu principles of linking the human mind with the Universal Mind and thus making contact with demons ...during meditation the New Age believer often uses a mantra, a mystical holy word of power, to invoke the demon spirit guide to come...it has been revealed...the mantra which TM [transcendental meditation] assigns is invariably the name of a Hindu god...The demonic power of these channeled spirits is far greater than the New Age believer can ever hope to bring under control.

As long as the individual does what the demon tells him, everything is fine. But once the person balks, and especially if he turns to the Bible or to prayer for deliverance, Satanic hostility breaks out as the angry spirit furiously attempts to whip the subject back into line. Yet, in the end these demons are no match for the sincere person who repents and calls on the name of Jesus."[11]

Another New Age practice is *visualization,* where a person conjures up an image of a spirit he wishes to contact. This may be enhanced by focusing one's eyes on an object such as a candle flame, a crystal or a mandala. A mandala is most often a circular pattern "(the circle represents Satan and the karmic wheel of reincarnation and birth) comprised internally of a scene or symbols reflecting New Age themes."[12]

---

[11] Texe Marrs *Mystery Mark of the New Age,* p .111-115
[12] Texe Marrs of ark Secrets of the New Age, *Mystery Mark of the New Age,* p .113-114

New Age Plan

1. The **One World** system must be formed stating that man is destined to progress toward a state of Godhood.

2. **Unity,** with belief that both man and the planet are living organisms and that the love of man must include an understanding and love of *our planet as a living being.*

3. **Creation of a World Body** governed by an elite group of twelve wise men, constituting a "World Government which will act for the good of all humanity."[13] .

4. **World Mind -** creation of elite rulers to be given "sufficient power and authority so it can synthesize or unify all aspects of life, including religion, art, and science."[14].

Is this not what technology is seeking to do now: synthesize all aspects of life by digitizing everything, have it all connect to the internet, have us merge with technology or implant a neural lace device in our brains so we can connect to the internet, aka *World Brain?*

The New Age Bible

There will have to be a new Bible to accommodate the New Age World Religion. Initially there will be toleration of of continuing Christian and Jewish traditions but eventually there will be requirements for all religions to conform to the New Religion. "What will happen to present day religious groups?…Religions of today probably will continue to function initially much as they do now…As concepts of the world religion are scientifically validated, learned and spread about, present

---

[13] Vera Alder *When Humanity Come of Age* p.20
[14] Texe Marrs *Dark Secrets of the New Age,* p. 170

religions will begin to make changes and evolve into centers for the world religion."[15]

"The New Age has long sought to destroy the Bible of the Jews and the Christians. Alice Bailey has accused the God of the Old Testament as being unworthy of man's worship. In 1947 she wrote that "all sane, sincere, thinking people should repudiate the Old Testament and its presentation of a God full of hate and jealousy." She termed the Christian belief in heaven and hell unacceptable doctrines designed to "keep people in line with…fear and threat."[16]

Universal contempt for the Holy Bible among New Age leaders is convincingly demonstrated by David Spangler who has stated, "We can take all the scriptures, and all the teachings, and all the tablets, and all the laws, and all the marshmallows and have a jolly good bonfire and marshmallow roast, because that is all they are worth."[17]

New Age dogma is expressed under nine major doctrinal cornerstones:

➢ **Mystery teachings**
➢ **Occultism and Eastern mysticism**
➢ **Psychology/powers of the mind**
➢ **Science and technology as revelation**
➢ **Hedonism**
➢ **Evolution**
➢ **Pantheism**
➢ **Selfism**
➢ **Leadership by spiritually superior beings [demons in disguise][18]**

---

[15] Lola Davis, *Toward a World Religion for the New Age*, pp. 187, 188
[16] Alice Bailey, (Lucis Publishing Company, 1947) *Problems of Humanity* pp. 142, 143
[17] David Spangler, *Reflections on the Christ* (Scotland: Findhorn Publications, 1982), p. 73
[18] Texe Marrs Drak Secrets of the New Age pp. 189, 190

Karma/Reincarnation

The law of karma demands that individuals suffer an pay in this life, or in a later reincarnated life, for one's shortcomings. Reincarnation is the belief that your spirit inhabits another body after you die, and you continue the journey towards Godhood. This makes no logical sense, as we are thousands of years into this progression and men should have all evolved into this godhood state, if they had been constantly improving.

Psychology/Powers of the Mind

This is the belief that everyone can unlock magical powers and perform miracles, reinforcing the idea that we are "gods" and the self is all important. The use of psychedelic drugs for enlightenment is promoted.

Pantheism

"Pantheism will be at the core of the New Age Bible. Pantheists deny the existence of a personal God, maintaining that the universe itself and everything in it is "God." Since God is in everything, everything is God. Therefore, the sun is God, Mother Earth is God, the moon, stars, and galaxies are gods. They are alive. And if the planets and stars are living gods, man is subordinate to them. It is therefore his sacred duty to revere these divine, living beings.

This belief in a divine sun, earth, and moon leads many New Agers to worship these planetary bodies as deities. The full moon ritual is especially popular, as is the passing of seasons...The doctrine that man is an evolving god, but that *he must be obedient to superior evolved man-gods* will be an important feature of the New Age Bible. This teaching will ensure the dominance of the Antichrist and his demonic aides. Perhaps the major drawing card of the New Age World Religion is its seductive flattery that man is a deity. But ironically man will find that in seeking to be his own master, he has become the slave of one far greater in intelligence and supernatural power.[19]

There are many modern words in your home Bibles now. The attack on scriptures by the enemy is astounding, and the denial by "learned" scholars, ministers, pastors and clergy is just as astounding. Many people have gone to their pastors to tell them of the Bible changes, only to be rejected outright, and often shunned and told to leave the church. This could be a case of cognitive dissonance, ignorance or deception. I am sure that they all come in to play.

Pastors have a role to play, and that is to preach the Word of God from the scriptures and if anything calls the scriptures as being malleable, they believe their position is to defend. Another serious belief they have is that the scriptures cannot change and point to several verses in the Bible that can loosely be connected to that concept, but in reality, they do not speak of that at all. Many pastors have this belief, as we all once did, that if you see something - it is true. We previously had no idea that something written down or an object, could change from one form to another. I once spoke to a pastor who said, "That couldn't happen!" in support of this very belief. However, as the Bible does show, there are many supernatural occurrences ranging from Moses' staff (now Aaron's) changing into a serpent as well as the ungodly soothsayer's staff

<hr>

[19] Texe Marrs *Dark Secrets of the New Age* pp. 198, 199, 200, 201, 202

turning into a serpent , to Jesus' walking on water, to water being turned into wine and more.

It has also been recently understood by people who see the Bible Changes that the Word of God is not the scriptures, but Jesus himself as stated in John 1:1. So when they say the "word of God cannot change" when referring to the Bible, in actuality they are saying that Jesus Himself and what He said cannot change. Not that ink on paper can't change.

> ### Rev 22:18¶
> *For I testify unto every man that heareth the words of the prophecy of this book, <u>If any man shall add unto these things,</u> God shall add unto him the plagues that are written in this book:*
>
> ### ☑ Rev 22:19
> *And <u>if any man shall take away from the words of the book of this prophecy,</u> God shall take away his part out of the book of life, and out of the holy city, and from the things which are written in this book.*

The above passages in Revelation admonish anyone who adds or removes words from the Bible, proving that it is possible to do so. There is not an invisible force field of protection around the Bible. We know that witchcraft can make people rich and successful, can hurt other people and I think could possibly be causing these changes. Do we understand it? No, but do you understand how the television projects images and sound into your house? You don't, but there it is.

People who only had radios for communication decades ago would have thought the TV was some sort of impossibility.

The Bible says God would shorten the days in the end so maybe this is why. Perhaps things get so crazy at the end of this age that Satan tries to go back in time to put off going to the Lake of Fire. Has he done it, yet only partially - leaving residue behind?

Time Manipulation

In regards to time, it has been shown that we don't even know what year we are in. Evidence proves that our entire past timeline has been falsified and faked. We know this because of the fantastic cathedrals and elaborately constructed marble buildings all over the world. They tell us that they were constructed in a year or two during the late 1800s. That is a time when there were no power tools, no trucks or cranes, and just horse and buggy. Heck, even the roads were not paved. They had harsh winters. The horses would have had to be fed and many of them harnessed to even drag the marble and granite to the site. Plus, many of the nearest quarries were hundreds of miles away. And how did they lift the heavy pieces of marble 2, 5 or even more-stories high? And then elaborately carve them so well you would think they came out of a mold?

So we are supposed to believe that these cowboys managed to create these magnificent buildings that we can't even construct today? Even if we could come close to it, how long would it realistically take? 5, 10 or 40 years?

Furthermore, there was and is a concerted effort to demolish most of these buildings from the past, for instance, in the Chicago World Fair, where an entire city was razed after the fair was over. Oh, they were made out of paper mache.

Give me a break. The adjoining canals to the buildings along would have required extensive foundations just to be able to withstand the fair. So, we have been lied to about our entire history. They say that between 700-1,000 years has been added. We could realistically only be in the year 1024. Think about it - we are only a dozen generations past Jesus' first coming on this earth.

Why would they want to cover up our timeline?

Let's start with the Flat Earth. Why would they want to cover that up? Well, along with the flat earth with a dome around it, you can't have any space. And if you can't have any space, then you can't have aliens flying around in spaceships, especially the ones they expect to land and tell us they are our creators. Also, if there is no valid space exploration, you couldn't funnel $50 million dollars off the American people everyday for basically propping up an elaborate hoax. What easy money that is to pocket!

Then we know they are covering up artifacts and skeletons from Giants. Why would they want to cover that up? For one thing, that would destroy their theory of evolution, and for another-it proves that what the Bible said in the Old Testament concerning the existence of giants was real. Easy-peezy.

In the next chapter, we will explore how our entire timeline of history is also falsified.

Chapter 9

Timeline Corruption:

How the Millennial Reign of Christ May Have

Come and Gone

"Silence is a lie that screams at the light."
— *Shannon L. Alder*

Has the Millennium of Jesus Christ's reign on earth come and gone? Has the lion already laid down with the lamb? Are we now in the period of the wolf dwelling with the lamb? No doubt we are living in a time of great deception and born into a society built on lies.

As the onion is peeled back, we see that the earth is flat, that reality is malleable and most churches are indoctrinated religious institutions that bow to the evil government. And if that

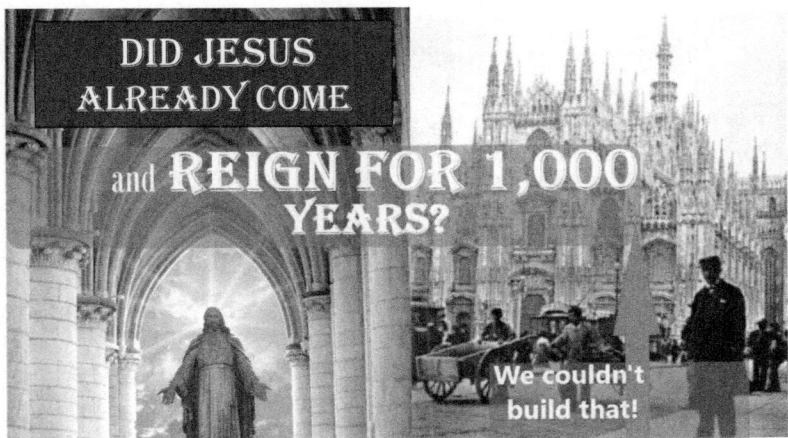

weren't enough, I am here to propose to you that our historical timeline has been altered by 700-1,000 years in an effort to conceal the theory that Jesus' Second Coming occurred at approximately 70 A.D. and reigned with the saints for 1,000 years in the period known as the "Millennium".

I will be presenting information and using quotes from a recent book titled, "Welcome to the Little Season," and "Lucifer's Flood", both by Alan Conford.

> *Revelation 20:2-3. And he laid hold on the dragon, that old serpent, which is the Devil, and Satan, and bound him a thousand years, And cast him into the bottomless pit, and shut him up, and set a seal upon him, that he should deceive the nations no more, till the thousand years should be fulfilled:and after that he must be loosed a little season.*
> *Revelation 20:7-8. And when the thousand years are expired, Satan shall be loosed out of his prison, And shall go out to deceive the nations which are in the four quarters of the earth, Gog and Magog, to gather them together to battle: the number of whom is as the sand of the sea.*

The Time is at Hand

Philippians 4:5- Let your moderation be known unto all men. The Lord is at hand.

1 Peter 4:7- But the end of all things is at hand: be ye therefore sober, and watch unto prayer.

Revelation 1:7- Behold, he cometh with clouds; and every eye shall see him, and they also which **pierced** him: and all kindreds of the earth shall wail because of him.

How else could those who actually pierced Jesus' side with a spear, see Him coming in the clouds, if it didn't happen when they were alive?

Matthew 16:28 - Verily I say unto you, There be some standing here, which **shall not taste of death,** till they see the Son of man coming in his kingdom. (If we take this literally, then Jesus had to have come back in that generation.)

Matthew 23:46 - Verily I say unto you, All these things shall come upon this generation.

Matthew 24:34 - Verily I say unto you, **This generation shall not pass,** till all these things be fulfilled.

Luke 21:32 - Verily I say unto you, This generation shall not pass away, till all be fulfilled.

Revelation 22:20 - He which testifieth these things saith, Surely I come quickly. Amen. Even so, come, Lord Jesus.

"...realistically, do you not think that when Jesus said things like, "Repent, for the kingdom of heaven is at hand", he was addressing the folk in his presence, and not some future generation a couple of thousand years down the line? And still being realistic, do you not think that Jesus meant exactly what he said at the time? And do you not think that his disciples realized that Jesus was referring to their own generation?

Why else would those who came to faith in Christ that day, sell all of their worldly possessions or give them away, unless they believed the end was nigh, so to speak?

Acts 2:44-45. And all that believed were together, and had all things common; And sold their possessions and goods, and parted them to all men, as every man had need. Or could it be that the Apostles knew exactly what they were talking about? That they expected the return of Christ in the not too distant future?

John also warned the seven churches in Asia, that the "time is at hand", whilst Jesus himself said; "Behold I come quickly." Not just the once, but six times. Now why would Jesus emphasize his soon return to the seven churches, if it were not true?

... John wrote the very last book of the Bible. Yet in the very first verse of the very first chapter of the very last book of the Bible, John warned of "things which must shortly come to pass." He was also instructed not to seal the words of prophecy, for the time is at hand.

Revelation 22:10. And he saith unto me, Seal not the sayings of the prophecy of this book: for the time is at hand.

Yet here we are more than two thousand years later, and our pastors and church leaders, with good intent I'm certain, are still telling their congregations to keep looking up, for surely, Jesus will be returning in the clouds very soon. Which is exactly what Jesus promised the folk that he spoke to back in 33 AD, a clear-cut sense of immanency which John then conveyed to the seven churches of Asia."[20]

Revelation 22:10. And he saith unto me, Seal not the sayings of the prophecy of this book: for the time is at hand. John also warned the seven churches in Asia, that the "time is at hand", whilst Jesus himself said; "Behold I come quickly." Not just the once, but six times.

"The majority of Christians today believe the coming world war will be that referred to as Armageddon in the Book of Revelations, but that particular war

---

[20] Alan Conford *Welcome to the Little Season* p. 75 -78

occurred long ago during the times of Jacob's trouble. It has been disguised in our history books as being the fall of Babylon aka Jerusalem, as foretold by both Jesus and John, and the fall of the Western Roman Empire.

It is quite likely that the fall of this vast empire was a far more sudden event, rather than a gradual decline over two hundred or more years, as we've been led to believe. Either way, the coming world war is the final battle, referred to in the Book of Revelations as that of Gog and Magog."[21]

"In fact, all the evidence, and there is plenty of it, would strongly indicate that the likes of you and I, along with the few generations before us, have all been born into the open-ended period of time referred to as "the Little Season" in the Book of Revelations. A time of unprecedented Satanic Deception, which sounds much like the times we are living in now.

Although Jesus didn't explicitly state that John would not die prior to His return, the disciples understood exactly what Jesus meant. For whilst many of them, including Peter, were to expect a martyr's death, John was told he would remain alive until the coming of the Son of man.

John 21:23. Then went this saying abroad among the brethren, that that disciple should not die: yet Jesus said not unto him, He shall not die; but, If I will that he tarry till I come, what is that to thee?

So, if John was to remain until His coming, and secular history is correct that Jerusalem fell in 70 AD, then John was changed in an instant, and raptured to meet the Lord in the air, most likely from 68-70 AD.

Tradition on the other hand, would have us believe that John died of old age whilst in exile on the Isle of Patmos, but tradition would also have us believe that

---

[21] Alan Conford *Welcome to the Little Season* p. 63

he didn't complete the Book of Revelations until circa 95 AD. The internal evidence of the Scriptures however, silently declares this would have been impossible. For just like Jesus had done, John also foretold the destruction and fall of that great city, Jerusalem, aka Babylon, proving that the Book of Revelations was completed prior to 70 AD.

Little wonder then, that in the first verse of the first chapter, of the last book of the Bible, John records "things which must shortly come to pass."[22]

"It would seem that Judgement came upon Israel during the seventy seventh generation from Adam, when Jesus returned in the clouds, as was foretold by the prophet Daniel and John in the book of Revelations.Welcome to the Little Season."[23]

Signs in the Sun, Moon and Stars

"As for signs in the heavens, in 59 AD a lightning bolt struck Nero's dinner whilst it was being served, and a total eclipse occurred the same year at his mother's funeral. In 65 AD a comet appeared in the heavens along with a sword-shaped star, and both remained visible for a whole year.

In 69 AD another comet was seen, and the same year, the moon was eclipsed twice, just three days apart. Witnesses claimed it was first blood, then appeared black, followed by other colours. To top it all, two suns were recorded being seen in the sky that same year. Whilst two suns being seen simultaneously sounds impossible, it is a known phenomenon, although it's not a duplicate sun, but a large and very bright moon.

---

[22] Alan Conford *Welcome to the Little Season* p. 78
[23] Alan Conford *Welcome to the Little Season* p. 91

Other miraculous phenomenon were reported by historians during the Jewish wars, including a virgin cow giving birth to a lamb, a large solid metal door opening by itself, supernatural voices saying they were leaving the temple, which was followed by "an unearthly tumult and wind".

In Revelation 19 A spectacle witnessed in the sky over Israel which marked the start of the Jewish revolt in 66 AD .

In his history of the Jewish War, Josephus writes: On the one and twentieth day of the month Artemisius, [Jyar,] a certain prodigious and incredible phenomenon appeared: I suppose the account of it would seem to be a fable, were it not related by those that saw it, and were not the events that followed it of so considerable a nature as to deserve such signals; for, before sun-setting, chariots and troops of soldiers in their armor were seen running about among the clouds, and surrounding of cities Tacitus also recorded this amazing event in The Histories 5.13.

In the sky appeared a vision of armies in conflict, of glittering armour. A sudden lightning flash from the clouds lit up the Temple. The doors of the holy place abruptly opened, a superhuman voice was heard to declare that gods were leaving it,and in the same instant came the rushing tumult of their departure.

Notice what Eusebius of Caesarea says in his Ecclesiastical History (Book 3, Ch. 8.) For before the setting of the sun chariots and armed troops were seen throughout the whole region in mid-air, wheeling through the clouds and encircling the cities.

This was most likely the fulfillment of Jesus' prophecy; "And when ye shall see Jerusalem compassed with armies, then know that the desolation thereof is nigh". (Luke 21:20.)"[24]

Archaeological Evidence of Buildings Melting with Fervent Heat-Was this what Happened at the Battle of Armageddon?

10 But the day of the Lord will come as a thief in the night; in the which the heavens shall pass away with a great noise, and the elements shall melt **with fervent heat, the earth also and the works that are therein shall be burned up**.

Rocks or Burn Marks?

---

[24] Alan Conford *Welcome to the Little Season* p. 93-94

Perfect Square Windows!

The Melted Bricks of Fort Zverev, in Russia.

Fireclay Bricks melting between 1,600°C and 2,800°C

How Much Time Would It Take To Carve This?

For more extensive videos depicting melted buildings throughout the world, go to TheTruthseeker69 channel on Rumble. Or Meltology-101 on Youtube.

What the Tribulation Looked Like Under Nero

"There's little doubt that Nero fulfilled the role of the Beast, and is remembered for crucifying the Apostle Peter up-side-down, feeding Christians to the lions, nailing them to crosses, lighting them on fire to serve as street lights for chariot races, and dressing them in animal skins to be chased by a pack of dogs.

Nero killed his brother, his mother and three of his wives, killing his last wife to be with a young boy. He also married several men who he alternated masculine and feminine roles with.

Early Christians being killed in early art

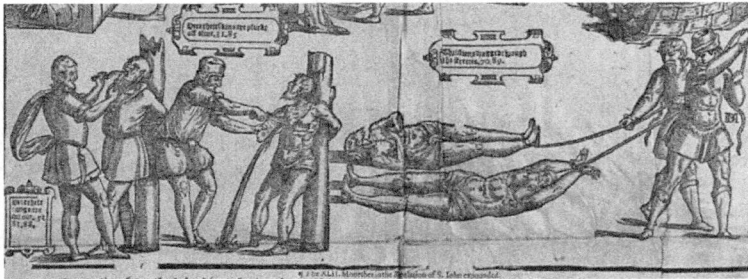

Under the reign of Emperor Nero, and over a five year period from 62-67 AD, the apostles Andrew, Bartholomew, James, Matthias, Paul, Peter and Thaddeus were all executed, and in 67 AD, after two failed attempts to murder him, Nero exiled John to the isle of Patmos, where he wrote the Book of Revelations. By 66 AD each of the 12 apostles had been martyred, and having been falsely blamed by Nero for the great fire of Rome in 64 AD, an unknown number of Christians were brutally slaughtered."[25]

"There were endless trials and tribulations, and thousands upon thousands of deaths for the Israelites prior to Jesus returning in the clouds. Which he had foretold of course, most likely around forty years earlier. There's no doubt whatsoever, that the people living in Israel at the time, endured and suffered the time of great tribulation, as warned of by Jesus in Matthew 24:21.

---

[25] Alan Conford *Welcome to the Little Season* p. 171

Yet it needs to be understood, that Scripture does not describe a 7 year Tribulation; it describes a period of 7 Seals where 4 Horsemen ride and a period of 7 Trumpets (begins at Revelation 8) called the Great Tribulation, lasting 1260 days or 42 months. The last day is the 7 vials/bowls of God's wrath which was the Second Coming of Jesus, and most likely shortly before, the dawn of the Millennium.

Futurists would disagree here, as I once did, by saying, "of course there will be 7 years of Tribulation". It says so in the Bible. But they can't tell you where it says so. For it is an understanding that comes from interpreting the 70 weeks recorded by Daniel as being 70 weeks of years. Simply put, 69 weeks of years ended with the death of Jesus, followed by an open-ended age of Grace, with the final 70th week being the 7 year tribulation, which they claim has not yet happened, but will do shortly.

But if the 70th week is still in the future, as claimed, then why did Jesus say "the time is fulfilled" in Mark 1:15? If there is a 2000+ year gap between the 69th and 70th week of Daniel, why doesn't Daniel, or any other scripture mention it? Because the presumed massive space of time between the 69th and the 70th week comes from Bible study notes, which are the word of man, and not the word of God. Study Bible Notes began in earnest with con-man Cyrus A Scofield, the Zionist Congress and the Bible Revision Committee in the 1880s."[26]

Early Christian Being Killed by Lions in the Coliseum as Entertainment

---

[26] John Conford *Lucifer's Flood* p. 94,95

Could it possibly be that when adding the "missing" seven hundred years back into the timeline, that 1776 was the true date for the end of the millennial kingdom?...if we were to assume the little season runs for 250 years, when added to 1776, we arrive at the year 2026."[27]

"How did he come to the 250 years length of The Little Season? If you look at the annual season, there are four, so 1/4 of 1,000 years is 250.

CHRISTIANS GIVEN TO THE LIONS IN THE ROMAN AMPHITHEATER.

Yet starting from 53 AD, two earthquakes occurred in Rome and two at Laodicea, whilst others were recorded at Campania, Chios, Colossi,Crete, Hierapolis, Judea, Miletus, Samos, Smyrna and finally at Jerusalem in 70 AD, fulfilling the prophecy of earthquakes in divers places.

The Mark of the Beast

With all the confusion that is going on in the world right now, it's easy to understand why so many Christians associate the mRNA vaccines with the mark of the beast. But this prophecy was fulfilled back in the days of Nero, for it was a

---

[27] John Conford *Welcome to the Little Season* p. 171

document called the Libelous, which had to be presented upon any transaction being made, whether buying or selling.

Receiving within their forehead was symbolic with those who worshiped the beast (emperor Nero). Receiving it within their hands was symbolic with those who took it just to survive. With all the confusion that is going on in the world right now, 1776 May Have Been the End of the Millennial Reign Josephus correct when claiming 5,000 years of world history had already passed by the start of the first century AD?

2025 -2026 are Pivotal Years

Deagel 2025 Forecast by Country			
Country	Population 2017	Population 2025	Populatio
United Kingdom	63,390,000	14,517,860	-77.1
Ireland	4,770,000	1,318,740	-72.4
United States of America	316,440,000	99,553,100	-68.5
Puerto Rico	3,640,000	1,165,780	-68.0
Germany	80,590,000	28,134,920	-65.1
Luxembourg	514,862	199,020	-61.3
Israel	7,710,000	3,982,480	-48.3
Libya	6,000,000	3,253,820	-45.8
Iceland	339,747	195,927	-42.3
France	67,100,000	39,114,580	-41.7
Spain	47,370,000	27,763,280	-41.4
Bahrain	1,410,000	837,800	-40.6
Cyprus	1,220,000	791,720	-35.1
Australia	23,230,000	15,196,600	-34.6
Angola	29,310,000	19,564,500	-33.2
Switzerland	7,990,000	5,342,540	-33.1
Denmark	5,600,000	3,771,760	-32.6
Belgium	11,490,000	8,060,900	-29.8
Austria	8,750,000	6,215,000	-29.0
Ukraine	44,570,000	31,628,980	-29.0

Could it possibly be that when adding the "missing" seven hundred years back into the timeline, that 1776 was the true date for the end of the millennial kingdom? Accompanied by a devastating series of mud-floods across many parts of the earth?

And the release of Satan from the bottomless pit, the approximate start of the Little Season? The beginning of a time of great Satanic deception for all the nations of Earth? Speculative maybe, but **if we were to assume the little season runs for 250 years, when added to 1776, we arrive at the year 2026.**

I am not, nor have I ever been a date-setter, but have felt for a considerable period of time now, that 2022-2025 are the pivotal years for humanity. Deagel predicted in 2020, that the United Kingdom would see its population decline by 77.1% by the year 2025"[28]

But What About the Dates on Old Coins and Artwork?

THIS COIN IS SAID TO BE 1 700, BUT THE CHARACTER BEFORE THE 7 IS NOT A 1

Why the need to change dates? Because everything couldn't be wiped out, such as coins, building with dates and artwork. It appears that **coins minted before the 1800s have a letter "i" or "j" in place of the 1.** The buildings were commonly labeled in Roman Numerals, and the M, which is 1,000 was added to the beginning.

By adding 1,000 years to the date, a vastly complex building built in the year 700, under Christ's reign, would now read 1700, which adds validity to the idea that the Dark Ages did not have any accomplishments. This proof can be seen in the video below, named 1000 Years Was Added to our Calendar - Our Timeline Was Changed.

[28] Alan Conford *Welcome to the Little Season* p. 171

This is surmised to mean **Iesus, Jesu and Iesu, in Latin** and other languages. In addition, it would be a matter of course for them to now use the power to change the reality itself, such as the dates on old artwork, via the phenomenon known as the Mandela Effect. They have already changed the artwork itself, such as the *Creation of Man,* by Michelangelo, which used to have God's finger pointing diagonally from the upper right, down to man, signifying He was greater than man, as I illustrated in Chapter 2.

Why Do Current Events Look Like an Impending Tribulation?

"The events we can see going on in the world around us, I believe, are man's attempt to fulfil the prophecies which were already fulfilled over 2,000 years ago. Whilst it would appear the perpetrators are following the blueprint of Scripture to achieve this, under the flag of Molech, the God of Zionism and modern-day Israel, is NOT the God of the Bible. For everything points to the fact that we are living in the Little Season where Satan has assumed the role of God.

Jesus warned the first generation of believers and unbelievers alike, that Jerusalem and its temple would be physically destroyed. He referred to that great city as, "spiritually Sodom and Egypt", whilst Peter referred to Jerusalem as Babylon. (1 Peter 5:13.)

When writing the Book of Revelations, John recorded the fall of Babylon, that great city, aka Jerusalem, as being one of the "things which must shortly come to pass." The point being that although Jesus, John and Peter referred to 'that great city' in spiritual terms, the fulfillment of prophecy was both literal and physical.

John also warned the seven churches in Asia, that the "time is at hand", whilst Jesus himself said; "Behold I come quickly." Not just the once, but six times. Now why would Jesus emphasize his soon return to the seven churches, if it were not true?

When reasoning from the Scriptures, the internal evidence silently declares Jesus has already returned, just as he promised to. But it all depends upon whether or not we take the Scriptures literally, unless the surrounding context dictates otherwise, of course. It also depends upon us not arguing against the Scriptures, from our own traditional understanding of the end times.

Or put another way, if there is no Biblical evidence to support our long-held beliefs, then we should question whether or not that belief is based purely upon tradition. For example, is there anywhere within the Scriptures which would even suggest that the promises Jesus made to those in his presence, would NOT be fulfilled during their lifetime? If not, then we must conclude that Jesus kept those promises he made, rather than put them on the back-burner for another 2,000 plus years.

For there is nowhere in Scripture to suggest Jesus would postpone his second coming for at least another 2,000 years. That super-long delay is merely a doctrine invented by man, and one which is not supported by Scripture. There is nowhere in the Bible which says a third temple must be built in Jerusalem,even though the rabbis have been talking about it for decades. It is merely an invented doctrine of man, promoted by the false ideology of Zionism.

For nigh on thirty years, I dismissed John's writing of "things which must shortly come to pass", because it didn't suit my inherited end-times understanding. But when reading the gospels, the epistles and the Book of Revelations with a fresh pair of eyes, It slowly began to dawn on me, that I'd been hoodwinked. It was a very humbling experience I might add, having prided myself for years, as one who believed every written word of God."[29]

The Dark Ages Was Really Christ's Millennium Reign on Earth

Satan inverts everything, as we can see so clearly now. If something is labeled "transparent" it means it is "concealed". If another thing is "safe and effective", it means it's "dangerous". Banning gay and transvestite pornographic books is "banning books", as in "banning free speech". Speaking the truth is "hate-speech". So it is no wonder that if the millennial reign of Christ's light on this earth were labeled by the ruler of this world, it would be the "Dark Ages".

"The Dark Ages for example, meaning the last two thousand years of world history is largely a fabricated construct. Whilst not easy to get one's head around, I really don't think we can have things both ways.

Either the events of the Book of Revelations were fulfilled shortly after they were recorded, as Jesus said they would be. Or they were not. This would include the thousand year reign of Christ…".[30]

Revelation 20:3. And cast him [Satan] into the bottomless pit, and shut him up, and set a seal upon him, that he should deceive the nations no more, till the thousand years should be fulfilled:and after that he must be loosed a little season.

"In other words, it could rightly be said, that having been released from the depths of the Abyss, this was the return of, or the second coming of Satan. Saturn

---

[29] Alan Conford *Welcome to the Little Season* p. 91-97
[30] Alan Conford *Welcome to the Little Season* p. 98

represents Satan, and according to Annie Besant, former leader of the Theosophical Society aka the cult of Saturn;"

"Saturn will rule during the age of Aquarius."[31]Turns out we are entering the Aquarius age now.

...those of the first resurrection in their supernatural bodies, were the builders during the Millennial kingdom, and left behind all the amazing free aether energy gathering structures, which the deceivers have since led us to believe were constructed as places of worship. "[32]

What Happened at the End of the Millennial Reign?

"Revelation 20:5 reads; "But the rest of the dead lived not again until the thousand years were finished". Notice the Bible doesn't say the rest of the dead received a bodily resurrection, just that they lived not again until the thousand years had ended. It was the first resurrection alone, who were raised from the dead in their new spiritual bodies, and also prior to the start of the millennial kingdom.

There is nothing in Scripture to suggest "the rest of the dead" were actually resurrected to life. Is it just possible I ask myself, that God permitted the spirits of the unsaved dead to inhabit the physical bodies of the first generation of those born into the post-millennial world? This might also include all the unrighteous souls, who would finally accept the gospel of Christ and be saved?

This would legitimately explain, why we're effectively told the dead lived again, with no mention of them being resurrected to life. It may also explain the

---

[31] Alan Conford *Welcome to the Little Season* p. 115
[32] Ibid p.114

numerous old photographs from the nineteenth century in which the people seem to be completely out of place within their local surroundings. Paris for example.

It's extremely hard to believe that this generation of folk with unmade streets and a mode of transport and technology which is so primitive by today's standards, were responsible for building the awe-inspiring architecture surrounding them. In fact, it seems like these people are distinctly out of place when compared with both the size of the city and its huge and impressive buildings. Who built these amazing structures? And where did all the people in the photograph come from?

Is it possible they are the descendants of "the rest of the dead" who arrived into an age where an infrastructure already existed? Wouldn't you agree that something's not quite right here, and there appears to be something awry with the time-line?

And why are there so many old photographs of major cities, with stunning architecture and dirty unmade streets, that seem to be almost empty of people? It almost appears that the generation of folk seen in the photographs recently arrived on the scene and inherited these majestic buildings, rather than being the ones responsible for their original construction. And if so, who were the true builders? And where did they go?

This question has led to two trains of thought. Firstly, that those of the first resurrection in their supernatural bodies, were the builders during the Millennial kingdom, and left behind all the amazing free aether energy gathering structures, which the deceivers have since led us to believe were constructed as places of worship etc.

Secondly, this incredible architecture was in fact, the work of the evil Tartarians, who were assisted by an unknown race of giants. I am just one of a growing number who believe that because the architecture and stonework in most major cities across the world all bear a similar hallmark, it would suggest they were all constructed by the same unified and advanced civilization. A people with the ability to harness the power of electro-magnetism.

I'm not advocating the belief in reincarnation as such, nor is the concept taught in the Bible, but if we take Revelation 20:5 literally, then "the rest of the dead" lived again after the thousand years had finished."[33]

"...we are not told how long after the millennium this resurrection takes place... there are those who believe that an entire generation of the dead were resurrected immediately after the millennial reign came to a close, but such a concept would amount to reincarnation. A highly popular belief, but one not supported by the word of God. We do not get a second chance at life."[34]However, because a person's death is by appointment, followed by the judgement (Hebrews 9:27), we can only assume this second, and final resurrection occurs at the very end of the world, and the final judgement at the great white throne. (Revelation 20:11.) But whether or not there is another rapture beforehand for believers in Christ, we are not told. Personally, I

Paris - elaborate building

[33] Alan Conford *Welcome to the Little Season* p. 115-116.
[34] John Conford *Lucifer's Flood* p. 92.

suspect there will be, but that is just my own opinion.

Take a look at the buildings purported to have been built in Paris, when there was no power tools or cranes.

What if the history of Western Civilization is both drastically shorter and dramatically different than the new false historic narrative conveniently superimposed onto the old world infrastructure?

In the video below, an elaborate city hall building was purported to be built in a year. When AI was asked about the logistics of constructing that building in the 1800s, and how long would it take, AI answered that it would take about 5 or more years.

"What if certain agencies have been re-writing history? Could it be that so-called 'Universal Classic World History' prior to the sixteenth century, is a carefully crafted construct of lies and deception, fabricated in the 16th-18th centuries upon the 'firm' foundation laid down by an assortment of Italian scholars, Roman clergy and humanists from the 14th -15th centuries?"[35]

We are being lied to about all these buildings being built in the age of horse and buggy, when even brick making machines were not yet invented:

---

[35] John Conford *Lucifer's Flood* p. 93

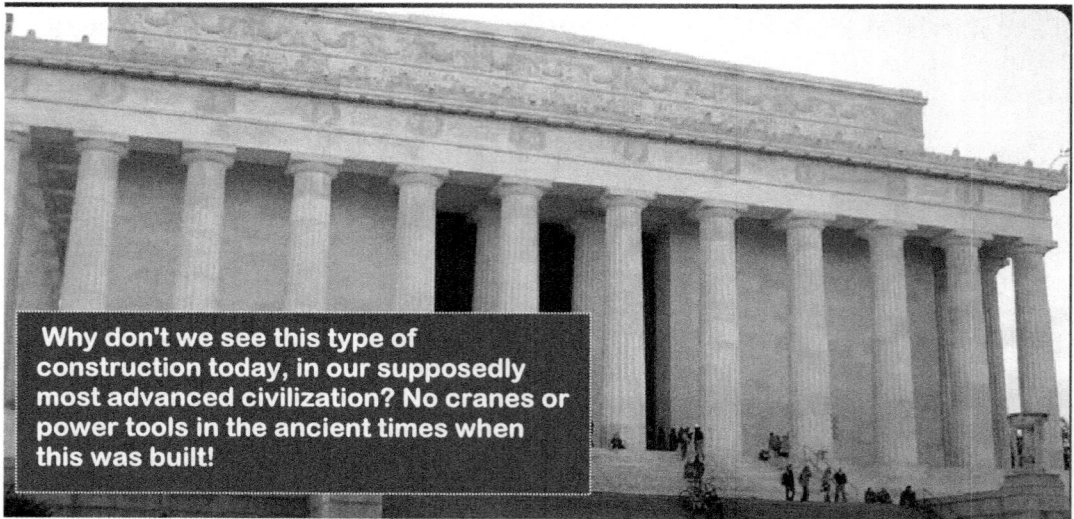

Why don't we see this type of construction today, in our supposedly most advanced civilization? No cranes or power tools in the ancient times when this was built!

Why don't we see this level of quality in carved statues today?
We don't create this type of craftsmanship today!
I thought we were supposed to be the most advanced civilization ever?
I thought we were "evolving" and instead, it seems
that we are going backwards.
People are dumber, craftsmen are in short demand, art consists of a few large brush strokes on a canvas, music is not even music, but shouting and rapping.

Or, "Everything we know about "the rest of the dead" is contained within this one sentence, but we do know they were not part of the "first resurrection",i.e.

those who are Christ's at his coming. (1 Corinthians 15:23 .) The very term a first resurrection demands at least a second however, and there are those who believe that an entire generation of the dead were resurrected immediately after the millennial reign came to a close, but such a concept would amount to reincarnation.

A highly popular belief, but one not supported by the word of God. We do not get a second chance at life. However, because a person's death is by appointment, followed by the judgement (Hebrews 9:27), we can only assume this second, and final resurrection occurs at the very end of the world, and the final judgement at the great white throne. (Revelation 20:11.)." [36]

Satan's Little Season

It would seem that you and I, and the few generations before us, have all been born into the time period known as the Little Season. A people who inherited the architecture constructed by those in their new spiritual (not spirit) bodies, who once reigned on the earth for a thousand years. For how long the "little season" will last, who can tell? But over its

---

[36] John Conford *Lucifer's Flood* p.92-93

duration, who can deny that the clown world we inhabit has increasingly become more bent and twisted?

For under the influence of the god they worship, this world is being run by the Luciferian elite, the controllers, psychopathic liars and paedophiles. And they just become more and more brazen."[37]

PALACES WITH NO BATHROOMS

Palaces such as the one in Versailles, France had no bathrooms.

Palace of Versailles

The excuse is they didn't have the know-how to construct them. Elaborate plumbing systems were in place that brought water into spouting fountains, yet supposedly at least 10 centuries after Rome (where they had a toilet system) they couldn't figure it out?

Palace of Versailles

Look at the grandeur of the architecture and tell me they couldn't figure out how to construct a lavatory. The theory is, these palaces were made to house the resurrected saints,

---

[37] John Conford *Lucifer's Flood* p. 117

who were now in their incorruptible bodies, needing no waste management systems.

Palace of Versailles

In addition to that, the old domes and spires on the cathedrals have been thought to have generated free energy. The same dome and spires can be seen in old structures all over the world:

The spires are said to have generated free electricity

Soil Liquefaction/Mud Floods

"After the flood of Noah, God placed a rainbow in the clouds as a token to mark the covenant he made with every living creature, that never again would the waters of a flood destroy the earth.

Genesis 9:13. I do set my bow in the cloud, and it shall be for a token of a covenant between me and the earth.

Nevertheless, Jesus warned how the last days for Israel would be reminiscent of the days of Noah, and the prophet Daniel foretold how the end would come with a Flood. Daniel 9:26. And after threescore and two weeks shall Messiah be cut off, but not for himself: and the people of the prince that shall come shall destroy the city and the sanctuary; and the end thereof shall be with a FLOOD, and unto the end of the war desolations are determined.

Maybe this was a localized flood of water, but we are not told. Or is it possible this was the first of a series of multiple mud-floods? For we know from scripture that the last days for Jerusalem aka Babylon, were accompanied by a great earthquake. (Revelation 11:13.) God also warned of a time when due to its very foundations being shaken, the earth would reel to and fro like a drunken man. (Isaiah 24:18- 20.)

Soil Liquefaction commonly referred to as Mud-floods is a very real phenomena, which occurs when saturated or partially saturated soil substantially loses strength and stiffness in response to an applied stress such as shaking during an earthquake. And there is plenty of evidence for mud-flooding having affected nations right across the earth. The difficulty is pin-pointing exactly when these multiple mud-floods occurred. Has it been a whole series of individual events over the centuries? Or mud-flooding which occurred in multiple countries, and more or less simultaneously?

I take very seriously the belief among many researchers that there was a relatively recent worldwide mud flood liquefaction event that wiped out an advanced civilization, and then there was a subsequent historical reset of the timeline by those responsible for invoking the cataclysm. Apart from one thing.

A cataclysmic mud-flood did not wipe out a former advanced civilization as many believe, rather a time of catastrophic judgement occurred as the millennial kingdom came to an end, and the kings and priests of Jesus Christ voluntarily vacated this earthly domain. We are not told if the kings and priests left this realm for heaven, or whether the "camp of the saints" exists at a hidden location somewhere on the earth. It would seem to be the latter mind, for it is written that a time will come, when "they" [the nations] went up on the breadth of the earth, and compassed the camp of the saints about". (Revelation 20:9.)

…many events that we've been led to believe have taken place in antiquity may in fact, have been as recent as only a few hundred years ago. In which case, our perception of the historical timeline has been grossly distorted, to put it mildly.

At times it seems how we are all skating on the veil of history, while the truth is right beneath our feet. Take the excavations of Rome for example, for an internet search reveals some very interesting images.

We've been led to believe the excavation work began in the late nineteenth century, and maybe it was to an extent. But the majority of the work was undertaken between 1938 and 1942, under the direction of Benito Mussolini. Like most cities across Europe, modern-day Rome sits atop the infrastructure of a society that once existed before it. We are told the original structures were either demolished, or buried to become the foundation for the city we have today. But we are not told where the thousands of tons of earth came from, and as can be seen from the photographs, we're not talking about a layer of 3 or 4 feet of dirt, but a depth of 20-30 feet or more.

Where did such vast amounts of excess earth come from, if not the result of a former mud-flood?"[38]

Now in light of the research that suggests 700 years, maybe less, maybe more, have been inserted into the first millennium, perhaps the medieval crusaders weren't that chronologically confused after all. Perhaps it had literally only been a few generations between the time of Christ and the first crusade."

Russian mathematician and professor at Moscow State University, *Anatoly Fomenko*, says we really know little at all about anything prior to 1100 AD, and even suggests that from around this time period, people knew full well they were gradually climbing back to normality, in the wake of a major catastrophe.

"Either way, as humanity slowly progressed, there must have come a point in time from where they were left to rely on the historical accounts of those under the stewardship of the rulers of nations, the powerful Church of Rome, various secret societies and the educational institutions that each had their own agendas. By the time of the printing press, all bets were off. Printers could print anything, without the need for handwriting experts to prove the validity of the paper or ink, etc.

From all accounts the history over the first millennium remains a bit of a mystery. The truth is, we can only speculate as to precisely where we are in the timeline, and when the mud-flood occurred, for we really just don't know. Whatever the primary cause, it appears that most countries across the entire earth were affected by soil liquefaction on an unprecedented scale.

---

[38] John Conford *Lucifer's Flood* p.122-4

Whether the massive brick and stone constructions left behind by the builders sank into the ground under their own weight, due to a quick-sand effect, or whether they were buried or partially buried by rivers of liquid mud, I wouldn't know. Others suspect the ground water was struck with some form of frequency oscillation causing the soil to expand and swell, which then rose around the structures.

Either way, tens of thousands of these "old world" structures were later discovered and inherited by those who remained on the earth, and the generations born unto them. And no, this incredible architecture was not designed by an army of visiting aliens, but by a unified society who were very much aware of, and able to harness the power of free energy, in the form of electro-magnetism.

Maybe the people who inherited this architecture were the rest of the dead who lived not again until the thousand years were finished, but that is pure speculation. As too is the possibility that at least some of "the rest of the dead" who lived again, became the powerful and filthy rich robber barons, who would end up founding the secret societies, the intelligence agencies, the United Nations, the world organizations and controlling pretty much everything.

The USA took a completely different approach when dealing with the unfathomable amount of excess earth, mud and dirt. This was achieved under the guise of raising entire cities such as Kansas and Chicago, by anywhere from 12 to 20 feet above their original level. Like multiple cities across the earth, both Chicago and Kansas City also suffered major fires, most likely, each one a controlled burn event. Thus destroying much of the evidence of a previous world part-buried beneath our own. In fact, I believe some parts of the former underground city in Ellinwood, Kansas, are still open to members of the public.

The Destruction of Thousands of Elaborate Buildings during the World Fairs of the late 1800s

The Worlds Fairs Spanned Hundreds of Acres of Highly Intricate and Elaborate Buildings, only to be torn down.

"Thousands of remarkable old world buildings, were systematically destroyed over the course of the mysterious World Fairs, which were held during the nineteenth and early twentieth centuries. Under the pretext of having been recently constructed, an achievement carried out in an impossibly short space of time, these architectural wonders, reminiscent of ancient Greece or Rome, were displayed to the public for the very last time. For the public were told that these spectacular buildings were only ever constructed on a temporary basis, and the vast majority were razed to the ground within six months from the closure of the Exposition.

Palace of Electricity at late 1800s World Fair

World fairs were set up for indoctrination purposes and as an excuse to tear down these huge elaborate buildings, which by rights should not have existed."[39]

"The horrors of human savagery planned since the Feast Day of Lucifer on Aug 15, 1871, for WWIII by 33 degree Freemason and Satanist Albert Pike, are about to begin. Stir-Crazy war generals guiding psychotic world leaders into WWIII is part of God's pre-written plan. God is in total control of the timeline and warning us every step of the way; we just need to be able to hear Him.

For this coming war is not the war of Armageddon, as most Christians suppose, but the final battle against Jesus Christ, the war of Gog and Magog. In this sense the rabbis are right when declaring the coming world war to be that of Gog and Magog, but for all the wrong reasons, For their expectations are based upon Ezekiel's prophecies in the Old Testament. Not on John's prophecy in the New Testament, which says Gog and Magog takes place after the millennial reign

---

[39] John Conford *Lucifer's Flood* p. 126-131

of Christ, and after the Little Season. The time-frame we almost certainly exist in today.

The point being, we are NOT the generation Jesus promised to return to. Jesus kept the promise he made to the first generation of believers in Christ," [40]

"It would be good to think that as the little season comes to an end, a world-wide outpouring of the Holy Spirit might take place, causing all the nations to repent and turn back to God. But the Bible as good as informs us that this will never be, for we're told that Satan will deceive every nation on earth.

Exactly how things will pan out, and how this world will finally end we are not told, other than how the world's nations, collectively referred to as Gog and Magog, will be deceived to such an extent, they will gather together for the final battle on earth.

We are told how a multitude without number, from the deceived of the nations will traverse the earth and completely surround the camp of the saints and the beloved city. At which point all will be engulfed in a maelstrom of fire from heaven. The final Holocaust. Revelation 20:8-9. And [Satan] shall go out to deceive the nations which are in the four quarters of the earth, Gog and Magog, to gather them together to battle: the number of whom is as the sand of the sea. And they went up on the breadth of the earth, and compassed the camp of the saints about, and the beloved city: and fire came down from God out of heaven,and devoured them.

The scriptures tell us that Satan deceives the entire world, therefore it would be quite logical to believe that when the nations of the world gather together for the final battle on earth, it will be for all the wrong reasons.What if Satan were

[40] John Conford *Lucifer's Flood* p. 169

able to deceive the nations into believing, that the real threat comes from elsewhere? That the governments of the world are only doing the bidding of those who inhabit the camp of the saints, let's say?

Will humanity seek to make war on Christ and his saints, as the Bible suggests? I doubt the "beloved city" refers to any physical city that we are presently aware of, although I have considered whether or not it may be located beyond the extremities of the known earth.

Will the nations be deceived into believing this to be an alien invasion from the depths of space, and the true enemy of mankind?"[41] Currently, researchers postulate that the "camp of the saints" may actually be at the North Pole, an area which no one is allowed to go to. They say that the northern lights are actually reflections from heaven. That the city may be hovering above the North Pole, in the air. My NASB Ryrie Study Bible comments on Rev. 21:2 about the heavenly city: "During the Millennium the New Jerusalem (described in detail in Rev. 21:9-22:5) apparently will be suspended over the earth…)

Isn't it curious that no one is allowed to go to, never mind to explore, both the North and the South Poles? Could the North Pole actually be the center of the earth, as shown in old, flat earth maps?

"After all, the Bible does refer to a "great nation" from "the sides of the earth" (Jeremiah 6:22) and Admiral Richard E Byrd on December 8, 1954, publicly announced the existence of an unknown landmass beyond the presumed South Pole. According to the Bible, the final deception will be so powerful that it will cause all the nations to come together as one, and this demon-driven human army

---

[41] John Conford *Lucifer's Flood* p. 221-223

without number will likely go to war against what is perceived to be a full-on threat to humanity.

Or is the "beloved city" more likely to refer to New Jerusalem the mother of us all, (Galatians 4:26) descending from out of heaven?"

Could it be that the reason the Mandela Effect's original purpose was to change the dates on ancient artwork and artifacts?

> *Could it be that the Millennial Period of Christ's Reign, when the lion laid down with the lamb, is over - and we are now in the reign of the wolf dwelling with the lamb?*

Perhaps that is what that Mandela Effect is trying to tell us.

Now let's back up to the original question. Why would they want to cover up our entire timeline? If Jesus came and reigned for 1,000 years, there was free energy and people were free to hone their artistic and craftsmen skills like the architecture proves, why hide that? If you were Satan being loosed out of prison after 1,000 years, you would not want anyone to know that Jesus kept His word and actually came. And that it was a fabulously glorious period of peace and prosperity under His reign. Instead, with a mission to deceive the world and gather together an army to take Jesus' city down at the Battle of Gog and Magog, you'd have to convince them of , well - something else.

Why not just deceive them into believing the exact opposite? There is no God, Jesus never came, and while I'm at it - you can't have any free electricity. Satan literally brought us back to the Stone Age and the only reason we have any prosperity today is because of the gradual work and discoveries by good people. But he is trying to reverse all that with all the Climate Change propaganda. It's so ridiculous. The wonderful age of light in which Jesus reigned is now called the Dark Ages.

If you knew that Jesus came, and reigned on the Earth as recently as maybe 200 some odd years ago - wouldn't that bolster your faith? You would know where we are in the Bible and not let Satan deceive you into fighting in some war which will be against Jesus and His resurrected saints.. Speculation has it that the Camp of the Saints is at the North Pole and if Satan convinces us that an alien invasion is happening there, he will get his worldwide war to take Jesus and the saints down. But we know what the Bible says will happen.

Anatoly Fomenko, head of the Math Dept in Russia, along with numerous other degrees, well versed in carbon dating and world chronology, states that all the Roman and Greek statues we see today are entirely fabricated creations during the Renaissance era, and that almost all history they tell us before the 1600s has been widely falsified to suit the agendas of changing the narrative of history.

How the timeline and history was corrupted. Explores the progression of church history and the occult, explaining why the occult religions such as Freemasonry had to go underground. Blavatsky and Crowley are shown as a big part of the occult re emerging.

So, as you can see, out history, timeline and time itself is being tampered with. Whatever the case may be, I believe Satan is behind the changes and it is an end time sign that we are entering into the very last days in which Jesus will return again, whether it is His second coming or the Great White Throne Judgement.

It is evident that it is high time to get right with God. In regards to how or if you should continue to read the Bible in light of the ongoing changes is a matter of choice. Some seasoned Christians prefer to rest in their previous knowledge of the Bible rather than learn different scriptures. I still advocate reading the Bible as the major themes, messages and teachings are still intact and it is a way of hearing God's voice for your life and spirit. If God can speak to us through secular music, unsaved people, circumstances that lead us to read or hear something, then He will absolutely guide you through the Bible to convey His messages. Of course, be aware that if you read anything that is blatantly against God's character, then do not take it to heart. If you haven't become astute in what is in the Bible, now is the time to catch up fast. We don't know how much longer it will contain God's words.

Friends, get on the right side of things now, while you still have a chance. If we are in the Little Season, and the length of that is only 250 years, we are seeing the literal end of this earth and the Great White Throne Judgement happening as early as within this decade. Get ready, get ready!!!

God Bless You all in your search for truth and your open-mindedness.

RESOURCES

Millennial Reign Already Came *Videos:*

1000 Years was added to our Calendar - Our Timeline was Changed by Autodidactic on Youtube

The Millennial Reign Of Christ & Satan's Little Season
https://www.youtube.com/watch?v=AeYnzAyMYMA

(COMPILATION) by Kingdom Within on Youtube
https://www.youtube.com/watch?v=NkdMU9OWdbw

Satan Unbound (Full Documentary) by Golden Age Past on Youtube
https://www.youtube.com/watch?v=zHCq5JMGKW0

Millennial Reign Already Happened Channels on Youtube:

- ❖ JTFollowsJC (and Rumble)
- ❖ Understanding Conspiracy (also on Rumble)
- ❖ BeyondtheVeil
- ❖ Golden Age Past
- ❖ There's No Place Like Home

Age of Historical Architecture Faked

- ❖ My Lunch Break Youtube and Rumble
- ❖ JonLevi   Youtube

Melted Buildings

- ❖ Meltology 101 Youtube
- ❖ TheTruthSeeker69 on Rumble

Mandela Effect

- ❖ TheSupernaturalBibleChanges.com (a website that hosts my articles)
- ❖ Wakeuporelse   Youtube and Rumble
- ❖ Residue for the Remanant   Youtube
- ❖ Nothing is As It Seems Podcast on Youtube
- ❖ Bluepacman13   Youtube
- ❖ JesusFreakComputerGeek   Youtube and Rumble and Bitchute
- ❖ Harbinger of the Harvest on Youtube and Harbinger_of_the_Harvest on Bitchute
- ❖ Moneybags73 Youtube
- ❖ Dose Of Reality with Brian S Staveley Youtube & Brian S Staveley   Rumble
- ❖ Changing Matrix   Youtube

Christian Truth

- ❖ Greg Hunter's USAWatchdog.com on Rumble and USAWatchdog.com
- ❖ Trunews on Rumble and Trunews.com website
- ❖ SGT Report on Bitchute and Rumble
- ❖ CBN News website
- ❖ TheEconomicCollapseBlog.com website
- ❖ TheScariestMovieEver on Youtube & KJOzborne on Rumble
- ❖ Ceiling Fan Man on Youtube and Rumble
- ❖ Canary Cry News Talk   Rumble
- ❖ The Healthy American, Peggy Hall on Bitchute
- ❖ Awaken with JP on Youtube and Bitchute (comedian who's so funny)
- ❖ XtremeRealityCheck   Rumble
- ❖ Richie From Boston on Bitchute
- ❖ DAYZOFNOAH on Bitchute
- ❖ Truthstream Media on Bitchute
- ❖ Become One That Can See   Bitchute and Ugetube
- ❖ Shaking My Head Productions   Bitchute
- ❖ Apocalypse_Watchman by MrE on Bitchute
- ❖ Awakened Saint on Youtube
- ❖ Face Like the Sun on Bitchute
- ❖ Politics-Owen Shroyer on Infowars/ Bitchute

About the Author

Carol Serpa is the author of over 500 articles, including being the main writer on the most prominent supernatural bible changes Mandela Effect website: TheSupernaturalBibleChanges.com. They also document the Bible changes in an interactive database. She has been at the forefront compiling the changes since its inception and interacting with the community on the ground level for over 5 years.

Originally writing for the website TheMostImportantNews.com, she switched to MandelaBibleChanges.com after learning of the Mandela Effect Bible changes. That website was the premier site on the topic at the time, but after 2 years was mysteriously taken down. For the last 3 years she has been writing for the above mentioned website but realizes that at some point, that site could also be removed. In light of Youtube censorship removing many videos from others on this topic, her belief is that a book is a good backup for protection against advancing and overt internet censorship that has recently overtaken this world.

Carol Serpa is recently retired and has one grown son, Jonathan. She has triple Bachelor degrees in Fashion Design, Education and Child Development and worked her entire life in the clothing manufacturing field and taught Design at the college and high school levels. She loves to create art and designed the cover of this book. She has written another book: *Beat Benzos the Natural Way* .

If you would like to contact her about any of these books, write to Carol here:

BeatBenzos@gmail.com

Printed in Dunstable, United Kingdom